D1553119

H·O·P·E·D·A·L·E

Urban Life and Urban Landscape Series

Zane L. Miller and Henry D. Shapiro, General Editors

H·O·P·E·D·A·L·E

*From Commune
to Company Town,
1840–1920*

EDWARD K. SPANN

Ohio State University Press
Columbus

Library of Congress Cataloging-in-Publication Data

Spann, Edward K., 1931–
    Hopedale : from commune to company town, 1840–1920 / Edward K.
Spann.
        p.   cm.— (Urban life and urban landscape series)
    Includes bibliographical references and index.
    ISBN 0-8142-0575-5 (alk. paper)
    1. Hopedale (Mass.)—History. I. Title. II Series.
F74.H74S63   1992
974.4′3—dc20   92-7194
                                                                    CIP

Text and jacket design by Nighthawk Design.
Type set in Caslon Antique and Pilgrim by
Graphic Composition, Athens, GA.
Printed by Braun-Brumfield, Inc., Ann Arbor, MI.

The paper in this book meets the guidelines for permanence
and durability of the Committee on Production Guidelines
for Book Longevity of the Council on Library Resources.⊗

9 8 7 6 5 4 3 2 1

To Suzan, Jason, and Laura

with love

Contents

Acknowledgments

I would like to thank the Research Committee of Indiana State University for its generous financial support. I also owe a debt of gratitude to those often unthanked but essential assistants of the scholar—librarians, especially the librarians at the Indiana State University Library, the American Antiquarian Society, and the Bancroft Memorial Library in Hopedale. My special thanks also to Jack T. Ericson for his work in compiling the Hopedale Community Collection on microfilm and to Paul Curran of Milford for his interest in my work.

Introduction

Hopedale, Massachusetts, is unique among American towns in that it was the site of two distinct attempts to create an ideal society, each representing a distinct phase in American history. It was partly for this reason that I decided to make it the subject of a separate book rather than incorporate it into my study of American radical social idealism, *Brotherly Tomorrows* (1989). In its first form, Hopedale ranks among the most successful communitarian experiments in pre-Marxian socialism made by Americans in the nineteenth century. Begun in 1842 as a struggling religious commune on a run-down farm, it developed into a thriving little village that won the attention of an ambitious entrepreneur, George Draper. Recognizing Hopedale's potential as an industrial site, Draper was able in 1856 to seize control of it and to expand its industrial base until he and his sons had created the nation's dominant firm in the production of looms for the cotton textile industry; the full story of Draper's coup against socialism in favor of capitalism is told here, for the first time, in chapter 9.

Under the Drapers and their partners, Hopedale became a model company town that provided benefits and a beneficial environment to its residents. During its peak years in the early twentieth century, it seemed to be the long-desired way to establish harmony between labor and capital. The nature of this experiment in welfare capitalism has been described by John S. Garner in his *Model Company Town*. Garner, however, does little to relate that experiment to the first period of Hopedale's idealism, without which there would have been no basis for either the Draper Company or its town.

Hopedale's earlier history calls attention to a special regional subculture that by the early nineteenth century had appeared along the Blackstone River in south-central Massachusetts and northern Rhode Island. This small world had its being in a local network of industrial villages that had sprung up to exploit the waterpower of the Blackstone and its tributaries. Although embracing some diversity of skill and ambition, these places were heavily dependent on the early textile industry. In a time of depression in that industry, the Hopedale Community was founded by some of the more idealistic as well as discontented inhabitants of the region, often craftsmen, petty businessmen, and other members of the small-town middle class, who sought a new social life for themselves in the familiar world of friends and families rather than on the far western frontier.

They drew their inspiration from the local religious community, specifically from Adin Ballou, who had developed a compelling spiritual vision from his experiences in the Blackstone region. Unlike most of Massachusetts, with its roots in Puritanism, this area had strong ties to the dissenting religion of Roger Williams and Rhode Island. From that background and from his involvement in Garrisonian abolitionism, Ballou developed his own social model based on what he believed was the one true Christianity Jesus had taught to his disciples, and especially on the critical doctrine of nonresistance. Convinced that God had, through Jesus, provided the principles for a truly good life to be achieved in this world, Ballou and his fellow Practical Christians determined to create a brotherly society based on the tenet that coercive force was not to be used against anyone, not even one's worst enemy. This belief could be found in various religious groups like the Shakers, but the Practical Christians who founded Hopedale extended it in a more radical direction by attempting to demonstrate that it would be possible for ordinary people to practice nonresistance without a sectarian isolation from general society.

Nonresistance, in this form, distinguished Hopedale from the rest of the world; in other respects the community was representative of the society around it. It exemplified the social radicalism that arose in response to early modernization, although its socialism was notably more flexible and pragmatic than most. Avoiding a commitment to one specific social plan, it experimented with varying forms of cooperative life, making itself a laboratory in which virtually every formula known to the times was put to the test. And it reflected the great moral ferment that enlivened New England during the half-century before the Civil War, a ferment associated with temperance, abolitionism, woman's rights, millenarianism, spiritualism, education, and other strivings to remake the world.

The Hopedale Community was also an effort by members of a small-town middle class to reshape small-town society so as to meet their cultural as well as economic needs, in the process protecting themselves from the tempting but also chaotic and corrupt world of big cities. Essentially, they tried—as many others were to try over the next century—to miniaturize the urban-industrial society developing around them so as to incorporate modern advantages into a stable community they could control. Toward this end, they often adapted practices common to the town developers of their day, demonstrating that Christian socialists could also be boosters and promoters.

Hopedale was thus a highly interesting social and religious adventure in search of a better tomorrow, an adventure inspired by perhaps the least adequately appreciated of the major socioreligious thinkers of his times, Adin Ballou. Given Ballou's central importance at Hopedale, it may seem that it was his personal experiment, but this was only partly true. Even more than his better known contemporary John Humphrey Noyes, he was less a dominating, charismatic leader than a practical visionary who led by rational persuasion and ruled by consensus, allowing for much active participation by his followers—women as well as men—in decisions affecting their lives.

Basically, this book recounts the efforts made by one extraordinary man and a group of ordinary people to work out the living details of a Christian socialism for themselves and, ultimately, for all America. Beyond that, it is also a story that recapitulates the history of idealism, of an inspired society successful enough to assure its own failure; and it is the story of how the religious devotion of some helped lay the foundations for the industrial wealth of others. Thus the history of Hopedale as godly community and as company town is a history of a social adventure that has significance for all seasons and ages.

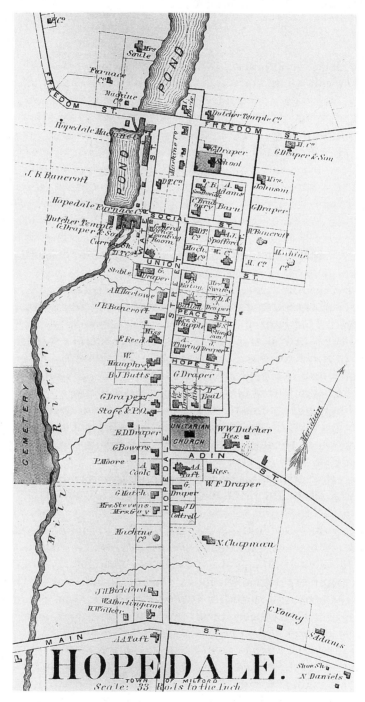

Courtesy of the American Antiquarian Society

1

The Road to Hopedale

The Hopedale Community was the most enduring of several efforts in New England during the 1840s to establish the good society in a corrupted world. It was an element in a great socioreligious ferment that inspired thousands of New Englanders to dream anew some version of the old Puritan dream of creating a truly godly community. Although overshadowed by Brook Farm, Hopedale as a social experiment outlived its better publicized rival by a decade. It, too, eventually failed, but only after the power of its governing faith had transformed a barren farm into a successful village—a village that eventually took the search for a good society into drastically different times. That it succeeded as it did resulted not from fortuitous circumstance but from the characters and the vision of the people who created it.

Why do such people—only the few—make the risky, difficult, and ultimately frustrated effort to establish the City of God in this world? Although the effort might be attributed to some irrational "fanaticism," the founders of Hopedale were generally rational people committed to a social vision that, while unimaginable to most of their contemporaries, had evolved from their immediate culture and experience during a time of religious ferment. This was especially the case with their longtime leader and spokesman, Adin Ballou, a man of modern reason as well as deep religious devotion.

Near the end of his long, creative life, Ballou was discovered by Leo Tolstoy, the Russian novelist and mystic, who predicted that he would be "in the future acknowledged as one of the great benefactors of mankind."[1] With this one exception, however, Ballou never achieved much public notice, in part because he spent virtually all

1

his years in a corner of New England that was obscured by the blaze of Boston and Concord and of Lowell and New Bedford. In terms of conventional success, Ballou judged himself a failure. "My hopes were too urgent and sanguine," he wrote in his *Autobiography*, "my standard and aim were set too high for immediate realization. So have I been defeated in some of my noblest schemes."[2] And yet he remained confident that he had, through reasonable deduction from concrete experience, found the God-given religious and social principles whose truth and beauty would ultimately convert the world.

Adin Ballou was born on 23 April 1803 in Cumberland, the most northerly town in Rhode Island, in an area heavily populated by the descendents of Maturin Ballou, a Huguenot and an associate of Roger Williams in the founding of the original colony.[3] By the early nineteenth century, the Ballou clan had begun to scatter in search of opportunity. One of them, James Ballou, moved first to the wilderness of New Hampshire and then to Ohio, where his daughter, Eliza, eventually became the mother of a future president, James Garfield. Adin's father, Ariel, however, chose to remain in his native region, where he was a man of substance, the owner not only of a large farm but of a sawmill and a cider mill. Although Cumberland was largely a farming town, it was not wholly isolated from changing times, since the Blackstone River on its western border furnished the waterpower for many of the early cotton mills established by Samuel Slater; the village of Woonsocket, less than ten miles from Ballou's birthplace, was soon to develop into an industrial center.[4]

Ariel Ballou himself invested some two thousand dollars in borrowed money in the establishment of a woolens mill on the Mill River immediately above its juncture with the Blackstone, a venture that also employed his eight-year-old son as a mill boy. Although Adin's factory experience lasted for only a few months, most of his life was destined to be spent in the mill towns of the Blackstone Valley and its tributaries. Decades later, a radical critic of industrialism was to write of the "brave little" Blackstone that "all the way between Worcester and Providence it is tugging at the wheel of Corporations, and summons its thousands of operatives to serve and slave under its despotism of machinery." In these earlier and simpler years, though, these towns retained a strong rural character that set them apart from the great manufacturing centers of the industrial age.[5]

Ballou's father was a disciplinarian who expected obedience and hard work from his children, but he was not indifferent to their needs. Adin, who early showed a bookish disposition, was given all the formal education the area provided, three months a year in the local school until he was fifteen. Although the boy had access to only a few books and newspapers, he made the most of them and of whatever other sources of education he could find. Eventually, he wanted to go to Brown University, only to be told by his father, "I am too much in debt." All Adin received was a last few months of formal education at an academy in Franklin, Massachusetts. Later he was to conclude that his inability to attend the university had saved him from falling into "some popular channel of respectability and renown." Instead of acquiring a conventional education, he was left free to form from his own experiences "the independent convictions, principles, and aims now so sacred to me."[6]

Ballou found his best school in the local world of religion, which came to a boil during his youth. When he was ten, the area was enlivened by the "Reformation," one of many local outbursts of revivalism that broke out in southern New England under the influence of the Second Great Awakening. The revival caused great excitement and produced nearly a hundred converts in Cumberland. Once the original enthusiasm subsided, most people slid back into their old ways; but even if it disappointed hopes for a complete change of heart, the revival had an enlightening influence on the town, producing what Ballou later called "a wholesome agitation of thought" that "awakened inquiry, investigation, and a progressive exercise of understanding."[7] Whatever its effects on others, this agitation opened a great religious channel for his developing thought that he would follow for the rest of his life.

In 1813 Ballou's awakened parents joined the Christian Connexion, a new dissenting faith that rejected any religious authority other than Christ and any test of church membership other than Christian character. This denial of the authority of clerics and of dogmas became the hallmark of Ballou's adult career, but what was of more immediate importance was the stand taken by this faith on the nature of the afterlife. The rebellion against orthodoxy often challenged the old view that sinners were condemned to eternal punishment after death, leading some radicals to reject the doctrine of endless punishment in favor of the idea that God would save everyone. The Christian Connexion, however, refused to accept universal salvation and adopted the more conservative idea that the souls of departed sinners would simply be annihilated, thereby preserving heaven only for the faithful.[8]

This "Destructionism" helped to stimulate young Ballou's interest in religion. By the time he finished his schooling in his sixteenth year, he seemed destined for the ministry. It was not a destiny that he was yet willing to accept, however. He had absorbed at least some of the widespread contempt for ministers, "a pitiable class" by the world's standards, and he had agonizing doubts about his own abilities to succeed in the pulpit. On the other hand, his parents were proud of his evident talent for religion, and he had no other career in prospect. The absence of a career acquired serious importance when at seventeen he became engaged to Abby Sayles, who was three years his senior. What to do? As would happen during later occasions of psychological distress, he found his answer in a vision: one night he awoke to see before him the glowing specter of his dead brother, Cyrus, who told him that "God commands you to preach the Gospel of Christ to your fellow man." Soon after, he forced himself to give a sermon at the local "Ballou Meeting House" (where his father was a deacon), which soon led to his appointment as minister of the congregation.[9]

Over the next few years the young preacher acquired local notice, particularly as a defender of Destructionism against the advocates of both endless punishment and universal salvation. When he was eighteen, he won more general attention when he published a critical review of the writings of Hosea Ballou, a distant cousin and a champion of Universalism. This review established him as a leading advocate for the Christian Connexion, but it also drew him into a lengthy debate with the Universalists, whose arguments began to weaken his belief in Destructionism. For the first time, Ballou was forced to submit his own convictions to one of the most essential tenets of his developing faith, that any belief should be subject to rational criticism. Later, in writing about these times he declared,

"My religion teaches me to be afraid of nothing but sin—to hear, read, examine—to 'prove all things and hold fast that which is good.'" After rereading the Bible in the light of the Universalist arguments, he publicly admitted that they were right and Destructionism was wrong.[10]

This proved to be more than a simple act of intellectual courage, since it antagonized his congregation; even his father threatened to disinherit him unless he recanted. Although he did not fulfill this threat, Ariel Ballou did support the decision of the congregation to disavow publicly his apostate son. Having been disowned by the Christian Connexion, young Ballou had no choice but to join the Universalists. This decision soon led to more conflict when the new Universalist began to preach in the small towns of southern Massachusetts. At Bellingham, he persuaded the authorities to allow him to use the town meetinghouse one week a month, only to become embroiled in a controversy with a local Baptist minister, who objected to any use of the house by one whom he condemned as no more than "a deist under a mask." The affair culminated in a ludicrous tussle between the two for control of the meeting place, which ended in Ballou's retreat but not his surrender. Characteristically, he responded with an act of peaceful aggressiveness. In his first published work, *The Furious Priest Reproved* (1823), the young minister launched a verbal assault on the Baptist preacher for failing to follow the example of "the meek and lowly Jesus" in the Christian policy of "love, tranquility, and order."[11] Throughout his career, he refused to be passive in his pursuit of harmony and peace.

Ballou was to find all too little love or tranquillity in these intensely religious times, but his decision to join the Universalists did lead him into a larger and more significant fellowship than he had known before. Although it had only a small following when measured against the established churches, Universalism was a growing faith that by the late 1830s claimed at least eighty ministers in Massachusetts alone. By 1823 Ballou had escaped from the narrow world of his boyhood to become the minister for the Universalist society at Milford, Massachusetts. He was to spend most of the next half-century within twenty miles of Milford.[12]

Universalism introduced Ballou to a general optimism regarding the world and the future. Its doctrine of universal salvation reflected its larger faith in the existence of a benevolent God who would, in the words of its 1803 statement of belief, "finally restore the whole family of mankind to holiness and happiness." Horace Greeley, another independent Yankee thinker influenced by Universalism, described its hopeful effects on him: "Once conceive that an Omniscient Beneficence presides over and directs the entire course of human affairs, leading ever onward and upward to universal purity and bliss, and all evil becomes phenominal and preparative—a mere curtain or passing cloud which hides for a moment the light of the celestial and eternal day."[13]

Ballou said later that his conversion came after he had experienced "a vision of the final triumph of good over evil." Universalism consolidated his maturing confidence that the world was inherently rational and progressive, the work of a God "of love and justice, of benevolence and truth." God had given to every person a soul, a dynamic and rational spirit, which he expected eventually to perfect itself. Souls were of inestimable value, created with the intention not that they should sin and be punished but "that they should exist and flourish in the enjoyment of happiness, and rise from knowledge to knowledge, from bliss to bliss through endless ages." In Ballou's idea of a spiritual economy, it was as foolish as it was malevolent for God to create souls simply either to punish or to destroy them. Rather, the Creator intended that they all participate in the ultimate attainment of universal holiness and happiness.[14]

Ballou, however, had more faith in Universalism than he did in the thinking of leading Universalists, many of whom held to what he called the "ultra" view that there would be no punishment in the afterlife for even the worst of sinners, the afflictions of sin being confined entirely to this world. He was uncomfortable with a doctrine that threatened his idea of moral responsibility and accountability. While he was prepared to accept the *eventual* salvation of all persons, his sense of justice rebelled at the idea that even the most unrepentant sinner would, with death, escape punishment. This, he believed, was an issue of "radical and vital importance," one that was soon to furnish another guidepost for his pilgrimage.[15]

He did little about it, however, until his private life abruptly changed. In 1828, while away from his family, he dreamed that his first wife lay dead beside a newborn baby. When he later described this dream, he called it a gloomy premonition, and such it proved to be. Less than a year later, three weeks after the birth of his second child, Abby Ballou died following a period of deteriorating health. Ballou was shaken by the loss, but not for long. A year later, he married Lucy Hunt, the nineteen-year-old daughter of the most prominent member of his congregation.[16]

There is no indication that he felt any guilt over having lost a sickly wife who was three years older than he and gained one who was not only eight years younger but better suited to his expanding interests. This change, however, may have intensified his growing interest in moral practice. Sometime between his bereavement and his remarriage he had succeeded after much prayer and effort in freeing himself from "the filthy, harmful, and reprehensible practice of smoking."[17] Over the next decade, his concern with practical moral behavior evolved into a deep commitment to what he came to call "practical Christianity."

However much this tendency was influenced by Ballou's home life, it was certainly fundamental to his resolution of the theological question that had dominated his earlier years. As a young minister, he had taken the leap from Destructionist to Universalist in his views of the afterlife. Now he resolved to make another leap by opposing the then dominant Universalist doctrine of no punishment for sin after death. He rejected this "ultra" doctrine on the grounds that it not only denied the moral responsibility of mankind but also weakened "the thread of continuity between this life and the next." In defense of what he believed was the essential moral order of God's creation, he argued that the sinful soul would suffer after death in order to purge it of its sinful tendencies; although God would "sooner or later" restore all people to their intended place in heaven, for sinners it would be later rather than sooner. Ballou believed that this "Restorationist" view made for a dynamic moral order in which humankind, guided by the precepts of Christ, would participate in realizing God's ultimate plan for "a full end of sin and misery" throughout creation.[18]

In 1830 he began to publish a Restorationist weekly, The *Independent Messenger*, with himself as its editor, beginning what proved to be thirty years of religious journalism. His need for a press to print the *Messenger* soon brought him into partnership with the first of those who would later help him form the Hopedale Community, George W. Stacy, previously publisher of the *Groton Herald*. After pledging any profits "to the establishment of a liberal literary institution for the education of youth," Ballou began his newspaper with the promise that he would devote it to religious truth, free inquiry, civil and religious liberty, and efforts "to amend the hearts, enlighten the understanding, refine the sentiments, and ennoble the minds of mankind."[19]

Less than a month after he began this new venture, Ballou's largely ultraist congregation at Milford fired him. Essentially exiled from Universalism in general, he soon found a new home and friends. In 1831 he and his fellow rebels organized the Massachusetts Association of Restorationists to promote belief in "Future Rewards and Punishment, to be followed by the Final Restoration of all men to holiness and happiness." Outside of Restorationism, Ballou had also begun to attract the interest of various other liberal Christians, especially some of the Unitarians in the area, and within a few months after his firing he was appointed minister of the First Congregational (Unitarian) Church at nearby Mendon. While he continued to insist that he was only defending Universalism from the "modern" perversions of the ultras, he had in fact left it behind him.[20]

Mendon was to be his home for the next decade. Although this town on the Mill River was then one of the largest and most thriving in southern Massachusetts, his new church was neither large nor thriving, having lost most of its membership to a conservative revival in the area. Over the next years, Ballou was able to rebuild it, chiefly by attracting those who, for varied reasons, "had drifted away from the established institutions of religion." He was an energetic and innovative minister who, among his other works, persuaded his congregation to abandon their traditional Yankee prejudice against the celebration of Christmas and to have a special evening service in honor of Christ's birth.[21]

These were often trying years. In February 1833 his two sons died from scarlet fever, leaving him the only comfort of a bereaved father: "Where immortal spirits reign / There shall we meet again." It is notable that when he later wrote of this tragedy, his thoughts were of the earthly future as well as the afterlife: "The causes, preventives, and cure of disease will no doubt be better known in future ages than at present, and such knowledge will, I believe, deliver our human race from most of the pain, suffering, and premature death that now afflict it." Knowledge did not come fast enough, however. In the summer of 1833 Ballou was comforted by the birth of another son, who, along with his daughter, Abbie, became his pride—only eventually also to lose this boy to disease, at the very beginning of manhood.[22]

Tragedy intensified his interest in a practical Christianity. In 1831 he had written that "we deem true morality the natural *offspring* and only demonstrable evidence of pure religion." He came to believe that the only real Christian was one who conformed both his spirit and his earthly behavior to moral principle. Initially, this meant little more than the morality of conventional Calvinism. After having broken himself of the habit of using tobacco, he became a confirmed advocate of total abstinence from any kind of alcohol except for medicinal purposes, and he took an increasing interest in "moral reform," meaning opposition to every form of sexual "licentiousness." Increasingly, though, his moral concerns came to involve not simply the improvement of individual human character but also the betterment of the human social condition in the interests of freedom and happiness. Through total abstinence in particular, he was exposed to dreams of a radically better world, to a millennial vision of a happy land freed from corrupting and debilitating drunkenness.[23]

His first expressed social concern reflected his fundamental conservatism. In 1830 he condemned much of the public press for spewing out "torrents of falsehood" threatening to the good order and welfare of society, and he proposed the formation of "Newspaper Temperance Societies" to boycott those newspapers not committed to truth and morality. Ballou's social interests took a radical turn, however, when he discovered abolitionism. Previously, he had considered slavery to be a distant sin beyond his immediate moral concerns, but the often violent persecution of abolitionists in the 1830s convinced him otherwise. Before long, he concluded that John Wesley was right in condemning slavery as "the sum of all villainies," and he joined the ranks of the Garrisonian abolitionists. This movement significantly broadened his thinking regarding freedom and equality. Having decided that the essential wrong of slavery was that it prevented personal moral development, he became an advocate of equal freedom and responsibility for all regardless of race or sex, thereby giving new depth and meaning to his belief in the brotherhood of mankind. By the end of the decade, his thoughts had shifted from heaven to earth, toward the hope of attaining, through the reform of society, freedom for all men and women to strive for holiness and happiness in this world.[24]

This tendency was brought into focus by his discovery, through Garrisonian abolitionism, of the doctrine of nonresistance. Nonresistants believed that God, acting through Jesus, had introduced a revolutionary new principle into human society by supplanting the old Hebraic practice of "an eye for an eye" with the injunction to love all, even one's enemies. In their view, the new law forbade physical resistance against anyone, including one's most threatening foes. They were not passivists, since they believed in the aggressive use of spiritual force, the active promotion of the good and true against every kind of sin. Physical force, however, they repudiated in any form, from the armed violence of war to attempts to coerce a person into doing anything he was not willing to do.[25]

Initially, Ballou found the doctrine too radical for his tastes, but as he had done with other new ideas, he examined it in the light of both faith and reason and soon concluded that it was right. In 1839 he appeared at the annual meeting of Garrison's New England Non-Resistance Society, where he gave such an effective exposition of the doctrine that he was accepted as one of its leading advocates. Over the next few years, he developed nonresistance into a coherent moral philosophy, notably in his book *Christian Non-Resistance* (1846). He attempted to make the simple biblical principle "resist not evil" into a practical basis for human behavior. God, he believed, had chosen through Jesus's character and words to express a basic truth which if practiced by men would establish a Christian paradise. Nonresistance, in his view, was not simply a test of one's preparation for the afterlife but the practical basis for the kind of life that God had intended for man on earth and in a regenerated world.[26]

Ballou rejected the prevailing contention that violence was often a necessary and natural act of self-defense on the grounds that the practice of responding to evil with evil only enflamed the danger. He agreed that self-preservation was a natural instinct, but he denied that injurious force was the way to preserve life. Over the course of recorded history, "how happens it that, according to the lowest possible estimate, some fourteen thousand millions of human beings have been slain by human means, in war and otherwise?" Not all the uncontested murders and robberies in history could have produced anything like that havoc. In general, the armies, crusades, prisons, and gallows through which profane men had attempted to conquer evil had only produced more corruption and misery. The best hope for humanity, then, lay in a full commitment to nonresistance.[27]

Although he did accept some use of nonviolent force—to restrain a maniac, for instance—Ballou believed that the world could be saved only by moral power, which "operates on the affections, passions, reason, and moral sentiments of mankind and thereby *controls* them without *physical force*." Moral power was pervasive and creative, even in contrast with the legitimate force of government:

> Moral power unites male and female in marriage, multiplies human beings, subdues the earth, increases wealth, forms neighborhoods, and builds cities. Political power takes the census, levies taxes, trains soldiers to do its fighting, and assumes the office of protecting the people. Moral power educates the people intellectually, religiously, morally, socially, and industrially. Political power tickles their ambition, uses up their substance, and punishes a few of their grosser crimes.[28]

He rejected the prevailing political institutions of existing society. At the beginning of the decade, he had expressed the hope that "our most excellent form of government be perpetuated with all its ultimate blessings." Now he concluded that it was a Christian's duty to withdraw from government because it supported war, slavery, capital punishment, and other acts of violence. To hold office or even to vote was, therefore, to sanction violence.[29] On the other hand, he did not advocate either resistance to government or even a complete disassociation from it. A Christian could make use of legal titles to property, patent inventions, and pay general taxes, provided that such things did not make him an accomplice in violence.

Ballou was careful to disavow the extreme anarchist implications of nonresistance: "We are not anti-socialists, nor insurrectionists. We know mankind are by nature social beings, and will associate somehow. . . . The method whereby social organization in a nation, state, or community executes its aggregate will is government." [30] He could at least dream of a truly Christian government and of a politics not of injurious force but of redeeming love and moral power.

Whatever his hopes for government, however, he was becoming much too radical for most of his Restorationist colleagues. When the Restorationist Association held its annual meeting in 1837, he submitted a series of resolutions for moral reform that began with the declaration that "it has pleased God in these latter days to awaken the special attention of the people to the prevailing vices, iniquities and corruptions of the age, and to excite them to extraordinary efforts for the reformation and improvement of their fellow men." Many of his colleagues, however, seemed more interested in building a new religious denomination than in acting like Christians, and the resolutions were not submitted to a vote. By 1839 his new commitment to nonresistance deepened the split between himself and the conservatives, virtually assuring the breakdown of the Restorationist Association. [31]

Again, however, he won new friends and associates, men and women who this time would accompany him to the end of his pilgrimage. As his local reputation grew, his home at Mendon became, as he called it later, "a sort of cabinet or place of resort for all kinds of reformers," among them a number of people who shared his deepening devotion to a practical Christianity. Although Ballou was the leader of the group, he was far less a dominating figure than the first among equals, influenced by the ideas and enthusiasms of the others. Generally, this group was made up of the siftings from the reform-minded middle class of the Blackstone Valley, young townsmen of some talent and ambition who mixed with their religious concerns at least some anxiety over the depressed times that followed the Panic of 1837. [32]

The most fateful of this group, since he became the most persistent mainstay of the Hopedale Community, was Ebenezer D. Draper of nearby Uxbridge, a textile town whose principal mill had been thrown into bankruptcy by the panic. Eleven years younger than Ballou, Draper, the son of a Yankee inventor, combined a deep interest in morality with some practical business experience. In 1834 he had married Anna Thwing, who also was to become a significant member of Hopedale, as was her brother, Almon—another man with notable practical skills. By 1837 Draper's involvement with both temperance and abolitionism had led him to join Ballou's Mendon congregation, beginning a friendship that was to last for nearly fifty years. It was probably through Draper's influence that William W. Cook, a young resident of Uxbridge and later a successful florist, joined the group.[33]

The Uxbridge group brought a variety of skills and interests that made the building of Hopedale possible, but they were overshadowed in the beginning by several young ministers who constituted what Ballou called the "progressive" wing of Restorationism. Among them was his earlier associate in religious journalism, George Stacy, who had become a Restorationist minister at Carlisle, Massachusetts; in 1837, before his conversion to nonresistance, he had served for a term in the state legislature. Probably the most aggressively individualistic of Ballou's associates, Stacy was an ardent come-outer who hoped to liberate society from what he called "mental slavery" to sects and organized churches.[34]

Another minister who hungered for freedom was Daniel R. Lamson. A restless soul, Lamson had begun his ministry at Berlin, Massachusetts, in 1834, but by 1840 he was teaching school in West Boylston, where, so he claimed, he and his wife were persecuted for their religious views. Ballou found a far steadier associate in Daniel S. Whitney, a lifelong advocate of temperance, abolitionism, and rights for women. Although he eventually left the Hopedale experiment, Whitney was long remembered by Ballou as "a man of intelligence, sterling rectitude and honor," who made notable contributions to the cause of a practical Christianity.[35]

Ballou's staunchest ministerial ally was William Henry Fish, a fellow Rhode Islander. Born in Newport in 1812, Fish became a Restorationist soon after meeting Ballou in 1834. Three years later, with the latter's support, he became minister of a mixed Restorationist and Unitarian congregation at Millville, where he had frequent contacts with his mentor at nearby Mendon. Like the others, he was a devout abolitionist and nonresistant. More than the rest, he was a visionary who saw in the radical religious ferment of his times the promise of a radically better life for man: "Our age is certainly a peculiarily interesting one," Fish wrote in 1840. "Does it not bear a strange resemblance to that in which the Savior dwelt in the flesh, than any one that has preceded it for centuries?" He did not believe in a literal reappearance of Christ on the Blackstone or anywhere else, but he was confident that the rising agitation against evil signaled the return of Christ's regenerative spirit, whose influence could create a heaven among men. "Human life, I know," he wrote in 1844, "might be as beautiful and as blessed as the 'angels'—a life of prosperity, of peace, of improvement—a life of intelligence and love."[36] That was the founding spirit of Hopedale.

The road to Hopedale began to open in 1839 when, under the influence of nonresistance, Ballou and his loyal band decided to make a determined commitment to actually living their ideal of a thoroughly Christian life. At least since his acceptance of total abstinence in the early 1830s, Ballou had pondered the problem of converting intentions to do good into actual practice. He concluded that what was needed were clearly defined specific acts of virtue to which the individual would uncompromisingly pledge to conform his behavior. Not trusting the ability of the isolated person to maintain this commitment, he had also decided that some form of voluntary cooperation was needed to support individual moral behavior. In the spring of 1839 he met with Fish, Lamson, Stacy, and Whitney to work out a detailed plan of Christian moral conduct, "a faithful epitome of what is laid down in the New Testament to guide the practice of professed Christians." The result was a prolix "Standard of Practical Christianity," which they pledged to follow in every particular; signing the pledge with them were two laymen, William W. Cook and Charles Gladding, a young tailor from Millville.[37]

The new Practical Christians declared that "our grand object is the restoration of man, especially the most fallen and friendless. Our immediate concern is the promotion of useful knowledge, moral improvement, and Christian perfection." They then listed the things that as Christians they were pledged not to do, a list that clearly reflected the influence of the moral reform movements to which they had committed themselves in the 1830s, especially total abstinence, abolitionism, and nonresistance. Eventually, they condensed their statement into a more readable "Declaration," which bound each signer

> never under any pretext whatever to kill, assault, beat, torture, rob, oppress, defraud, corrupt, slander, revile, injure, envy or hate any human being—*even my worst enemy*; never in any manner to take or administer any oath, never to manufacture, buy, sell, or use any intoxicating *liquor as a beverage*; never to serve in the army, navy, or militia of any nation, state, or chieftain; never to bring action at law, hold office, vote, join a legal posse, petition a legislature, or ask governmental interpositions in *any case involving a final authorized resort to physical violence*; never to indulge self-will, bigotry, love of pre-eminence, covetousness, deceit, profanity, idleness, or an unruly tongue; never to participate in lotteries, games of chance, betting, or pernicious amusements; never to resent reproof or justify myself in a known wrong; never to aid, abet or approve others in anything sinful but through divine assistance always to recommend and promote with my entire influence the holiness and happiness of mankind.[38]

Ballou and his friends intended the "Standard" to be a platform for a true Christian church as well as a basis for their own personal action. In their view, they were not attempting to found a new religious sect. Rather, they had compiled truths on which Christianity, riven by arid sectarian conflicts over doctrinal matters, could be reunited so that it might resume its mission to regenerate the world. To disseminate their views, they began, in April 1840, to publish a biweekly newspaper, the *Practical Christian*, devoted to "a faithful exposition, defence, and promulgation of Primitive Christianity." Included in the first issue was the Standard of Christianity supported by a thicket of footnoted references to passages in the Bible; the first paragraph alone had nineteen footnotes. As editor of the fledgling paper, Ballou admitted that its backers were "few in numbers and feeble in resources," but he found much hope in the essential righteousness of their cause.[39]

Undoubtedly, the Practical Christians hoped to reap an abundant harvest of recruits from the growing number of religious rebels in New England who had "come-out" from the established religions.

Under the spur of anxious but hopeful times, the come-outers had determined to take their pursuit of holiness outside of what they took to be corrupted churches and a corrupt society, following the biblical injunction "come out of her my people, that ye partake not of her sins." When in August 1840 the radicals gathered for a "Christian Union" convention at Groton in northern Massachusetts, some of the Practical Christians attended. They were disappointed, however, by the manifest lack of unity among the delegates and by the limited interest in their cause.[40] In other respects, too, the first year of their missionary effort seems to have had little effect beyond a few conversions in the immediate vicinity.

For more than twenty years, they were to cling to the hope that they could transform the governing spirit of the existing social order and so make the practice of true Christianity possible, but these early disappointments seemed to indicate that society had rendered people blind to the Christian promise. The oppressiveness of conventional religion hit close to home when in 1840 Lamson's wife, Mary, was expelled from her church because of her Unitarian views. For this as well as for other reasons, Ballou had also begun to feel oppressed by a situation under which "we of the nominal Christian ministry and church *lived down* faster than we could talk up true righteousness."[41] In existing society, then, how could even the devout be able to conform their own lives to the Standard of Practical Christianity?

By 1840 these disappointments and the economically depressed times had begun to inspire thoughts of coming-out from the existing order and of creating new social conditions suited to a holy life. In September 1839 Ballou had concluded a long speech on nonresistance by attempting to picture how a nonresistant majority would manage the affairs of society: "They will propose measures, discuss them in friendship, and come to a conclusion in favor of the best— without wounding personal vanity or breeding a quarrel with each other's selfishness. The law of love and wisdom will prevail without strife, and all be eager to contribute their full share of expense and effort." At the time, he intended nothing more than a rather pious illustration of the practicality of nonresistance, but illustration led easily to thoughts of actually demonstrating that such behavior was possible. Initially, the Practical Christians considered buying a farm to serve as "a sort of missionary outpost," but the idea soon grew into a dream of establishing independent communities for all of the faithful.[42]

Ballou first unveiled the dream in the 15 September 1840 issue of the *Practical Christian*, after noting that there had been much discussion among "our brethren" on the subject of establishing communities. The leading idea, he said, was to establish "a compact neighborhood or village of practical Christians, dwelling together by families in love and peace, insuring themselves the comforts of life by agricultural and mechanical industry and directing the entire residue of their intellectual, moral and physical resources to the Christianization and general welfare of the human race." Although Ballou did not try to provide all the details of such a community, he did emphasize that it would be firmly grounded in the Standard of Practical Christianity. He concluded the article in a burst of millennial enthusiasm:

> If one such community could be established, the number might be indefinitely multiplied over the whole face of the earth, till at length the kingdom of the earth should be absorbed into the glorious kingdom of our Lord Jesus Christ. Then the reign of ignorance, selfishness, pride and violence will be terminated among men, and the whole great brotherhood of our race dwell together in peace, under the immediate government of Him, to whom belongeth the kingdom, power and glory forever.[43]

By this time Ballou had become convinced that God had made such a millennial state available to humankind. However, having decided, as he said later, that "we must try to build a new civilization radically higher than the old," he and his followers had to confront the problem of actually beginning the first community.[44] How could the Standard of Practical Christianity be realized in practical social form? And how could a group as limited in its earthly resources as it was in numbers find the money needed to launch even the holiest social experiment? The effort to resolve such questions delayed the beginning of Hopedale by more than a year; the answers were imperfect, but they proved good enough to inaugurate one of America's more successful attempts to create a community at peace with its God.

2

A Christian Socialism?

The founding of the Hopedale Community was part of a much larger striving in New England and elsewhere to find a new basis for society. By 1840 economically depressed times had excited efforts to escape from defective social institutions as well as from corrupted churches. In 1846 William Henry Fish wrote that "the community enterprise" had been initiated simultaneously in various places "by men who had never had any intercourse or acquaintance with each other." Fish believed that this expressed a growing hunger for some fundamental social reform:

> The old order of society had come to be felt, by many of the most progressive class of minds, to be selfish and burdensome, and they could not, with easy consciences, longer sustain it—at least without trying for something better. They saw that labor was unequally divided—that property was—that nearly all the conveniences and luxuries of life were; and that this was wrong—*unquestionably wrong*.

Horace Greeley, a leading "progressive" mind and editor of the *New York Tribune*, made the same point when he included Hopedale among various experiments in "Socialism," a new term that he defined as an effort to apply "Christianity to the Social Relations of mankind."[1]

It was much easier, however, to condemn existing society than it was to agree on the fundamentals of the new social order, as Adin Ballou quickly discovered. When Ballou published his preliminary plan for a community in September 1840, he excited the interests of other progressives, notably George Ripley and his fellow Transcendentalists, who had grown increasingly uneasy with the gap between the ideal and the real. Ripley, who was in October to announce his resignation from the ministry and soon after to launch Brook Farm, apparently had already begun to discuss the idea of a model community with the Practical Christians. On 18 October Henry Wadsworth Longfellow, a rather befuddled bystander, reported that the "Out-and-Outers" had "formed a holy alliance with the Transcendentalists. Out of this fermentation of mind has sprung up a new plan, namely to form a new community, to be called 'The Practical Christians.'" Whatever chance there was for an alliance, however, was nullified by the refusal of some of the Transcendentalists to accept the Standard of Practical Christianity as the required basis of the community, although Ripley himself seemed disposed toward such a test.[2]

This disagreement involved a critical question that was frequently to disrupt socialism over the next century. Although many might dream of a society founded on brotherhood, they disagreed over who were qualified to be members of that brotherhood. Transcendentalists rejected the Standard as a condition for membership because they believed it exalted conformity to law over spirit. Their position was stated by Elizabeth Peabody in Emerson's *Dial* in 1841. Peabody praised Ballou's plan as reflecting "a deep insight into the Christian ideal" but criticized the Standard as failing Christ's ideal of a "world-embracing church" open to all: "This can be founded on nothing short of faith in the universal man, as he comes out of the hands of the Creator with no law over his liberty but the Eternal Ideas that lie at the foundation of his Being." For Transcendentalists like Emerson, even exalting Christ as a model of human behavior limited what they believed was the infinite potential of the human self, which should be freed from the confinement of all creeds and institutions.[3]

The Transcendentalists were among various critics who decided that the Practical Christians were simply another religious sect whose membership requirements would exclude the great majority of the human race from a paradise that rightly belonged to all. Ballou insisted, however, that these requirements were nonsectarian, since they did not demand adherence to Restorationism or to any other of the various theologies that had long disrupted Christianity.

Above all, they were not dogmas to which the mind must conform: at Hopedale, there was to be freedom of thought and belief, the continuation of a dissenting tradition that extended back to Roger Williams, and one on which Ballou depended in his own search for ultimate truth.[4]

If there was to be a community of "free minds," though, its members were obligated to do "what was clearly right," since the good society could be realized only when people conformed their *behavior* to a clearly defined code of conduct. Ideally, conduct would be animated by the spirit of Christian love, but there had to be a practical basis and guide for that spirit. While some progressives believed that right behavior would result naturally from the liberated self, Ballou held that practical righteousness depended on the discipline of self, on a committed effort to rise above the imperfections of human nature. Convinced that the Standard required only the behavior that God had intended to produce human happiness and holiness, he saw nothing sectarian about making it a condition of membership: "Is he a sectarian because he wishes to found a community from which war, slavery, etc. are utterly excluded?"[5]

If society were ever to be regenerated, it would have to begin with a rightfully organized association of "all-sided saints." Ballou and his associates insisted that the ideal community depended ultimately on the moral commitments of individuals rather than on social contrivances, but they also believed that humans were social beings who needed some form of social organization.[6] Having decided to make the Standard the basis for their radically new civilization, they wrestled with the problem of creating a social framework for their moral principles. They investigated various plans of social organization, held frequent discussions, and in late January 1841 completed their "Constitution of the Fraternal Communion," a general plan for a national association of "Christian commonwealths" that they expected sympathetic Americans to form throughout the nation.[7]

They had to resolve the particularly difficult problem of the ownership and management of property, a central problem for both Hopedale and social radicalism in general. "The question of property will divide us into odious parties," wrote Emerson in September 1840. "And all of us must face it & take our part. A good man finds himself excluded from all lucrative works. He has no farm & he cannot get one." In industrializing and modernizing New England, individual and local autonomy was giving way before a new economic order in which virtually everyone was becoming dependent on forces beyond his or her control.[8] During the depressed times that afflicted many areas by the late 1830s, some thinkers were led to reconsider established ideas regarding property. If, as it seemed, the rich and powerful were devoting their possessions to their own aggrandizement at the expense of their fellow citizens, what could be done to assure the average man a share of property? In a society increasingly dominated by the wealthy few, how best to protect the welfare of the straitened many? By 1840 these questions, which were demanding attention throughout the modernizing North Atlantic world, had begun to attract the notice of religious radicals in the Blackstone Valley.

Ballou and his associates were generally conservative on economic matters, but they concluded that the times demanded an answer to the property question if their Christian commonwealth was ever to become a reality. Although they continued to emphasize the necessity of individual moral commitment, they were coming to believe that even the dedicated could not live truly Christian lives so long as property was left to the exclusive control of individuals. The growing gap between rich and poor, as well as the selfish striving and antagonistic competition for wealth, made for a society in which the practice of human brotherhood was impossible. The scramble for individual property, Ballou wrote later, was "engendering discontent, ill-will, resentment, animosity, hatred, and sometimes the spirit of revenge and open violence."[9] If a society of loving, moral citizens was ever to become a reality, some way had to be found to Christianize and socialize property, to make it work for rather than against the Standard of Practical Christianity.

One way was already familiar to social radicals. In previous decades, they had looked to common ownership, to the collective possession of property for the good of all on the basis of personal needs. Robert Owen had experimented with this common-stock idea at New Harmony with disastrous results, but the idea had been put into notably successful practice by the Shakers, whose communities involved both common ownership and the basic communistic formula of wealth distribution: from each on the basis of ability, to each on the basis of need.[10] Since the Shakers had seemingly grown ever more prosperous during previous decades, their communism won considerable attention from religious and social radicals, including the Practical Christians. In early 1841 one of Ballou's followers told him that the common-stock principle was "a sovereign cure for covetousness" and that individual rights to property could not exist in a Christian commonwealth.[11]

Ballou and most of his associates, however, were the products of a provincial middle-class culture oriented toward individual initiative and property. When Ballou first proposed the idea of Christian communities, he specifically rejected the Shakers as a model, in large part because he believed their system suppressed individual freedom and responsibility. Previously, he had made individual moral obligation the cornerstone of his Restorationism; now he made it an essential ingredient of his ideal community: "We go for unabridged *individuality* of mind, conscience, duty and responsibility." The next years deepened his aversion to communism into an outright loathing. Common-stock property, he wrote in 1841, "must have keepers and stewards, whom so much power will exalt and corrupt, whilst the majority habitually dependent for their food, clothes, and other comforts on the direction of these managers, will cower down, grow servile, lose all force of individual character, and finally become dull, unthinking drudges."[12] If communism was to be rejected, though, what then could guide the use of property toward Christian ends?

The Practical Christians tried to answer this question in their Constitution for the Fraternal Communion. On the one hand, they made "the honest acquisition of individual property" a basic goal. On the other hand, they limited that individual property to shares in a Christian joint-stock concern that would actually own and manage the land, residential properties, and productive enterprises of the community. Individual members of the Communion could buy or sell shares, and each would receive profits from the community proportionate to the number of shares he or she owned. In theory, all shareholders would have reason to contribute their work and talents to the enterprise, while at the same time the collective control of property, guided by the requirements of the Standard, would assure that individual energies would serve the happiness and holiness of the whole community.[13]

This form of Practical Christian socialism was to endure. Much less durable was an attempt to bring property into harmony with the principle of equality, to which the Fraternal Communion was pledged by its constitution: "All members of every community shall stand on a footing of *personal equality*, irrespective of sex, color, occupation, wealth, rank, or any other natural or adventitious peculiarity." Although the Shakers had practiced, and the Garrisonian abolitionists had supported, the principle of racial and sexual equality, this pledge was far ahead of any other constitutional commitment to equality at the time. Hopedale would long abide by it. It was soon to retreat, however, from the attempt to translate equality into economic terms by means of the constitutional provision that each member be paid a "uniform rate of wages" regardless of the nature or results of the work; similarly, members were to pay a uniform rate for housing, food, and other necessities.[14]

The fact that the constitution established any rates of reward and payment at all indicates that the Fraternal Communion had no intention of committing itself to pure communism, but even this partial commitment to economic equality was too extreme for Ballou, who said later that he had agreed to the wage provision only out of deference to the views of some of his associates. At the time, though, he did his best to defend it in the last part of his lengthy "Dissertation on the Fraternal Communion" published in three successive issues of the *Practical Christian*: "Thus the strong bear the affirmities of the weak—the more capable assist the less." It would, he said, assure that women would have equal pay with men, encourage the less competent to do their best, reinforce the benevolence of the more capable, and avoid the jealousies and resentments associated with unequal wages.[15]

Having completed their grand plan to regenerate the world, Ballou and his associates had to confront the need for hard cash to begin their first community. They were few and relatively poor, but they convinced themselves that the essential righteousness of their cause would bring success: "The *elect* of God for any great work of reform, are always *few*." To begin their work, they succeeded in getting three thousand dollars in subscriptions to the joint stock of the

Fraternal Communion; nearly half of the fifty-dollar shares were taken by Ballou and four of his followers in Mendon, and another quarter by two men in nearby Uxbridge. Like other would-be founders of communities, they soon discovered that their plan won more attention from those in need than from those in the money, and they ended their first year of effort with a distinctly warlike complaint that secret adversaries were "pulling every wire and turning every stone to defeat us."[16] By the summer of 1841, however, they had raised enough support to purchase a place for their experiment.

They considered buying a tract of cheap land in the West, but they decided to remain in their native region, "surrounded at a little distance by the estates, dwellings, and villages of our fellow men, where we can at all times hold intercourse with our relatives, friends and neighbors." In September they announced that they had contracted to buy a 258-acre farm located on both sides of the Mill River within the limits of the town of Milford. Although both the land and the buildings had been run down by decades of neglect, the farm had one notable asset, a twenty-four-foot fall in the river that could supply the waterpower sufficient for small-scale manufacturing. Waterpower not land was to be the central physical influence on their future; from the beginning, the City of God to which they aspired was to be a godly version of the mill towns that had marked the progress of their region. Long before, the place had been known as "the Dale," so they christened it Hope Dale. By the fall they had hired a surveyor to lay out the streets for the projected village and had issued an appeal for donations of "money, or cattle, or books, or building materials" to help begin its development.[17]

In March 1842 Ballou resigned his ministry at Mendon with a long discourse on the changes that had taken place in his thinking over the previous decade, changes that had led him to conclude that the Christianity of the Sermon on the Mount "must be made practical, both individually and socially, in respect to all the great interests of life, in order to realize salvation in ourselves and bring about a restoration of all things." After declaring "I am a Fraternal Communionist," he brought his family to Hopedale to join the people who were gathering there. By June twenty-five adults and twenty children had crowded into the broken-down buildings of the farm to begin the work of creating a Christian paradise: "There came to the Dale a few Pilgrims of Zion / A band faint and feeble whose hope was in God."[18]

They came chiefly from the primary recruiting ground for Practical Christianity, an area of eastern Worcester County that extended southward from Boylston and Berlin to Mendon and Uxbridge and to Millville near the Rhode Island border. They were farmers, artisans, and small-town business and professional men, dreamers and realists, who shared the hope of creating a better world at least for themselves. Even the generally hardheaded Ballou could fantasize the town they would build: "There are various stores, mills, factories, barns. . . . Children, youth, young men and maidens have their becoming amusements, and choirs of music send up their symphonies, but vice and violence, and unseemly rudeness are put far away."[19]

Although they were forever short of the money needed for their work, these Yankee pioneers soon put nearly twenty acres of their farm under cultivation, repaired the dilapidated buildings, and constructed a new structure for a dormitory, a schoolroom, and an office to print the *Practical Christian*. They also began the construction of a large two-story mechanic's shop "with dam and water power sufficient to operate the more necessary labor saving Machines usual to such establishments." Before the end of their first year, they were planning to build a combined chapel and schoolhouse.[20]

Men, women, and children joined in the work. Even Ballou, their elected president, took on a share of the physical labor in addition to serving as minister, missionary, and the editor of the *Practical Christian*. In the Fraternal Communion, officers were the "official servants" of the people, and so he dedicated himself to such work as ditching and constructing the dam. At times the labor was so exhausting that he would lie down on the ground, wishing he would go to sleep and never awake, but he soon returned to work. He said later that during this year, he found his greatest respite in visiting nearby churches to preach funeral sermons.[21] Although not all the members were so conscientious, the group was able to demonstrate some of the constructive power of committed collective labor when it is wisely organized and led.

The pilgrims of Hopedale were less successful, however, in dealing with themselves. At the beginning, their idea of the Fraternal

Communion involved an intensely collective life: the housing provision of their constitution gave exclusive attention to the construction of "mansion-houses" designed to accommodate a hundred or more people as members of one extended family. They recognized that intimate living, with its denial of the secrecies that protected personal sensitivities and foibles, was likely to breed resentment and contempt. As Ballou was later to put it, they were challenging the entrenched idea that "ordinary civilized society with its partition walls, its class distinctions, its conventional barricades, and compulsory insularities, allows mankind quite as much unity and closeness of association as they will safely bear." They hoped that adherence to the Standard of Practical Christianity would refute that idea, since "what occasion is there for quarreling, or even hard feelings, among a body of people who are determined never to quarrel at all?" [22]

During the first year the crowding of some two score adults and children into one "time-shattered" farmhouse put that hope to the test, and for a time it passed, in part owing to the capable management provided by two women who became mainstays of the community. One was Lucy Hunt Ballou, a determined and intelligent woman who years before had demonstrated her mettle when she had broken off her education at a women's academy in Providence to nurse her seriously ill husband-to-be back to health. Once her initial reluctance to join the community had been overcome, she became its energetic "Director of housekeeping." The other was Anna Thwing Draper, the wife of Ebenezer Draper, an independent-minded but amiable woman with a special talent for calming troubled social waters. [23] Devoted to all aspects of Practical Christianity, she was the woman most often elected to some position of influence within the community. The Ballous and the Drapers formed a close and enduring friendship that served as the sustaining heart of the Hopedale experiment.

Even the noblest of dispositions, however, could not eliminate the frictions of intimate living. "We have found ourselves in close contact with each other," it was reported in June, "and of course had ample opportunity to know each others weaknesses, failings and besetting sins." For a time, it seemed as if adherence to the Standard might assure harmony, but the interaction of sometimes eccentric personalities took its toll, and in less than a year several members had withdrawn.[24] One of the original investors in the joint-stock association, Sally Borden, had come to Hopedale to recover from the nervous breakdown that had temporarily confined her in the state insane asylum; she found no respite and withdrew to a decade of physical and mental torment that ended only with her death at age forty-three. Hopedale remembered her as an early friend. It was equally ready to forget Clothier Gifford, a self-proclaimed "practical phrenologist," who apparently joined the community in the hope of finding a permanent audience for his views. By early August, after his obstinate eccentricities had irritated most of the membership, Gifford departed with the announcement that he was planning to form a community on an "entirely different" plan. When he ignored requests that he resign his membership, he was formally expelled from the Fraternal Communion.[25]

The experience with Gifford helped persuade the community to suspend the admission of new residents, but this decision simply intensified internal discord. By the fall, what had initially seemed to involve little more than expected differences in personality was becoming a far more serious disagreement over Hopedale's fundamental principles between two of the men who had formulated the Standard of Practical Christianity. On the one side was Daniel Lamson, who pushed the ideal of fraternal community to a logical but threatening extreme. If the spirit of Jesus truly governed the community, Lamson had written in 1841, then "it will be our highest pleasure to do good to one another." At Hopedale, he interpreted this to mean that the poorest and least capable should have their needs met first and fullest. He took up the particular cause of new mothers, insisting that they receive regular wages for taking care of their babies. When the majority agreed to this policy, he then used the principle "the last shall be first" to demand that the weakest be given the best of the community's limited housing space.[26]

Lamson soon made himself a great irritant to Ballou, not least because of his insistence that as Practical Christians, all were bound by the Standard "to do good as we have opportunity unto all mankind, to feed the hungry, clothe the naked, minister to the sick." To those who like Ballou were exhausting themselves to establish the community, he was pushing this element of righteousness at the wrong time and, as was duly noted, to his own special advantage. Not only was his wife then nursing a baby but in April, during planting time, he had conveniently absented himself to Providence, Rhode Island, in order to get a new wooden leg, having at some point lost a lower limb. A man of greater sense and sensibility might have recognized the need for discretion, but Lamson insisted on pressing the issue to the point of condemning the already over-worked Ballou for not giving more attention to nursing mothers.[27]

By October Ballou had decided that Lamson and some others were determined to convert Hopedale into a common-stock community where the least capable and productive would be favored. Although he did not reject religious communism as an ideal, Lamson's version of it offended Ballou's sense of equity as well as his belief in the es-sential importance of individual responsibility: a voluntary com-munity based on love was "heavenly and will yield heavenly peace," but there was nothing heavenly about a system that forced honest labor to support "idlers and loafers." Previously, he had given little thought to the way that wealth would be distributed at Hope-dale. Now he was forced to formulate a principle of distribution in harmony with his idea of Christian socialism. Within some general limit to be agreed upon by the community, he concluded, every per-son should receive a just compensation for work performed, and the poor should be assisted as a matter of religious duty, not because they had a formal right to the wealth of the productive. To adopt Lamson's position would only create a false right for the lazy and irresponsible to "perpetrate virtual robbery by piecemeal," assuring the ruin of any community.[28]

At a special meeting of the community in October 1842, Ballou was able to gain the three-fourths majority needed to purge the Con-stitution of the Fraternal Communion of both communism and ex-cessive communalism. Six months' experience with communal liv-ing persuaded the majority to scrap the idea of mansion houses and collective work in favor of a provision allowing individual members to build their own houses and transact their own business so long as they were not "notoriously inconsistent with the principles of this Association." In place of equal wage rates and living conditions, all workers were to be "allowed a fair compensation according to the nature and productiveness of the service rendered" up to a maximum of a dollar per day, and everyone would be enabled to purchase what he or she needed at a price as close to the original cost as possible. In response to charges that "a money-loving, aristocratic spirit" was behind these changes, it was also agreed to limit dividends on the joint stock to 4 percent; the remainder of any profits were to be either divided equally among the workers or given to the community for its joint use.[29]

Ballou denied that these changes betrayed the original design. He argued that they provided a balance between personal individuality and the social cooperation needed to realize its nonresistance goals. The common commitment of individuals to behave as Christians would assure adequate protection for the unlucky and the under-endowed without inhibiting the efforts of the more capable. Moreover, the original guarantee that everyone would enjoy "a footing of personal equality" was given a practical basis in the maximums set for both wages and profits, which would protect the community from "those fictitious and extravagant compensations" that had created the false and unbridgeable inequalities of conventional society. This experiment with the principle of limited rewards had great social potential and was to endure as a basis for the community, although Ballou was later to regret that it had not been developed more fully.[30]

The rejection of his ideas led Lamson to abandon Hopedale for the Shakers, whom he soon proclaimed to be more Christian than his old associates. Eventually, though, dissatisfaction with his new friends led him to condemn them in his *Two Years Among the Shakers* (1848), a book that Ballou said had, considering the character of its author, given him a better opinion of the Shakers. Lamson's "crooked career" made him probably the only man Ballou ever really disliked.[31] Greater charity awaited another seceder who held to the communist ideal, Charles Gladding, one of the original signers of the Standard. After resigning in protest against the change, Gladding attempted to model his life on that of the Good Samaritan, giving so much of himself to the unfortunate that he assured his own personal failure, and eventually he fell fatally ill. Suffering from tuberculosis, he returned to the Practical Christian fellowship, there "to pine and die" among his old friends in 1854 at the age of forty-two.[32]

The departure of these and other dissidents did far more to strengthen than to weaken the experiment. Remaining was a core of committed and productive members who were to lay the foundations for a successful community. Aside from Ebenezer Draper, who had some talent for business, they included Henry Lillie, a carpenter and millwright; Samuel Colburn, a baker; Lemuel Munyan, a sometime woolens manufacturer; Butler Wilmarth, a physician; and Edmund Price, a hatter. They all seem to have had little gift for success in the outside world (even Draper was eventually to fail outside), but they formed an assemblage of talent and experience that made Hopedale's success. It was to such men and women that Ballou referred when in his report on the first year he declared that while the rejection of communism would discourage many from coming to Hopedale, new members would likely be "persons who depend on their own capability, industry, and frugal economy, rather than on the resources, systematic management, and magic economies of an associated mass."[33]

This hope influenced the admissions policy of the community. Aside from pledging to uphold the Standard of Practical Christianity, applicants for membership were expected to supply detailed information regarding their education, skills, financial standing, and various other attributes before the community voted on their applications. Even then they were usually not admitted to full membership until they had lived for up to a year at Hopedale, where their usefulness and compatibility could be determined. In 1842 the Fraternal Communion created a recruiting device in the form of a projected system of "inductive conferences," classes on Practical Christianity to be established anywhere within the reach of Hopedale's ministers, which would prepare interested people for membership:

> Welcome the sterling mind,
> The generous trustful heart,
> The head to diligence inclined,
> The hero of a noble part.[34]

A policy of selective membership made for a coherent community. It also made, though, for a small one. A year after the communist secessions, the *Practical Christian* estimated that the community consisted of some one hundred members and their dependents, only forty-five of whom actually lived at Hopedale. Limited accommodations and opportunities prevented even a desired growth of population, especially in the range of skilled workers required for economic development. Ballou said later that Hopedale suffered from an excessive diversity of business undertakings created to accommodate the various skills of its members.[35] Whatever the accuracy of his memory on this point, it is evident that the early community lacked some of the workers and industries needed to fulfill its ambition to become a commonwealth in miniature.

Efforts were made, therefore, to recruit selected workers, including a carpenter from Grafton and a boot- and shoemaker from nearby Milford, as well as various mechanics for the fledgling machine shop. This program grew into a larger industrial plan intended to expand the range of business. In 1844 the community appropriated a hundred dollars for a hatting business, purchased some of the equipment needed for a blacksmith shop, appointed a committee to make arrangements for box making, and considered the idea of producing a newly invented "air-tight cooking-stove."[36] The stove business failed to materialize, and the desired skills were not always obtainable, but such policies did contribute significantly to Hopedale's development.

By 1844 two years of striving had begun to produce results. In May Ballou said that Hopedale was yet of "little consequence in the great world" and that its aims would take years of dedicated effort to achieve, but he expressed pride in the progress it had made. And his little community had begun to attract outside attention. In November the New England Non-Resistance Society commended it for its successful application of the principles of nonresistance. To satisfy the curiosity of the world, the *Practical Christian* printed the report of Hopedale's financial condition for 1844, which estimated that the assets of the joint-stock association exceeded its liabilities by $456.91 and predicted "a constantly increasing prosperity." Among the assets were four hundred acres of land, three dwellings, a mechanics shop, and a combined schoolhouse and chapel whose basement provided space for a community store. Not included were seven houses, each on half-acre plots, that were owned by individual members rather than by the community. What had been only a run-down farm less than three years before showed fair promise of becoming a prosperous industrial village.[37]

Thus by 1844 Hopedale seemed to be succeeding in its intention, stated in 1842, to combine "all the advantages of a well ordered village of free-minded, conscientious individuals, and of a close association of capital and labor, without the disadvantages of either." Its system amalgamated three forms of property. Its joint stock owned the land and most of the other productive assets. Individuals had possession of their own houses and yards as well as personal effects under the general regulations of the community. And the maximum limits set on both wages and dividends were expected to yield a surplus profit from community enterprise, thereby creating a common fund to be used for the benefit of the needy, for education, and for the general good. Under this system, both labor and capital would be free to reap a just return for their efforts in productive cooperation with each other, while all members and their dependents would be protected against life's adversities. Thus, the goals of socialism would be attained without giving "idlers and loafers" any right to the wealth of the productive and without limiting individual freedom.[38] Once the community conformed its life to the Standard of Practical Christianity, its members would be both cooperative brothers and free, responsible individuals, each and all energetically engaged in the common pursuit of holiness and happiness.

In reality, though, Hopedale did not entirely satisfy its leaders. Although it had made notable economic progress, it fell far short of realizing Ballou's hopes in 1841 that a cooperative community would so efficiently utilize its "money, time, strength, skill, learning, and everything else" that it would not cost "a quarter of what it now does to feed, clothe, educate and maintain our families." It had not yet produced the promised 4 percent return on its joint stock, much less the hoped-for common surplus to be used for the common good. The cost of constructing the schoolhouse and chapel, the central building of the community, had been met largely by individual donations, more than half from outside.[39]

The industrial policy initiated in 1844 promised eventual surpluses through quickened economic development, but the recruitment of skilled workers also helped create another problem that threatened the very essence of the Hopedale experiment. When the community rejected communism in 1842, it allowed individuals to do business on their own account, opening the way for individual enterprise. Under this policy, Nathan Harris, a carpenter and one of the first residents at Hopedale, contracted to build three houses for other members. Whatever its immediate benefits, however, individual business served to weaken the collective, joint-stock business of the community and to drive a wedge into its society. When the community attempted to regulate Harris's work, he resigned his membership and settled outside the village, dispelling some of the hope that Practical Christianity alone could control "selfish egotism."[40] The recruitment of needed new skilled workers threatened to compound the danger.

If Hopedale was to grow without losing its soul, something had to be done to stem the growth of the individualism unleashed by the rejection of communism in 1842. How to preserve and to actualize the ideal of brotherhood during the passage from pioneer times to maturity? How to reorganize one last time so as to swing the pendulum back toward collective life? By the end of 1844 Ballou and his associates believed they had found the answer. The resulting reorganization, even in its failures, was to have a lasting influence on Hopedale's character and future.

3

The Well-Regulated Economy

The search for some form of property to serve both individual and communal good ranged far beyond the limits of Hopedale village. At least for its leaders, the village remained what it had initially been intended to be, "Fraternal Community No. 1," the first of an ever-growing number of Practical Christian communities that would eventually transform the world. It was to be, as Ballou put it, a "powerful concentration of moral light and heat" that would inspire all those who were dissatisfied with existing society to create Christian commonwealths of their own. By 1843 there were signs of progress in that direction. The *Practical Christian* published a report that a "Society of Practical Christians" recently formed in Pittsburgh was planning to establish a community in western Pennsylvania.[1] This plan came to nothing, but it reflected a growing public interest in the formation of cooperative communities.

In New England the new spirit produced not only Hopedale and George Ripley's Brook Farm but John Humphrey Noyes's society of Christian Perfectionists at Putney, Vermont, and the more secular Northampton Association in western Massachusetts. Although each of these communities was founded on different principles, all were laboring, said William Henry Fish, "to realize the Kingdom of God on earth." Fish believed that they rode upon a rising tide of radical reform against what he and others saw as the inevitable tendency of existing society toward chaos, corruption, inequality, and misery:

> What a contrast would a well-regulated Community present compared with the present order of things—especially in large towns

and villages. None very rich and none very poor, none worn out with excessive toil, none idle, no children growing up in ignorance, and none without friends—*all*, young and old, male and female, prosperous and making progress in knowledge and Christian excellence.[2]

These communities were in fact part of a larger search throughout the North Atlantic world for some kind of cooperative society that could prevent the rampant abuses of property. This search was a natural response, in a world of uneven economic progress, to the concentration of wealth and power and the growing dependence of labor on capital for work. In 1849, Ballou gave his version of the problem:

> Capital is gaining power and influence every day. It is progressively assuming greater and greater importance throughout the civilized world. Who could prevent it, if he would; or would do so if he could? Property is good—indispensable in its place. . . . The problem then is to subject property to the great Christian law of love—to render it as powerful a means of promoting righteousness, peace, and happiness as it now is of promoting iniquity, selfishness, antagonism, war, violence, and misery.[3]

Broadly, the search was for some way to socialize property, to subordinate it to human needs and humane ends.

This emerging socialism promised to give new importance to Hopedale, but it also presented powerful competition, since most of the awakening American interest in cooperative communities was drawn to two European secular ideologies, Owenism and Fourierism, which soon dominated the debate over property. Almost twenty years after his failure at New Harmony, Robert Owen returned to the United States with the hope of awakening popular support for his form of communism. In 1845 he spent two days at Hopedale, where he won much admiration for his character but not for his cause. The greater part of the new cooperationism, however, was attracted to the more flamboyant but seemingly more practical doctrines of the French utopian Charles Fourier. Between 1843 and 1846 dozens of new communities were attempted along Fourierist lines.

Both movements raised questions of critical importance to Practical Christianity. Although Ballou admired Owen as a person, he detested the Englishman's communism and, even more, his doctrine that social circumstances were responsible for human character and behavior. In the spring of 1843 Ballou appeared at a "Property Meeting" of radical reformers in Boston in order to battle against the Owenite gospel. He spoke for individual property and moral responsibility, arguing that the cause of social evils lay neither in property nor in circumstances but in the heart of man. Any effort to reorganize society on the assumption that man was a "mere creature of circumstances," he said, was both undesirable and impracticable, since it neglected the need to reform the moral dispositions of individuals, which could be effected only under the influence of Christian nonresistance.[4]

Ballou also had strong reservations about Charles Fourier, particularly the Frenchman's emphasis on the need to free human passions from the repressions of civilization, but Fourierism was a form of collectivism that seemed to share his respect for individuality and individual property rights.[5] He assumed a significantly more positive attitude, therefore, when he and Daniel Whitney represented the Hopedale Community at a social reform convention held in Boston in late 1843 and early 1844. This largely Fourierist convention warmly received the Hopedale delegates, along with those from Brook Farm and the Northampton Association, as representatives of communities that had demonstrated some of the possibilities of cooperative life.[5] Heartened by the general optimism of the convention, the three communities agreed to hold a series of conferences among themselves with the particular aim of studying "the practical workings of their respective internal economies, with a view to mutual correction and improvement." During 1844 their representatives met first at Hopedale and then at Northampton.[6]

These conferences stopped before the close of the year, but not before they had furthered the interest in Fourierism, which Brook Farm had already adopted in the hope of giving its faltering economy greater energy and more effective organization.[7] As in earlier years, Hopedale's commitment to the Standard of Practical Christianity prevented any affiliation with Ripley's society, and that same commitment also separated it from the Fourierist movement in general. Whereas Fourierism emphasized the satisfaction of the passions, the Standard emphasized self-denial. Like the Brook Farmers, however, the Practical Christians were attracted to Fourierist plans for a well-ordered economic and social life in the form of the "phalanx." At a time of growing concern at Hopedale over the dangers of selfish individualism and of impatience over the slowness of development, the new scheme promised to provide for more effective and productive cooperation and to do it without resorting to communism, since it held to the same principles of joint-stock ownership and limited profits that had already been adopted.

How to have a cooperative society that would not weaken individual initiative and the will to work? In December 1844 the community adopted an elaborate "By-Law Respecting Industrial Organization" that provided for the organization of all resident members and their dependents into "Bands and Sections," each to engage in some specialized form of production under the general direction of an executive board. Every individual was to perform sixty hours of labor per week during the warmer half of the year and forty-eight hours during the remainder, with four vacation days per year. Whenever possible, each band was to consist of those members whose skills and interests matched its particular work.

In exchange, the community agreed to pay each adult member twenty-five dollars a year in spending money and to supply everyone with "house room, fuel, light, food, washing and mending, medicine, medical and nursing attendance, and conveyance by horse and carriage . . . fifty miles each per annum"; it was also to provide twenty hours per week of schooling to all children from the nursery to age eighteen. Profits from community industries were to be distributed first to the holders of the joint stock, up to the 4 percent maximum, and then to the general membership on the basis of the number of hours worked.[8]

Ideally, this well-regulated economy would enable the community to mobilize its full productive power for the good of all. With the expected wealth, everyone would be guaranteed all of life's essentials "through health and sickness," regardless of one's contribution. Here, it was hoped, would be the basis for a cooperative order that could resist selfish egotism and assure true Christian brotherhood, where "religion, reason, and humanity have full scope without conflict." On the other hand, this system would avoid the dangers of communism, since it provided for a return on capital and some rewards for labor. It also allowed for the individual possession of houses and house lots; those who had houses were to be given up to forty dollars a year in lieu of the housing provided to others.[9]

Ballou admitted that there were likely to be imperfections in this scheme, but he defended it as the basis for "the true social state" in which property "is so far *common* as to secure all the benefits of a united interest, and so far *individual* as to preserve personal rights from the encroachments of social tyranny."[10] On matters relating to property and economic organization, he and most other members were empiricists willing to test any system that promised to realize the dream of cooperative Christian brotherhood and to reinforce the behavior required by the Standard of Practical Christianity.

One member who did not accept this well-ordered scheme was Ballou's longtime associate in prayer and printing, George Stacy. An original signer of the Standard, Stacy had taken on most of the responsibility for publishing the *Practical Christian*, the biweekly newspaper of the movement, helping to make it a superior example of both radical and religious journalism. This work, combined with his missionary efforts for the cause, had removed him from the day-to-day life of Hopedale, a remoteness that he found comfortable, particularly since his wife had persistently refused to join the Fraternal Communion. As his instincts were more individualistic than communal, he was not disposed to accept the new scheme, particularly when he recognized that it would incorporate the printing business into its organization. In late 1845, therefore, he withdrew from the Fraternal Communion and established his own printing business in nearby Milford. Over the next decades, he succeeded in combining a devotion to abolitionism and temperance with interests in both business and politics, but he permanently abandoned the idea of any kind of community, Practical Christian or otherwise.[11]

In defense of his withdrawal, Stacy attacked the new system both as impractical and as a threat to individual freedom and integrity. If people were the Christians they were supposed to be, he said, it would be possible to have a loving and cooperative society without "the artificial and burdensome machinery" established at Hopedale; if they were not, then it was better to abandon any thought of "forced" communal organization and to concentrate on converting individuals to true Christianity. The new arrangements, he warned, would eventuate in "despotism," since the lazy and irresponsible would compel leaders to devise ways of forcing all to work. Better, then, that Hopedale entirely dissolve itself as a joint-stock community: "I am very certain that Christian neighborhoods would secure all the advantages now enjoyed or hoped for by communities without the useless *theorizing* and *petty tyranny* felt to be so essential."[12]

Stacy's criticisms, published in late 1845 in the *Practical Christian*, were a powerful intellectual challenge to the Hopedale experiment, not least because they evoked the community's own preference for individual integrity over social contrivances. The first response came from Clement O. Reed, a new member with distinctly Fourierist leanings and Hopedale's elected "Intendant for Manufactures and Mechanical Industry." Four years later Reed himself was to leave the community for New York City, where he played a leading role in founding an "extensive Bathing and Washing Establishment" designed especially for the poor. In 1845, however, he was satisfied with at least the idea of a well-ordered community. Although he conceded that the new organization was hardly perfect, he defended it as a "system of Christian equality" that would prevent the social evils engendered by individualism: "Here the strong help the weak." Whatever its defects, it was far better than leaving the average person to the untender mercies of "individual integrity" in a society based on the principle of every man for himself.[13]

Adin Ballou was reluctant to engage in a public dispute with his earliest convert. When Stacy complained of the lack of freedom at Hopedale, however, he was directly attacking what for Ballou was an enterprise as "dear to me as the apple of my eye." Probably because he shared Stacy's belief in the importance of personal integrity, he chose as his main line of defense an attack on Stacy's own integrity. Contrary to Stacy's portrayal of himself as a victim of communal oppression, said Ballou, the printer and roving minister had actually suffered little of Hopedale's early privations while drawing on its benefits, including a profit denied to its leading residents: after having invested only $15 in the community, "he is going away with more than $200 nett savings, to set up printing within a mile and a half of our press." According to Ballou, the immediate cause of Stacy's disquiet at Hopedale was a communal decision to ring a bell at 7:30 in the morning to summon everyone to work, a rule Stacy denounced, said Ballou, as *"factory despotism"* when it was simply a matter of good management.[14]

This exchange betrayed a decline in the religious enthusiasm that had inspired and sustained the Fraternal Communion in its early years. By the mid 1840s, religious radicalism in New England had begun to give way to more-secular forms of radicalism, and this had an effect on Hopedale, whose attitudes were also being influenced by a change of membership. In the first three years, nearly twenty members had left and an even larger number of new people had joined the community. Although new members like Clement Reed were committed to Practical Christianity, they were at least a step removed from the special conditions that had produced it in the late 1830s. For more than a decade, Hopedale would retain its special character and sense of mission, but the Primitive Christianity that had been its inspiring model was pushed further into the past, and the millennium that had been its compelling hope deferred further into the future.

In his address as president at the annual meeting of the community in January 1846, Ballou called Hopedale "a Bethlehem of salvation to the glorious social future" when "war is to cease, slavery is to cease, competition of interests to cease, false education, false religion, false government, false industry, false wealth, poverty and misery—all to cease." He said, however, that this future might be generations and even ages away. Of more immediate importance to him was the growing wealth of the community, particularly its joint stock, which had quadrupled despite the loss of "several thousand dollars" used to settle accounts with those who had withdrawn. He was particularly proud that the community had finally produced a profit and one large enough to pay the promised 4 percent dividend on its stock, not only for the year but also for the preceding years. Although this last achievement depended in small part on a $124 donation from Ballou's loyal friend Ebenezer Draper, it enabled the president to dream of a time when there would be profits beyond the 4 percent dividend to distribute among all the members.[15]

The first two years under the new system justified this optimism.

By 1846 Hopedale had become a "thriving little village" of some seventy residents with a dozen dwellings, a schoolhouse, a machine shop, and other facilities. And the community continued to improve its industrial base. It completed a second dam on the Mill River to increase available waterpower, added a sawmill and a blacksmith's shop, and experimented with a soap-making business. It also took steps to expand what proved to be its most important business, the manufacture of temples for power looms in the textile mills (a temple is a device that keeps the cloth in the loom stretched to the proper width during the weaving process); in March 1847 the trustees of the community voted "that the Blacksmith Branch charge the forging of Temples to the Machine Branch at 70 cents and that the Machine Branch charge finished Temples to Finance and Exchange at 180 cents for the present year."[16] This decision reflected Hopedale's growing involvement in the outside economy, where the expansion of the New England textile industry was creating a steady demand for the appliance. By early 1847 the village had begun to advertise some of its businesses—notably printing, carpentry, and shoemaking, in addition to loom temples—with the announcement that it had installed boxes in nearby Milford where orders for its goods could be deposited.[17]

Such policies expressed the will of a provincial middle class to create a manufacturing village shaped to their own needs and experiences. For most members, it was natural to look upon the mill towns of their native Blackstone region as forms of urban-industrial society comfortably shaped to a human scale. By adapting the mill village to Christian socialism, they hoped to avoid the future emerging at places like Boston and Lowell. On the other hand, they had no intention of basing their future on rural ways and on agriculture. Although they did do some farming, their thoughts were tuned chiefly to the new urban horticulture. In 1843 the community planted an apple orchard with 325 young trees shipped to it by a Practical Christian in Cincinnati, but its greatest effort went into its gardens. Its resident inspiration was the English-born Edmund Soward, a free spirit who had joined the group in 1843. An adept horticulturist, Soward willingly shared his plants and his knowledge with the other members; after his death in 1854, one member wrote, "When Spring and Summer and Harvest shall come around again—

the time for tomato-plants, for strawberries, for peaches—many will remember him."[18]

By 1846 Hopedale had a common garden and was offering gardening plots to anyone who might use them, even young boys. Of greatest importance, of course, were the plots owned by individual householders. To each householder who planted a garden, it provided from two to four cartloads of "good manure" per year and, to allow time for cultivation, exemption from twelve days of required work, in exchange for which the householder was to sell any garden surplus to the community at a fixed rate. In order to encourage each family to become as self-sufficient in food as possible, it also supplied those who were willing to raise poultry with fowls and with a bushel of grain per year for each hen.[19]

Under the system adopted in 1844, the community was also obligated to provide every adult with twenty-five dollars a year in clothing and pocket money and to meet every person's food, fuel, and lighting needs. Most of the goods were delivered on order from the community store to the resident's house; supplying these goods and delivering firewood were the responsibility of the Department of Domestic Economy. Although there were no formal limits on consumption, accounts were kept of the costs of meeting these needs, for the purpose, said Ballou, of "enabling all to understand what relations our expenditures bear to our income." In early 1847 this same accounting was applied to personal transportation, in the form of rent-a-carriage charges of nine cents per mile.[20]

Hopedale seemed well on its way to fulfilling Ballou's hope in 1841 that it would "feed, clothe, educate and maintain our families better than is now done by the middling class of society." And it had attracted some respectful attention from the outside world, particularly from George Ripley, whose Brook Farm had collapsed in 1846. Although Ripley considered the Hopedale system to be "non-scientific" by the standards of Fourierism, he commended it as "a model of a Christian church" whose members were demonstrating that it was possible for people to "arrange their social relations, on the principle of Christian brotherhood, far better than others can do it for them on the system of selfishness and antagonism."[21]

Ripley concluded his article, however, by quoting a lament from Ballou that the community had ended the year 1846 with "a considerable pecuniary loss," which prevented it from paying the 4 percent dividend. Ballou attributed this abrupt turnabout in part to an outbreak of sickness. Whereas in 1845 he was able to observe that no one had died at Hopedale, now he noted that death had become a familiar visitor: "We have been wasted by disease, bereaved by the *destroyer*, care-worn by anxious vigils over our emaciated friends, enfeebled in our industry, impoverished in our financial resources." The destroyer was typhoid, which caused the death of one woman and three children and depleted the health of a significant part of the small community. "Death has once more entered our fold," Ballou wrote regarding young Rebecca Brown, "and has taken one of the precious lambs of our fold." For nearly a month he had to suspend his editorial work for the *Practical Christian* in order to meet the labor needs of the community.[22]

Disease was only a part of the difficulty, though. By the end of 1846 Hopedale had also begun to experience troubles with its well-regulated economy that challenged its commitment to collective enterprise. Ballou and his associates knew the familiar argument that equal distribution of wealth encouraged laziness and irresponsibility, but they believed that they had found a way around the problem. Laziness, said William Henry Fish, was far more likely to occur in the old society, which allowed some to thrive without working while denying many the employments suited to their talents and interests. In contrast, a "well organized Practical Christian Community" would shame even the naturally lazy to work along with their brothers. Moreover, once it achieved its destined prosperity, it would be able to provide satisfying work for all: "Only a moderate degree will be required, and it will be performed, not merely to produce the immediate supply for the wants of the body, but to make for ourselves and our posterity a home of beauty, intelligence, refinement and love—'a kingdom of heaven on earth.'" In such a community of rewarding, transcendentally significant labor guided by the pervasive spirit of brotherly love, it would be natural for nearly everyone to do the best they could for the good of all.[23]

This happy state could only be achieved through sacrifice and hard work. In theory, the common commitment to Practical Christian behavior guaranteed both, and in fact there was much dedicated labor at Hopedale. By the end of 1846, however, Ballou had concluded that actual production was not enough to overcome the adversities of that year. In November he delivered a long discourse on the need for productive industry, declaring, "I hold idleness to be a sin; useful labor a part of Christian righteousness" and arguing that since people were social beings dependent on society, everyone had an obligation to labor for the good of all. He soon followed this exhortation with a detailed scheme for the better utilization of available labor power. In his annual address to the community in January 1847, he proposed a plan to render industry "more efficient, pleasant, and productive" and implied that some of the members had been more interested in filling their quota of work hours than in actually producing.[24]

As approved by the community, Ballou's plan included "a distinct branch of business . . . to be called Domestic Industry," which was to enroll all women and children for useful community work when they were not otherwise employed at home or at school. And for workers in the established production branches, there was a "special recommendation" that they meet each Saturday evening to discuss ways of making their work more efficient. Also approved was a complex plan to evaluate labor in terms of its actual productiveness rather than its "mere duration," the value of labor in each branch of business to be set by the community in dollars and cents. In turn, this led to an effort to fix the price of both goods and services; in February, for instance, the transportation branch was authorized to charge the other branches 12.5 cents per mile for the hire of horses and wagons.[25] At the same time, Ballou also tried to persuade his followers to consume no more than they produced by presenting them with what he described as "a very detailed report" on both the overall average costs of subsistence at Hopedale and "the specific costs of each family for ordinary supplies, for rent, fuel and other items."[26]

The evident intention of this scheme was to revive the promising tendency of 1845. The specific goal was to pay the 4 percent dividend, which was acquiring significance, not just for itself, but because it represented the breakthrough point beyond which lay the dream of a growing surplus of wealth.[27] If Hopedale could meet its obligations to those who had invested in it, it would be ready to demonstrate that a Christian commonwealth could guarantee to all its members the benefits enjoyed in conventional society only by an advantaged minority.

Unfortunately, this venture pushed the well-regulated community all too close to the "petty tyranny" and cumbersome social machinery against which George Stacy had protested in 1845. During the first half of 1847 Ballou and his associates struggled to give energy and efficiency to their social machine but with little success. As a member of the Board of Trustees, the elected five-member board that controlled Hopedale's property, Ballou found himself directly involved with a multitude of economic decisions on such matters as the sale of the community's bull and whether its "Fruit Branch be connected with the Garden Branch." In February the community's Intendant of Agriculture and Animals abruptly resigned in protest against the new arrangements, leaving the already overworked president to prepare for the planting season. While he was entangled in these details, Ballou was also attempting to continue his work as head of the Practical Christian Communion; and with Stacy's departure, he had been forced to shoulder the responsibility for issuing the *Practical Christian*, his principal pulpit in the world. By the spring, as he later recalled, a combination of physical exhaustion and mental pressure "seriously threatened an entire collapse of my system." [28]

The willingness of the strong to dedicate their talents to the welfare of the weak had its limits. As overburdened as he was, Ballou would undoubtedly have been willing to continue the experiment if it had begun to succeed, but he finally concluded that it was becoming increasingly "embarrassed by the friction of a complex industrial machine, multifarious counsel, protracted discussions, diverse judgments, and tardy cooperation." Aside from overtaxing the more enterprising members, the scheme's chief effect seems to have been to have made the less capable, responsible, and satisfied members even worse. [29] And Hopedale could find little reason for hope outside, since the popular enthusiasm for Fourierism, which had influenced it in 1844, had fizzled; Brook Farm had collapsed, as had most of the other phalanxes, which had been launched with expectations of great benefits from well-organized communal economies. It seemed to be time for a change in direction.

In June Ballou published a long disquisition entitled "Social Reorganization" in which he condemned society's failure to reconcile "*individualism* and *socialism*," leaving them "perpetually at war—blindly and madly consuming their resources in a quarrel which only renders a bad matter worse." His principal concern was to persuade his own community of its failure to find, as yet, the correct balance between the two principles. Although he was ready to acknowledge the importance of social influences on human behavior, he returned to his old emphasis on the essential importance of individual moral responsibility, and he listed the principal evils to be expected from an excessive emphasis on social organization: "over responsibility in the cares of management, irresponsibility and carelessness in the naturally unenterprising, friction of uncongenial intimacy, and the abridgment of personal independence."[30]

Apparently, most members of the community agreed that some fundamental change in its organization was necessary. They soon began to meet to determine what could be done, appointing a special committee to rewrite their constitution, and on 17 July 1847 they approved its plan of reorganization.[31] The result was an entirely new constitution that replaced the Constitution of the Fraternal Communion originally approved in 1841 and much amended since. Significantly, the new plan was designed not for some national communion of—in theory—many communities but specifically for the Hopedale Community. And its preamble boldly proclaimed an intention to establish a community "with as little as possible of mere human constraint, in which all members may be perfectly free to associate or separate their secular interests according to inclination and congeniality."[32] It was a landmark in Hopedale's history, bringing to an end the effort to create a Christian socialism exclusively on the basis of the collective ownership of property and the collective management of labor.

In line with this new policy, the community's Board of Trustees was instructed to sell off or rent out the productive property owned in joint stock to individual members. Consequently, the gristmill, sawmill, and machine shop were leased, and smaller businesses like shoemaking, transportation, and even the medical department were sold outright. Within a month Ballou announced that he had become sole proprietor of the *Practical Christian* and its printshop; as such, he said, he planned to relinquish "those cares and labors which have confined him so closely to the secular affairs of the Community, and will hereafter devote himself to the more general service of humanity as editor and publisher."[33] Although he remained as president of the community and one of its trustees, he was plainly quite content to escape from the well-organized life of the past.

He insisted, however, that this did not mean an abandonment of Christian socialism, nor did it. The community continued to own its farmlands, school, and that part of the village proper which had not been sold to individual owners, and it continued to operate its store, where groceries could be obtained at cost. Even some of those businesses that were to be sold or rented out remained under its control. In 1849, for instance, the community offered to rent its carpentry shop to any association of members willing to furnish employment at a "fair" wage and to turn excess profits over to the education fund; when it found no takers, it assumed direct responsibility for the carpentry business.[34]

Equally important, all property was controlled by those pledged to the Standard of Practical Christianity; no one who had not agreed to the pledge was allowed to own property or to reside permanently in Hopedale. Under the influence of Practical Christianity, it was at least likely that various individuals would voluntarily associate their interests for the mutual benefit of themselves and the community. Moreover, the community had in the preamble of its new constitution guaranteed that "no individual shall suffer the evils of oppression, poverty, ignorance, or vice, through the influence or the neglect of others," a guarantee that included employment for the able and charity to the disabled.[35]

Ballou rightly denied that Hopedale had become a mere "neighborhood" little different from conventional society. It remained dedicated to nonresistance and the other principles of the Standard, which formed the bedrock for its social experiments. At a time of growing misery and conflict in the world, the village could boast that it had no poverty, no crime, no drunkenness, no unemployment, no slavery, and no violence; nor did it squander its wealth on war, jails, or a corrupted and burdensome government. It continued to demonstrate to the world that it was possible to guarantee to everyone "comfortable subsistence, moral order, and all the great essentials of individual and social welfare." In these ways, it remained an example of Practical Christian socialism which, while recognizing individual possessions, had socialized property for the good of all, combining "the largest innocent individuality and the largest social cooperation."[36] As such, it pointed the way toward a solution to the great problem of the age: "Property must be Christianized. Otherwise it will Mammonize and Atheize nominal Christiandom."[37]

Eventually, property would triumph over love even at Hopedale, but the following years affirmed Ballou's faith. Having settled its fundamental questions, the community entered into its golden age, materially and morally. Although it fell short of a realized utopia, it did seem to demonstrate that Practical Christianity could eventually bring humankind to the gates of heaven, where righteousness, peace, and happiness would prevail.

4

Hopedale Village

In 1852 Hopedale completed the first decade of its development. What had been a woebegone farm had become a prosperous little town of nearly two hundred people. It had thirty-one houses, five mill and shop buildings, a printing office, a chapel and school, and various service buildings. Although it had no intention of becoming a farming community, it had through a series of land purchases nearly doubled its original "domain" of 258 acres. Beginning with less than four thousand dollars in assets, Hopedale had increased in value to over sixty thousand dollars, including both its joint-stock and individually owned property. Along with its farm, orchards, and gardens, it operated various small businesses: lumber, boots and shoes, cabinets, boxes, painting and glazing, printing, hardware, and, of special importance, power-loom temples. Much of this varied production was assisted by the force of the Mill River, which had a fall of nearly forty feet in its mile passage through the expanded community domain; some of its land purchases had been made to assure sufficient waterpower.[1]

Hopedale had begun as a struggling commune in an isolated dale separated from thriving Milford center by the imposing Magomiscock Hill, but in less than a decade it made itself into a local industrial center and part of a regional network of trade. Much of its region in southeastern Massachusetts experienced rapid modernization and development between 1845 and 1855, having recovered from the depression of the late 1830s. Textile mills in the area had grown in size and efficiency, producing a demand for Hopedale's loom temples. And the population of the town of Milford surrounding it had tripled from 2,500 to 7,500 people, increasing local demand for its foodstuffs and other commodities. The village made some effort to expand its outside connections. During the late 1840s it improved its roads both to Milford center two miles to the northeast and to towns to the south along the Mill River. It also contributed at least a hundred dollars to help bring a railroad to Milford, giving it access to Boston and to the industrial heartland of Massachusetts. By 1857 Adin Ballou was able to deny a newspaper charge that his followers had tried to isolate themselves from the world:

> Highways are open through the settlement in various directions. A regular express carriage plies several times a day between their main street and the aforesaid center [Milford]. Transportation teams owned in Hopedale are driven several times a week to and from Woonsocket, R.I., ten miles distant laden with freight. Thousands of dollars worth of produce, raw material, mechanical fabrications, horses, cattle, grain, flour and various kinds of goods are being annually exchanged in trade. Market loads of garden vegetables, in the season of them, are almost daily carried from our dale into the neighboring villages.[2]

This was the work primarily of those who in the context of their small-town Yankee world could best be described as middle class. Of twenty-four male community members listed in the United States census of 1850, nineteen were born in Massachusetts, Connecticut, or Rhode Island. Most were in the prime of life: ten were in their forties, and the rest, with two exceptions, were younger. They were predominantly family men: eighteen were married, and of these, fifteen had a total of thirty-four children. And they were men equipped with some education and a variety of practical skills: only four were classified as laborers, while fourteen were artisans, especially machinists and carpenters, mostly independent workers with some entrepreneurial instincts; five others could be classified either as businessmen or as professionals (two ministers and a physician).[3]

Instinctively, they were active town builders in an age of often extravagant town promotions. The return of prosperity by 1850 excited many Americans to boost the growth of places of every size in anticipation of direct gains for themselves. Generally, the people of Hopedale were not above seeing personal benefit in the development of their village, and they often acted like town boosters elsewhere. They had their own newspaper, the *Practical Christian*, which advertised their existence; they strove to add to their economy and to expand their ability to trade with the outside world; and as a community, they derived part of their collective income from the sale of town lots to their expanding membership.

The village was a special work of boosterism, however, by a special middle class. By 1850 the tide of religious radicalism that had arisen in the 1830s was fast receding into history, but its spirit had been incorporated into the town it had inspired. In 1851 Ballou described Hopedale as both "a Church of Christ" and "a Civil State, a miniature Christian Republic" within the state of Massachusetts and the United States, acquiescent to their laws but essentially independent of their corrupted governments:

> It has its own Constitution, laws, regulations and municipal police; its own Legislature, Judiciary, and Executive authorities; its own Educational system of operations; its own fire insurance and savings institutions, its own arrangements for holding property, the management of industry, and the raising of revenue. . . . It is the seedling of the true Democratic and Social Republic, wherein neither caste, color, sex nor age stand prescribed but every human being shares jointly in Liberty, Equality, and Fraternity.[4]

Sensitive to the anarchist implications of nonresistance, he and his associates emphasized that they were striving not for "no-government" but for "true government," a regime devoted to the principles of Christ rather than to the use of force. Those men and women who governed their behavior by the Standard of Practical Christianity were welcomed as citizens; those who did not were excluded from the community. Whatever the changes made in Hopedale's organization, the insistence that members pledge themselves to Practical Christian morality remained firm.

Within its moral walls, the community was a democratic republic whose members, male or female, had equal rights and responsibilities. Ballou, the heart and mind of the community, was undoubtedly the first among equals, the dominant influence on public decisions. His influence, however, depended primarily on general respect for his ideas and for his evident dedication to the community rather than on a commanding personality; no charismatic miracle worker, Ballou normally had his way because he shared the hopes and concerns of his followers. Although Hopedale's policies were normally those proposed by him and a few close associates like Ebenezer Draper, he had to persuade the community to ratify his major proposals at its various legislative meetings, where all members, male and female, were entitled to cast one vote each. At its annual meetings at the beginning of each year, the community elected its "official servants" to manage its executive business; in his original proposal in 1840, Ballou had written that these servants "shall be accountable to their constituents and subject to their instructions and removals at their pleasure," presumably a view on which the community was prepared to act.[5]

Most of the actual business of the community was done by an annually elected executive council that, with the president, was responsible for managing general economic and financial affairs. Its duties were diverse. Among various other things in 1846, for instance, it appointed Ballou to take charge of the grafting of fruit trees, attempted to find a "suitable horse" for community use, decided to purchase a waterwheel to power a new mill, and initiated an effort to establish a soap-making business. In 1849 it was instructed by the community to rent out the carpentry business—one of its many duties regarding the joint-stock property—and was authorized to levy a small tax on individual income, the revenue to be used for educational purposes. In the same year it established Hopedale's own postal service from the United States post office at Milford; this service was financed by requiring receivers as well as senders of letters to buy the special stamps of the "Hopedale Penny Post."[6]

Guided by their basic commitment to Practical Christianity, the people at Hopedale strove to create a superior version of the small towns they had known. They looked upon big cities as essentially evil. In 1840 Ballou urged parents to dissuade their young from pursuing their ambitions in cities: "The snares of vice and pollution, and infamy are more numerous and deceitful in populous places than in rural abodes." In such places could be found extremes of wealth and power threatening to hopes for the good life. "All great cities are probably unchristian from necessity," said William Henry Fish in 1846. "It is an artificial mode of living that cannot be sustained but by fraud, cunning and selfishness." Yet they were also aware of the advantages of city life, which were drawing people away from the towns and countryside; indeed, Fish's comment had been evoked by the visit of some twenty Practical Christians to Boston for the annual reform meetings scheduled there.[7] They dreamed of elevating the New England town into a new social form not only by Christianizing it but by incorporating into it the positive features of urban and industrial life, eliminating the need for cities and creating the conditions that would keep their children from migrating to distant places.

By 1844 the community had survived its early troubles and was able to begin the planned development of the village. At the annual meeting, the executive council was instructed to draft a plan for the layout of streets and lots—an already familiar practice of town developers but one with special conditions at Hopedale. Individual land sales were to be limited to a half acre or less, in line with the community's commitment to equality. Even more important, the council was instructed to sell grants of "perpetual title" only to members of the Practical Christian community pledged to the Standard and only on the condition that the property not be put to uses "notoriously inconsistent" with Practical Christian moral principles; to erect a tavern on a lot, for instance, would nullify the title to the property.[8]

Soon after this plan was approved, the council devised a street plan based on the then fashionable—and convenient—grid system of straight streets and right-angled intersections, a neat and simple geometry that repudiated the often disorderly street patterns of older places like Boston. It was notably prosaic in naming the three thoroughfares that ran parallel to the Mill River (respectively Water, Main, and High streets—with Main being half again as wide as the other two), but it enshrined the idealism of Hopedale in the names of the six cross streets (Freedom, Chapel, Social, Union, Peace, and Hope). Ballou built his house at the corner of Peace and Main streets; in 1846 he received permission to move some soil from Peace Street to his lot, provided that he replaced it with as much gravel for the street. As the plan was implemented, there were four principal residential blocks, each with four houses on half-acre lots, situated between Chapel and Hope, and Main and High streets, with most of the rest of the houses located nearby. The area along the river was assigned chiefly for industrial use because of the dependence on waterpower, and the block between Freedom and Chapel, and Main and High streets was set aside as a village square where the combined chapel and school was located.[9]

A few villagers continued to dream of a some kind of communal "mansion-house," an idea that was reinvigorated under the influence of Fourierism. "From the commencement of our enterprise," wrote Ballou's son-in-law, William S. Heywood, in 1853, "a unitary Mansion has been contemplated," and one "worthy of us in its architectural proportions and finish" would be constructed for those with a taste for collective living once the community acquired the money to build it.[10] The prevailing taste, however, was for the single-family household in the single-family house. By the early 1850s more than twenty houses of various styles had been erected. Most of them were built by private effort, but during the period of the well-organized economy the community itself assisted in the construction of several houses. In 1846, for instance, it agreed to "dig the cellar, haul the lumber and set the underpinning" of a house to be built for a new member. Whoever constructed them, Hopedale houses, including Ballou's, were plain and small; one was twenty-five feet by twenty-one feet and another thirty by fourteen. They were built of lumber from the community sawmill, at least until the 1850s, when several "gravel wall houses" were attempted, with rather dubious results. "These houses," wrote William Henry Fish, "sometimes *fall down* before they are finished, and when they are finished they don't always prove to be so *economical* after all."[11]

The greater part of village effort was directed toward public improvements. Over the years, streets and sidewalks were graded and graveled. In 1844 the community laid a "pipe aqueduct" to bring water from a spring a quarter of a mile away into the village for public and private use. In the same year, it voted to add a cupola to the chapel-schoolhouse and appointed Ballou to acquire a bell to be installed there. The following year it laid out a burial ground for the community on the other side of the Mill River, although little work was done on the cemetery until 1847, after the typhoid epidemic made death a reality. Eventually, the village constructed an icehouse and a woodshed for common use, as well as various work buildings.[12]

While concentrating on developing the village, the community also gave some attention to the rest of its domain, in part to try to balance Hopedale's industrial accomplishments. The villagers, said one, were too much "a mechanical people, laboring under disadvantages, perplexities, and troubles incident to that kind of pursuit." In 1850 Ballou urged greater attention to improving agriculture, for both religious and economic reasons: "Here we are to *gardenize* the earth—to restore *land* and *man* to their Eden-like condition."[13] As he recognized, however, the soil throughout the whole Milford area was not good for general agriculture or even for pasturage: "Our arable lands produce meager crops without frequent manuring." The new emphasis therefore had its greatest effects on the community's Horticultural Branch, particularly on its nursery, which, beginning in 1851, advertised that it had for sale "the most valuable varieties of Fruit Trees, Ornamental Trees and Shrubs, Plants, Roots, Flower Seeds, and Garden Seeds." In 1853 Ballou estimated that the nursery had between seven and ten thousand young trees being grown for sale in markets as distant as Boston.[14]

Agriculture of this sort was natural to a village people whose hearts and hands were in their gardens rather than on the farm. Much of their work went into the planting of shade and fruit trees and shrubs and flowers on their own properties, an activity that became village policy in 1849 when the community required all owners of house lots to plant and care for either shade or fruit trees on the frontage of their properties.[15] Over the next years Hopedale came close to the ideal of a village in a garden. In the summer of 1853 a visitor from neighboring Milford said that it was "one of the quietest and most Eden-like places we were ever in. It does one's soul good to ride through it on a June morning, and breathe the 'fragrance of a thousand flowers,' that cluster around and entwine the snow-white cottages and dwellings of the 'community.'" Two years later the editor of the Woonsocket *Patriot* took note of the "pretty dwellings and their surroundings" and praised Ballou as "the presiding genius of this 'Happy Valley.'" Ballou himself took great pride in this horticultural accomplishment, later calling Hopedale a "gem" among Massachusetts towns, where the passing years had only "heightened the prevailing loveliness and fascination of the scene."[16]

This was one Eden where Man was an active agent, striving through well-organized labor to improve his surroundings. In the early years the community was directly involved in improvement work, but the termination of the well-ordered society in 1847 required a new form of public labor. In 1849 the community created the Hopedale Industrial Army, in which all permanent residents were obligated to serve, with a mission to "promote the cheerful prosecution of public improvements and a generous assistance of persons needing occasional aid"; its male division was responsible for physical improvements. In line with Fourierism, it was organized into "efficient divisions and subdivisions, with suitable chiefs."[17] It was the peaceful army of nonresistance: one of its leaders, Edmund Soward, wrote in 1851 that its detachments were busy "not in the work of destruction but of construction, not rendering beautiful places dreary and desolate but rendering the wilderness beautiful as a garden, not polluting the earth with blood and covering it with the carcases of their fellow creatures but causing it to assume greater attractions."[18] The Industrial Army offered an idea that a later New Englander, Edward Bellamy, was to develop in his utopian novel, *Looking Backward*, into a plan for the reconstruction of America.

Unlike Bellamy's methodically organized labor force, however, the Hopedale Industrial Army was more a peace-oriented version of a local militia unit than anything else. Although all resident males were obligated for service, the army was generally unable to mobilize everyone for the few days of community work to be accomplished each year, and members were soon allowed to commute their obligations at the rate of eight cents per hour of required labor. Nor was the battle for improvement always well fought. After completing the community icehouse with much labor on a cold December day, the army discovered that it had built it in the wrong location. In another case the soldiers of peace beat a hasty retreat from their labors when it began to rain, except for their commander, who, "glittering in his shirt sleeves thro' the falling rain drops," continued to work; the event evoked a wish from Soward, one of the few members with a sense of humor, that community leaders would learn the science of meteorology.[19]

Whatever its foibles, the Industrial Army did exemplify some of the positive features of community service. Each year its members met to determine their future projects, most of which were accomplished energetically and with good cheer. On one hot summer day, the army, equipped with "a train of artillery in the shape of a good strong plough drawn by a powerful team," graded the public square, their thirst being satisfied by two women who "visited the field of action" with buckets of iced lemonade. The next day the army fought through the rain to complete a swimming area for the children of the community. Over the years between 1849 and 1854, various detachments graded streets and made sidewalks, dug a long ditch to drain a troublesome wet area, planted trees, built a community woodshed, laid out a playground, plowed and planted a widow's garden, and made numerous improvements in the cemetery and public square, proving, at least to their own satisfaction, that the shovel and the hoe were a mightier force than the sword and the musket.[20]

The Industrial Army was only one of several communal ventures conceived after the termination of the well-ordered society. By the late 1840s Hopedale had begun to take an interest in fire protection—but not in time to prevent Edmund Soward's home from being burned down in April 1851 with an uninsured loss of four hundred dollars. In response, the community decided to make itself into a "Mutual Fire Insurance Company" to guarantee against similar losses in the future and to uphold fire safety regulations, including one that required every head of family to keep a fire bucket in a convenient place. In the same year it also established a savings bank (with 4 percent interest on deposits) and enacted a small tax on property for a relief fund to affirm its pledge to protect all its members against poverty; the fund was to be administered by an annually elected relief committee responsible for providing material assistance and, if needed, labor to all who could not support themselves.[21] Earlier, the community had even debated the idea of "Health Insurance," but the idea was eventually voted down.[22] The record does not indicate the reasons for this rejection, but likely it was related to another health venture that Hopedale was about to support.

The new venture involved the water cure, a species of medicine peculiarly suited to the spirit of the community. Having decided that the corrupted churches and other prevailing institutions of society defied God's intentions, Practical Christians were inclined to be suspicious of conventional physicians, and with some reason. Although medicine had moved away from the old days of bloodletting and leeches, it had come to depend heavily on drugs, a "multitude of poisonous agents" like arsenic and lead that more than occasionally devastated the body. The use of such unnatural agents seemed to defy God's physiological design that people ultimately make themselves physically as well as morally perfect through the responsible care of their bodies. If, as was often believed, illness was caused by man's abuse of his physiological "system" through such bad habits as drinking and the use of tobacco, medicinal drugs were more likely to hurt than to help. "If I am sick and cannot live without dangerous medicines," wrote Ballou's son, Adin Augustus Ballou, in the late 1840s, "let me die. I am sure I had rather die and go to a holier, happier clime, then live broken down in body by so-called medicine." [23] A few years later, young Ballou was to die at the very beginning of his manhood, but his comment at the time was less a dire prophecy than an expression of hope, since by then Hopedale seemed to have found a better way to health and well-being in the form of the water cure.

The people of Hopedale were receptive to what they considered to be progressive medicine. In the earlier 1840s the idea of curing illness through the liberal use of water, especially in the form of cold baths, had been imported from Europe and was soon taken up by many of those dissatisfied with established medical practices. [24] By 1844 the idea had reached the village through the newly established *Water-Cure Journal*, published in New York City. In November the *Practical Christian* welcomed the first issue of the journal with the comment that "it is a pleasing reflection to contemplate the wisdom and goodness of the creator, in affording his children an abundant supply of water to heal the maladies of the body." The belief that the body could be redeemed through a water cure complemented the faith of religious progressives that God intended all to be saved and all to be happy. Universal salvation in this world and in the next, wrote one enthusiast, had its physical side: "The doctrine of being spiritually saved and physically damned will not produce a Millenium [sic], nor answer as a foundation for a truer order of society. Health—universal Health—only will produce the Millenium."

More practically, the new cure suited the temperance instincts of the villagers, particularly when they found evidence that water could be used as an effective home remedy, to be applied to the body as well as ingested. In 1845 Henry Fish, a member of the community, claimed that he had conquered a severe fever by taking three "sweats," after each of which he plunged into a cold bath. Fish soon proclaimed in the regular physiological column of the *Practical Christian* that the practices of "old school doctors" were being put to shame by the new reform approach with its "simple and true remedies" for preventing as well as curing disease.[25]

The water cure became more than a home remedy at Hopedale, however, thanks to the conversion of the village's resident physician, Dr. Butler Wilmarth. Some twenty years before, Wilmarth had begun a career in conventional medicine with no formal training other than a two-year apprenticeship with a physician at Amherst. Although he was able to achieve some local popularity as a country doctor at Leverett in western Massachusetts, he grew dissatisfied both with his career and with society. By the late 1830s he had become one of Ballou's most devoted followers, inspired by the hope that the combination of "the Bible and Science" would provide the knowledge "necessary for perfect human happiness." One of the early signers of the Standard of Practical Christianity, he had provided some of the money needed to begin Hopedale, but he attempted to continue his practice outside until 1844, when physical exhaustion and little profit persuaded him to join the community.[26]

Wilmarth hoped to maintain a limited medical practice at Hopedale supplemented by a "botanical garden" for the preparation of natural medicines. He soon discovered that the rapid spread of the water cure among the villagers left them indifferent to his skills, and he began to rethink his own views of medicine. By the late spring of

1847 he had decided to test the power of water to cure his own ailments by taking a course of treatment at the New Lebanon Water-Cure Establishment, one of many such facilities that were then springing up throughout the Northeast. In May he wrote to Hopedale that the establishment seemed "well calculated for breaking off pernicious habits and learning correct views of living in all things relating to physical man, and to a good degree to the moral and spiritual man also." A month later he announced that he was "about five-eighths converted" to water as a curative agent, at least if it were combined with the proper diet and behavior.[27]

Wilmarth was so thoroughly converted that by September 1847 he was advertising in the *Practical Christian* for people to buy stock in his proposed "Hopedale Water-Cure Infirmary," intended to be a boarding establishment for the sickly of the outside world. Despite his promises that the infirmary would cure a long list of nervous and physical disorders, he initially got little support, but eventually the community gave him some assistance. He was a popular figure at Hopedale, beloved for his flashes of high good humor and his sharp eye for the ludicrous side of human behavior.[28] Moreover, with the end of the well-regulated economy, his projected infirmary seemed to be the kind of business the village needed. When in 1849 the community again initiated a program to expand the range of its enterprises, it fitted up its largest house for the infirmary and granted six hundred dollars to begin the new business, the money to be raised by the sale of a special issue of its joint stock. By May 1850 the *Practical Christian* announced that Hopedale was prepared to accommodate twenty-five water-cure patients, noting that it was only thirty-two miles from Boston by railroad: "We have a free circulation of air through the Dale, abundance of good water, pleasant scenery, delightful walking grounds."[29]

Unfortunately, the hope of making the village a center of Christian health was doomed to disappointment by the darker side of Wilmarth's personality. Given to fits of depression and irritability, the doctor soon decided that he could not succeed in the water-cure business at Hopedale, and in 1851 he departed to "operate on a larger scale Hydriatically" as the resident physician at the New Graeffenberg Water-Cure Establishment near Utica, New York; two years later, the community was still trying to find a use for the vacant water-cure house, possibly as "a bathing place for Males & Females."[30]

In May 1851 Wilmarth was elected president of the American Hygienic and Hydropathic Association, but his career in the outside world was short. He became dissatisfied with his situation at Utica, and in 1852 entered into a partnership to open a new establishment at Westboro near Worcester, perhaps with some financial assistance from friends at Hopedale. Whether he would have succeeded in this new venture was never to be determined, since in May 1853 the train that he was taking to New York plunged off an open drawbridge into the Norwalk River in Connecticut, and this great advocate of the curative power of water was drowned along with more than fifty other passengers; his body was recovered and buried in the Hopedale cemetery, forever among friends.[31] Later, his widow, Phila O. Wilmarth, studied at the Female Medical College in Philadelphia and in 1856 advertised that from her home at Hopedale she was prepared to attend to the medical problems of the women of the surrounding towns.[32]

The water-cure disaster had little effect on Hopedale's penchant either for "progressive" ideas or for new ventures. In 1851, for instance, it decided to experiment with a plan to encourage its members to form various small associations to do "any particular kind of business" under contract with the community, the aim being to "let every man, woman, and child have a chance to excel in a small sphere, though they cannot in larger ones." To assist small enterprises of this sort, the community created the Hopedale Commercial Exchange, an association of members with trading skills, which was to buy the products of the enterprises and sell them in outside markets, exacting a percentage on the sales for itself; any money beyond an agreed-upon profit was to be given to the community for public use. Acting within the constraints of Practical Christianity, the Exchange was expected to "centralize, harmonize and stimulate every industrial and pecuniary interest of the community"—all this in a village of fewer than two hundred inhabitants.[33]

Although such experiments often failed, their cumulative effect was to encourage growth and innovation. During the late 1840s and early 1850s Hopedale attracted some new and talented people. William S. Heywood, for instance, was a young man with an interest in both moral reform and education; after marrying Ballou's daughter, Abbie, he became an associate editor of the *Practical Christian* and, with her, the founder of the Hopedale Home School, one of the more successful of the village enterprises. William Henry Humphrey, born in Ballou's native town of Cumberland, Rhode Island, was a sash maker and Garrisonian abolitionist who was later remembered as being "very righteous, but very *un* self-righteous." Dudley B. Chapman, originally a brickmason from Connecticut, soon acquired a local reputation as "a genius, especially in the chemistry of soap ingredients." By 1855 Chapman was advertising that he had successfully tested and was manufacturing at Hopedale "a *New* and *Superior* Article of SOAP" that "performs its service with but comparatively little labor, and without the least injury to the article washed."[34] From its small population, the village was able to generate a vitality greater than that of towns many times its size.

The dream of a miniature Christian republic appeared to be descending from air to earth. In 1852 the treasurer, Ebenezer Draper, reported that the community had ended the previous year with a profit rather than a loss and predicted that "very few deficits will come hereafter, unless by fire and flood." During another prosperous year, William Heywood was able to proclaim that "the Hopedale Community is a *Fact* of this nineteenth century. . . . It is, today, no mere fancy, no mere dream of a wild enthusiast, no utopia of the far-off future."[35] Finally, the community seemed to have found its way to a practical and dynamic Christian socialism in which social cooperation and individual freedom were brought into harmony. "Here exists a system of arrangements, simple and effective," wrote Ballou, "under which all capital, industry, trade, talent, skill, and peculiar gifts may freely operate and cooperate, with no restrictions other than those which Christian morality every where rightfully imposes."[36] Nonresistance and the Standard of Practical Christianity had proved themselves to be the bedrock on which to build a heaven on earth.

Hopedale's principal founder and inspiration was pleased, not least because some of these successes had occurred without his direct leadership. Although Ballou recognized that the work was not completed, he concluded in 1851 that the community had attained such strong foundations that his day-to-day leadership was no longer needed, and he resigned as its president and chief official servant after ten often anxious and exhausting years of service. His action would eventually prove to be the most hazardous experiment in Hopedale's history.

5

Fundamentals

The tenth annual meeting of the Hopedale Community on 14 January 1852 brought an "unprecedented attendance" of virtually every member. In part, the meeting conducted its usual business of electing its official servants for the year, including a new president, Ebenezer Draper, the former treasurer. The high point of the gathering, though, was the valedictory address given by the retiring president, Adin Ballou. Although he planned to continue as an influence and inspiration in the community, he abdicated his executive powers and responsibilities in the conviction that Hopedale had been able to devise "a system of social machinery which . . . will operate happily for mankind under the superintendence of any fairly honest and intelligent management." His years of sacrifice, he said, were amply rewarded by the earthly success of Practical Christianity: "To see what I daily behold in this orderly, tranquil, hopeful Dale—abounding in privileges and comforts and quiet dwelling-places—and to hear the whisperings of angels assuring me that this is but a single cluster of unripe grapes compared to the luxuriant vineyards yet planted—surely this is a reward not to be estimated in dollars and cents." [1]

Ballou emphasized the importance of general adherence to religious principles for the continued success of the community. He was careful to distinguish between essential and nonessential principles. On such matters as particular economic and social arrangements, there was room for disagreement and change: "Be characteristically an advancing people. Do not crystalize, do not petrify." On essential moral principles, on fundamentals, however, there was need for unity and obedience. Only by conforming to the principles preached and exemplified by Christ could humankind realize God's intention that all people be restored to the innocence and bliss he had intended for them on earth as in heaven. Christianity was not a religion of dogmas or ceremonies but of fundamental, immutable principles—"a religion for both body and soul, for the next world and for this world, for individuals as such and for society as such, for all peoples throughout all ages." These principles, which had carried Hopedale through its times of trouble and change, were the foundations for what might become a paradise in the world.[2]

In this discourse and elsewhere, Ballou maintained his most basic belief that the world could be saved only when individuals voluntarily conformed their behavior to these principles. Over the years, though, he had come to appreciate the importance of social influences on human action. In the great world of fraud and force, he said in 1850, there was little chance of living a truly Christlike life. It was necessary, then, for those who would be Christians in practice to associate themselves to form a society in harmony with their principles. Whatever its specific form, the true Christian society would be socialistic, "a state of society in which individual interests are harmonized into one common interest." In 1853 he specified the general objectives of Christian socialism as practiced at Hopedale: "There must be sufficient unity and cooperation to guarantee justice to all, necessary employment and subsistence to all, a decent education to all, and a tolerable moral culture to all."[3] Only under such conditions, freed from competition and conflict, would the spirit of Christianity flourish.

Although he accepted the need for some social arrangements, Ballou continued to insist that humanity would never achieve a higher social state until its members voluntarily conformed their behavior to moral principle. Any socialism that based its hopes on the premise that human evil resulted from an evil society alone would inevitably fail because it neglected the mainspring of human conduct, individual responsibility. No matter how perfect the society, it rested ultimately on moral foundations.

He refused, in this regard, to make a distinction between private and public conduct. Private virtue was not virtue unless it also governed one's actions in the social world. Indeed, the greater the success in achieving a virtuous private life the greater the duty to avoid any support for the world's wicked ways. In 1848 Ballou stressed the obligation of every virtuous man to "come-out" from a corrupted society so that his virtue would not be seen as support for "social and organic sins." Such a man should not become a permanent "stay-outer," however, since he had the obligation and opportunity to support the creation of a virtuous moral order.[4]

Ballou's ideal society was a voluntary community of individuals committed not only to living moral lives themselves but also to supporting each other's efforts to live a moral life; all should be willing to reprove their brethren for deviations from fundamental moral standards. Those applicants who refused to make such a commitment would be denied membership; those members who refused to honor it would, after sufficient warning, be expelled.[5] The key to the success of such a community was a clear, comprehensive, and practical code of behavior rather than vague moral pieties, so that no one would be left in doubt about his or her obligations. At Hopedale, this code was provided by the Standard of Practical Christianity and its abridgment, the Declaration, which remained unchanged, the moral bedrock for social change and innovation, throughout the history of the community.

Some elements of moral conduct were more general and fundamental than the rest. The most essential and most distinctive of Hopedale's moral foundations was its commitment to nonresistance. Members were bound to refrain from any injurious force not only among themselves but toward anyone under any circumstance. They might resort to noninjurious moral force, but even this could be applied only within the limits of the Christian obligation to treat the evildoer as a neighbor to be loved as oneself. Nonresistance also obligated all members of the community to abstain from outside political activity, since even the act of voting was an act of support for a government based on the use of force.[6] In the 1850s the *Practical Christian* twice broached the idea that civil government allow voters to specify publicly what political public actions they did not support, giving them the chance to absolve themselves from any complicity in immoral acts. Under such conditions it was theoretically possible for nonresistant voters eventually to eliminate injurious force from the governing process. In fact, however, Hopedale remained an isolated island set against a world of violence and force: "Man devours man," Ballou wrote in 1850. "Man continues to steal and rob and treat man as a chattel."[7]

Hopedale's virtuous isolation was given particular emphasis by the outbreak of the Mexican War in 1846. In the eyes of nonresistants, the war was an act of aggression by the United States, a bloody business deprived of even the usual justification of being a defensive war. Soon after war was declared, Ballou expressed the hope that it would end in defeat for the United States as the aggressor, and he made the by-no-means inaccurate prediction that victory would prove to be a greater curse than defeat: "Mark the prediction.—Your success will be the ruin of your country."[8] For support, the community could look outside to a few opponents of war, most notably the New England Non-Resistance Society. In 1843 Ballou had become president of the society and Hopedale its leading supporter. Near the end of the war in 1848, the society held one of its meetings in the village which concluded with the expressed hope that the war had begun "a great revolution of public sentiment" in favor of nonresistance. The war soon ended, however, and by 1850 the society had disappeared. For a time Ballou took some interest in the short-lived American League of Universal Brotherhood, but during the 1850s Hopedale became even more a lonely outpost of nonresistant principles.[9]

Hopedale's commitment against slavery as a particularly unchristian use of force gave it a longer but also ultimately more troubling outside relationship, with the abolitionist movement. The community's leaders remained committed to Garrisonian abolitionism. In 1844 Ballou and Ebenezer and Anna Draper were among the some 250 members of the New England Anti-Slavery Convention who supported a resolution calling for the dissolution of the American nation in order to free New England from any contact with slavery.[10] Ebenezer Draper served for a time as president of the Milford Anti-Slavery Society, and Hopedale hosted various abolitionist meetings, including, in August 1854, "a general Mass Meeting of the Friends of Universal Freedom" attended by nearly a thousand people who listened to speeches by Sojourner Truth and several white abolitionists.[11] Hopedale's commitment to abolitionism, however, was not as strong as its commitment to nonresistance, in part because slavery belonged to a world distant from the village.

More significant was another principle inherited originally from Garrisonianism: racial and sexual equality. There were apparently no black members of the Practical Christian community, hardly a surprise given the small number of black people in Massachusetts. In some cases the community modified its policy against nonmember residents to provide a temporary home for various blacks, including Lundsford Lane, who had bought himself and his family out of slavery, and Enoch Walker, a young free black laborer. In 1846 the community agreed to provide board and schooling to "a color'd girl" from Uxbridge at a rate, apparently charged to the town, of $1.50 per week.[12] In the early 1850s Ballou became the guardian of the sons of "my colored friend" James Johnson, who had died in nearby Millville. He attempted to place the younger son with some worthy family in which "*color* shall be no detriment," explaining, perhaps a bit uncomfortably, that he could not find a place for the boy at Hopedale because "we have such an oversupply of boys."[13] Overall, it seems evident that the Practical Christian commitment to racial equality, while real, was more a matter of principle than of fact.

The primary test of commitment to equality was the relationship between the sexes. In 1853 Ballou noted that women members had full equality with men, including an equal vote on community affairs. Two years before, he said that Hopedale had been founded on the principle that the sexes were "spiritually, morally and socially equal" and so were entitled to equal treatment.[14] The specific nature of equality, however, was strongly influenced by the sexual division of labor to which the members were accustomed. Early in 1842 the *Practical Christian* promised that Hopedale "will follow the order of unperverted nature, and endeavor to demonstrate the true equality of the sexes, without violating their mutual relations, or forcing either out of the sphere of usefulness ordained by the all-wise Creator." Especially during the first decade, this meant that women were involved primarily with their families in a community that emphasized the importance of family life. Although a few were single, most were wives and mothers; one of the first acts of the community in 1842 was to credit nursing mothers with the then-required forty-eight hours per week of work. Outside the home women had the right to vote in the community meetings, but with very few exceptions positions of authority were occupied by men.[15]

The most significant public role assigned to women during the first decade of the community illustrates this division of labor. In January 1847, during the crisis of the well-ordered economy, the annual meeting established a branch of "Domestic Industry" to employ women and children during their idle times in service work for needy members. This soon became the Hopedale Beneficent Society, the female branch of the Hopedale Industrial Army, which was later called the Hopedale Sewing Circle and Tract Society.[16] Meeting irregularly to sew and socialize, the Beneficent Society made clothing and various other items on order and for a price, the income generally being used for some charitable purpose or to support the publication of a tract such as "Away with War," printed for free distribution in 1848. At least occasionally the members expanded their work into a business by sewing clothes for public sale, placing their profits in the Hopedale Savings Bank. The Beneficent Society was not entirely segregated: in 1854 the secretary noted that "several gentlemen came in and our company was enlivened by music, singing, etc." Mostly, however, the women met to work and talk among themselves and to discuss matters of particular interest to women.[17]

In 1851 the members of the Beneficent Society voted unanimously in favor of employing a female physician at Hopedale. This may have had some effect, since during the following decade the village did have Emily Gay, a single woman and early member of the community who, with some assistance from neighboring physicians, taught herself the basics of homeopathic medicine. She was remembered as having a "naturally intuitive perception of maladies" which won the confidence of her neighbors: "Through sympathetic magnetism, and often a fund of volubility and cheerfulness, as well as through the 'little pills,' she commanded the increasing gratitude of many in Hopedale and vicinity." For a few years after 1855 she was joined by a more formally trained woman physician, Phila Wilmarth, the widow of the water-cure advocate.[18]

In the early 1850s the Beneficent Society also took up the discussion of woman's rights, encouraged in part by the national woman's rights convention at nearby Worcester in 1851. Although it is difficult to gauge the effects of this discussion, it seems to have encouraged an interest in extending the sphere of sexual equality in the village. At the same time, the reorganization of the community's government involved women more fully in its public affairs, especially as members of committees responsible for relief, morals, and education. Between 1850 and 1856 seventeen different female members were elected to such committees.[19] Although no woman was elected to an important executive position, the 1850s significantly expanded the public role of women at Hopedale with no apparent opposition from the men.

Abby H. Price was the leading spokeswoman for equal rights at Hopedale. Mrs. Price and her husband, an unsuccessful hatmaker, had originally joined the community in 1842. A member of the New England Non-Resistance Society and the author of at least ten hymns and various pieces of verse for the community, she was a talented woman whose abilities earned her election in 1843, at age twenty-eight, as the community's secretary, the one exception to the male dominance of major offices in the 1840s. Some unspecified "family cares" led her to withdraw temporarily from Hopedale, but by 1848 she had returned and was elected secretary-treasurer of the newly formed Beneficent Society. Early in 1851 Mrs. Price gave a long speech before the woman's rights convention in Worcester in which she claimed for women the same rights as men had, including participation in all the affairs of government and "suitable and well-compensated employment" to give them financial independence. The convention, well attended by women from Hopedale, approved a set of resolutions along these lines, giving special emphasis to voting as the "corner-stone" of the movement.[20]

In her speech Abby Price expressed general satisfaction with conditions at Hopedale, citing it in support of her demand for equal political rights: "In the little commonwealth where I live all persons have equal rights in public deliberations. Men and women are alike recognized as having a common interest in public offices and measures." In an address given at Hopedale in 1852, she said that "here woman has no restrictions imposed because she is a woman, but has a fair chance of being all she is capable of doing." But she also noted that equal rights had increased the burdens of women with homes and families; she herself had four children. To liberate woman from the tyranny of washing and ironing, therefore, the community should provide a "combined household, where she might be occasionally relieved from the care of the family—and be free to exert her nobler powers unfettered." The idea of cooperative domestic work had already been sanctioned by such national feminists as Elizabeth Cady Stanton and Amelia Bloomer.[21]

The male leadership at Hopedale postponed indefinitely the plan for a combined household, but in theory at least, it supported greater opportunities for women. Lucy Stone, the "gifted advocate of Universal Humanity," was well received when she gave two lectures on woman's rights at Hopedale in late 1851. Two years later William Henry Fish applauded both the ordination of a female minister and the publication of a feminist newspaper. Although Ballou's nonresistance principles left him with little enthusiasm for the woman's suffrage movement, he did open the pages of the *Practical Christian* to its advocates, publishing Abby Price's demand in 1853 that the state of Massachusetts eliminate the word *male* from its voting requirements.[22]

Ballou showed greater enthusiasm for another of her projects, dress reform. A critic of the world's fashions, he had an instinctive distaste for the elaborate and confining dresses decreed for women. Women as well as men, he said in 1840, should be "dressed rationally, comfortably, modestly." A decade later he published Price's speech as president of the "Bloomer Costume Convention" at nearby Milford in which she advocated the new bloomer dress: "Woman has serious and important duties to do, and has no business to envelope herself in useless drapery." At least a few women at Hopedale experimented with the bloomer costume in the 1850s. One member who wore the new dress while she worked declared that it was essential for liberation: "The elevation of women to pecuniary independence can only be accomplished by increasing her strength of body and mind, and it is very evident the present slavery to fashion induces both physical and mental weakness." When some twenty-five bloomer-clad women from Hopedale and vicinity attended the woman's rights convention in Worcester, they attracted such a crowd that the police had to be called in to maintain order.[23]

Overall, with the exception of the Shakers, Hopedale came as close to equality between the sexes as any place in America.

Women as well as men were also equally obligated to conform themselves to Practical Christian morality. In becoming members, they vowed never to use violence in any form, never "to violate the dictates of pure chastity," never to trade in or use an intoxicating beverage, "never to indulge self-will, bigotry, love of pre-eminence, covetousness, deceit, profanity, idleness, or an unruly tongue," never to participate in games of chance or "pernicious amusements," and never to aid or abet others in any sinful act.[24] These were not simply moral goals but moral requirements of daily behavior at Hopedale.

Most members saw nothing oppressive about these requirements, which they believed embodied the progressive morality of their reform culture. "In a truly Christian Community," wrote William Henry Fish, "every one may enjoy as much freedom and individuality as is conducive to the *general* good, including his own."[25] Universal compliance with the requirements would result in a world without violence, slavery, inequality, arrogance, laziness, drunkenness, or sin in general, a world without war, armies, social parasites, prisons, or saloons. Whatever the limits on freedom, virtually all would achieve a greater freedom from the oppressive burdens and restrictions of the corrupted world. Moreover, Hopedale leaders were not narrow-minded bigots. When a woman in a neighboring town committed suicide, for instance, the *Practical Christian* refused to condemn the act as sinful: "Enlightened reason and humanity begin to perceive that such events happen both to the righteous and the wicked, and that they are the results of disease in the nervous system." Ballou detested tobacco smoking, but he reminded himself not only that he had once smoked but that tobacco had "so many respectable and even good hearted devotees, that I must not deprecate thy worship too harshly."[26]

No exception was made, however, in regard to the requirements established in the Standard of Practical Christianity. When a woman abolitionist was reported to have drunk a little wine in celebration of the antislavery cause, the *Practical Christian* condemned her for disregarding the need for total abstinence: "It is a great mistake to imagine that one good cause can be promoted by retarding another."[27] All the required behavior was to be practiced all the time if heaven was to be established on earth: "A continual unscrupulousness in little things undermines all moral principle," Ballou warned. "Righteousness is an aggregate of the littles of life." He was too much of a realist, though, to believe that most people could easily make themselves the "all-sided saints" that his heaven required. How, then, to protect the moral foundations of Hopedale or any other Practical Christian community?

In theory, Hopedale had already found the answer in its strict membership requirements. The community was to be limited to responsible individuals who had voluntarily committed themselves to abide by its moral principles. Surrounded by people who had made the same commitment, each individual would find it easy to practice and difficult to violate basic principles. Generally, there would be no conflict between individual freedom and duty, since every person would naturally choose to do what was right. In those few cases where human weakness overcame commitment, there would be those around who would reprove and correct the lapse. Only in rare cases would it be necessary to apply the supreme penalty available to a nonresistant community, disfellowship and expulsion. In the true Christian state, said Ballou in 1851, "nine out of every ten offenses now committed would be prevented, nine-tenths of the remaining one-tenth would be repented and forgiven without being bruited abroad. Nine-tenths of the last fraction would be peacefully settled by private and friendly arbitration." In such a situation there would be no need for the coercing, punishing machinery of government.[28]

But reality was not the ideal. As Hopedale grew, it acquired numerous inhabitants who had not committed themselves to its moral order. In 1853, of 223 inhabitants, only 76 were members. Many of the rest were children not yet ready for membership, but 22 were probationers who had yet to prove their commitment to principle, and 52 were essentially outsiders. These last people were a matter of considerable concern, especially as possible bad examples for the children. In 1849 a community meeting had voted "that the protracted residence of persons on the Community domain who are not sympathetically interested in our objects, principles and social order has a demoralizing tendency and ought not to be encouraged." However, the village had had trouble finding all the labor it needed among its members and had been forced to recruit outsiders "for the convenience of Industrial operations," making so many exceptions to its policy of exclusion as to virtually nullify it. In 1848, for instance, it advertised for a blacksmith and five farmhands; in 1851 a hired farm laborer drowned while attempting to swim in the community's millpond.[29]

Growth also threatened to attract members of doubtful commitment. In 1851 the *Practical Christian* announced that people who wanted a secure and easy life were not welcome at Hopedale: "We want men and women of noble, generous Christianized souls, who come to us from convictions of duty and religion." Yet the very success of the village and the decline of religious enthusiasm outside increased the chances that at least some of the new members would be slack in honoring their commitments. "We are not sufficiently distinct from the world," warned Abby Price in 1852. "We are not yet that peculiar people . . . that we should be in order rightly to glorify our professions."[30]

History was familiar with societies whose moral bases had been sapped by their prosperity. If Hopedale was to endure as a living model of Practical Christian socialism, some way had to be found to strengthen its moral foundations. In the early days of the Fraternal Communion, its Intendant of Religion, Morals, and Missions had been generally responsible for supervising the moral order; in 1846, for instance, the community instructed the Intendant to prevent some of its boys from fraternizing with the hired men.[31] That role seems to have been secondary to missionary work, however, and in any case, the office was abolished with the termination of the well-regulated economy in 1847. In 1848 the community first attempted to resolve the problem by instituting monthly meetings "for Christian discipline & improvement" which all members were expected to attend, in addition to the two religious meetings held every Sunday. In April 1849 the community tightened its control over children by requiring that they be at home at night and that their parents keep them from "habits of injuring, annoying or teasing their playmates."[32]

The circumstances of the expanding community persuaded Ballou of the need for some form of "moral police," and in 1850 Hopedale created "the Council of Religion, Conciliation and Justice," an annually elected body that was to implement decisions made by the monthly moral improvement meetings. The council was responsible for screening prospective members and for supervising behavior in the village. It was "to reprove, admonish and endeavor to correct all anti-Christian customs, habits and practices springing up within the Community; to advise, mediate, conciliate and adjudicate in all cases of controversy between member and member, and between members and officers of the Community," all of its decisions being subject to appeal to the community itself. Its five members always included two or three women, generally the leading wives of the community like Lucy Ballou and Anna Draper; Mrs. Draper served for five of its seven years.[33]

The council gave special attention to the children of the village, posting rules to regulate youthful behavior and lecturing parents on their responsibility for governing the development of their offspring. In one case it also intervened on behalf of a woman abused by her drunken husband, threatening him with expulsion unless he changed. In theory, it could delve into every corner of life: "We think it proper to remind you," it declared in 1854, "that we are not here in this community, as mere neighbors. . . . But we are here as a great family of brothers and sisters bound together by a common interest, pursuing together, a common end. . . . We ought to feel free to advise, counsel, and admonish each other as we would if bound together by ties of consanguinity."[34] In the communal family there were to be no secrets.

This new moral regime did not please all. Indeed, it was a factor in the decision of several members to leave the community in the early 1850s in protest against what one called an excess of "governmentalism." Two, Clement Reed and Horatio Edson, had joined in the mid 1840s, but another was one of the original stalwarts of the Fraternal Communion, Daniel Whitney, whose departure left only William Henry Fish among those ministers who had helped Ballou formulate the Standard of Practical Christianity. Although Ballou accepted Whitney's resignation with some bitterness and much regret, he took pride in his old friend's later career as a reformer, particularly his "manly" advocacy of woman's suffrage at the state constitutional convention in 1853.[35]

There was neither pride nor regret involved in another departure from the new moral order: in April 1853 the community expelled Matthew Sutcliffe on the grounds that for five years he had aggressively refused to abide by its rules, proving thereby that he was "out of all real fellowship with its principles, polity, discipline, authorities and brotherhood." The English-born Sutcliffe, who told the United States census taker in 1850 that he had no occupation, was troublesome not least because he owned Hopedale's only boarding-house for permitted workers; one charge against him was that he had acted in "a tyrannical and vexatious manner" toward his tenants, even threatening to use physical force. The experience with Sutcliffe was undoubtedly one reason why the council in 1854 urged the community to be more careful in its admission of new members: "Better . . . that we should remain for a long time exceedingly small in numbers than that we encourage the dangers of amalgamating with the old order of society by voluntarily lowering our Standard."[36]

Sutcliffe was only the lesser of two shocks to moral order experienced in 1853, a far greater one coming from perhaps the oldest threat to earthly paradise, human sexuality. In line with his emphasis on a rational morality, Ballou in some respects took an enlightened view of sex; he said in 1854 that no man or woman should marry "without a tolerable knowledge of that part of human physiology which treats of the sexual peculiarities, functions, relationships and necessities, as existing both in male and female." He was also ready to accept the idea that sexual intercourse, beyond its reproductive side, helped strengthen, albeit in a minor way, the marital relationship. He was unbending, however, in his insistence that nothing violate "the dictates of pure chastity." For him, there was to be no sexual intimacy outside marriage, nor was there to be any unbridled sexuality within marriage, since he believed that a reckless sensuality did far more to destroy than to sustain a loving, considerate relationship between husband and wife. Marriage was a permanent relationship, a "sacred union" to be formed only with care and to be broken only by marital infidelity.[37]

Ballou reserved his harshest judgments for "free-love," a doctrine all too fashionable among outside progressives, which he believed was no more than a screen for sexual promiscuity: "It deceives the understanding, perverts the conscience, vitiates the affections, ultimates in sin, destroys domestic happiness, and tends to universal disorder."[38] Since Hopedale took pride in its openness to progressive ideas, the defenders of its moral order were especially concerned about the possible intrusion of the free-love doctrine, and in 1853 they were given reason for their concern by one of their more prominent members, Henry Fish (no relation to William Henry Fish), the auditor of the community during its early days and later the head of the Hopedale nursery.

Sometime in the early 1850s Henry Fish had become interested in the welfare of a Mrs. Seaver, a new member whom he had taken into his home probably as an act of charity, since she was described as "a great sufferer from domestic troubles, diseased bodily and mentally." Eventually, his interest in Mrs. Seaver became too deep for his wife, who complained to the Council of Religion, Conciliation and Justice. An investigation convinced the council that there was fire to the smoke, and it reprimanded the guilty twosome. The incident might have ended there if they had not then defended their relationship on the basis of the free-love doctrine, an open defiance of their pledge to uphold pure chastity and an immediate cause for their dismissal from the community.[39]

Unfortunately for everyone, the affair also cost Hopedale one of its most talented members, Abby Price. According to her own account, Mrs. Price had tried to prevent what she took to be an innocent relationship from becoming a public scandal, only to be charged by the council "with knowing too much to keep dark." Offended by the reprimand, she left the community for the Raritan Bay Union, an experiment with a tamed version of Fourierism in New Jersey, of which Clement Reed was originally the Treasurer; the Raritan Bay community eventually failed, but neither Price nor Reed returned to their old friends, even though Reed had buried three of his children in the Hopedale cemetery. Abby Price, whom Ballou long remembered as "an intelligent woman, with a literary and poetic genius," died at Red Bank, New Jersey, in 1878 at the age of sixty-four.[40]

The incident was a major crisis for the small community. Hopedale responded by adopting ten resolutions "unequivocally" affirming pure chastity. The first resolution defined chastity as prohibiting "adultery, fornication, self-pollution, and lasciviousness, not only in external act, but also in purpose and in cherished desire." The last expressed abhorrence of free-love theories and practices in any form, including "social refinement, individual sovereignty, physiological research, and philosophical progress." The community also issued a list of fifteen regulations intended to tighten control over the behavior of residents, especially of children, who were prohibited from being on the streets after nine o'clock and from playing except at designated times.[41] Perhaps because it was anxious to keep out the wrong people, Hopedale made no attempt to conceal its tightened moral controls. "There was nothing so public and general, nothing so private and personal," said the *Practical Christian* in 1854, "that it may claim exemption from criticism and judgment" in a society where religion was expected to "cover the whole field of human thought, feeling, and effort."[42]

These restrictions could be defended as required by Hopedale's mission "to bring order out of confusion and beauty out of deformity." They also had the effect of distorting Hopedale's character in the eyes of outside observers. Early in 1854 one journal associated with free love took note of the prosperity and general progress of the village only to condemn it for its lack of freedom:

> The most puritanical blue laws that ever disgraced the statutes of 'the land of steady habits' were not more oppressive and destructive of all spiritual and affectional growth and enjoyment than the rules and regulations, espionage, scandal, and tyranny of the directors of this association. . . . This petty, miserable, pervading social tyranny, felt more or less in all our society, culminates at Hopedale.

Ballou republished this attack in the *Practical Christian* with little comment except to urge all those who wanted sexual freedom to stay away from the community.[43]

Such criticism, unfortunately, had a point. Efforts to regulate conduct did not square well with an experiment founded on the voluntary commitment of its members, a matter that Abby Price had touched on in 1852 before the scandal when, after praising the "improvement in moral discipline" made in the previous year, she said that the community gave too much attention to outward conformity and too little to "the spiritual element, that earnest faith, that enthusiasm, which would increase our power . . . over the world." Hopedale's prosperity, the turnover in its membership, and the ebb of the religious enthusiasm that had inspired it had begun to create an atmosphere in which conformity was easier to expect than true moral commitment.[44] Thus was Ballou's miniature Christian republic of devout Christian moralists becoming a society, recapitulating in little more than a decade the fate of every inspired social innovation.

In its own miniature way, however, it remained an extraordinary thing, a distinct creation set apart from the world and at least a little closer to heaven. If it was drifting from the moral enthusiasm of its primitive years, it was also reaching a time when its members could begin to reap the promised benefits of their toil, not only material benefits but the promise of one of their hymns:

> May every year but draw more near
> The time when strife shall cease
> And Truth and Love all hearts shall move
> To live in joy and peace.

Its religious commitments may have softened, but it had, even with its restraints, created conditions that allowed its members greater freedom to develop than they could have found outside. In its constitution Hopedale had bound itself to create a state "in which no individual shall suffer the evils of oppression, poverty, ignorance, or vice through the influence or neglect of others."[45] If in 1853 it seemed preoccupied with vice, it had not forgotten the rest of this pledge.

6

Moral and Mental Culture

Moral control was only a part of Hopedale's strivings for a Practical Christian society. Ballou accepted human depravity as a fact to be resisted, but he also believed that ultimate human goodness and happiness was God's intention and Man's obligation. Whatever the corruptness of people at any one time, their souls "are progressively ascending . . . through better and better forms, as by gradual process of purification, to higher stages of excellence." The process of purification was not an easy one, especially in regard to those who seemed doggedly resistant to moral improvement. In 1850 the *Practical Christian* said that the community had on some occasions received a few "vicious" people with the intention of reforming them only to injure itself without effecting a change, partly "because we had among us no skillful, experienced, and fully competent moral physicians." It resolved to abandon the attempt.[1]

Ballou believed, however, that the truly vicious were only a small minority. Once enlightened to the promise of Practical Christianity, most humans would voluntarily commit themselves to the struggle for moral progress. Through the committed and guided exercise of their individual wills, they would cultivate the good and suppress the bad in their natures, at least when they were removed from a corrupting society to a "rational Christian union" like Hopedale, where cooperation rather than competition would prevail. If Ballou believed in the need for "an orderly well-regulated neighborhood," he linked this to a concern that everyone be afforded "decent opportunities for religious, moral, and intellectual culture" so that each individual could freely develop his or her full moral and mental potential.[2]

80

Life at Hopedale was often somber, especially during its pioneer years, but the community did attempt from the beginning to add an element of joy to its earnest strivings for improvement. In 1843 it announced that it was establishing the custom of "noticing the birthdays of the members . . . by an evening gathering, hymns, prayer, and personal congratulations. We have found these occasions truly affecting, profitable, and refreshing to our better feelings." It also gave much attention to the subject of amusements, especially for children, a particularly perplexing matter for its leaders. On the one hand, they were suspicious of the often brutal, lewd, enervating, and time-wasting entertainments of the corrupted world; on the other hand, they recognized that there was a basic human need for some healthful diversion and merriment to provide occasional release from the serious business of life.[3] How, then, to invent amusements that would nurture rather than detract from moral development?

This question became the particular concern in the 1840s of Daniel Whitney, the official servant for educational affairs, who became, as Ballou later called him, "a kind of Purveyor of Amusements." Whitney spent much time inventing and arranging various sports, games, and other entertainments, his most notable effort being an attempt to establish monthly "festivals" where members met to sing, give speeches and readings, and play some games. This effort to consolidate communal feelings on a monthly basis seems to have faltered even before Whitney abandoned the community, but it did yield some more-permanent results, including an annual May Day festival that Whitney helped inaugurate in 1848 with a hymn, "Wildwood Flowers":

> And why should we not love the flowers
> That grow about this Dale of ours
> Sweet tokens they will ever prove
> Of our dear Father's precious love.

In 1850 a sympathetic visitor observed one May festival, celebrated with music and singing in the Hopedale chapel: "Across one end of the room is a table covered with refreshments, and with vases filled with fresh flowers. On the seats are the men, women, and children, looking so bright, so loving, intelligent and happy."[4]

Hopedale also celebrated the major traditional holidays in its own distinctive way. In 1845 some eighty people sat down at a long table in the machine shop to have Thanksgiving dinner, after which they sang hymns especially composed for the occasion. Eventually, the community even got around to commemorating the Fourth of July, despite its associations with war and riotous behavior, by emphasizing its connections with the rights of man rather than with nationalism. Without drunks and firecrackers, the community met to celebrate its own devotion to the divine principles of freedom. Such festivals, wrote William S. Heywood, "receive their characters from that which is useful substantial, true, and therefore have a permanancy and value peculiarly their own."[5]

Hopedale's most momentous celebration was Christmas, held in December to commemorate not so much Christ's birth—which was supposed to have been in the spring—as his example. It was a conscious defiance of New England's religious past, when Puritans had spurned Christmas as a heathen holiday. In 1854 Heywood began his address to the assembled residents by making "a very unpuritanical wish," that they have a Merry Christmas, one that would combine an earnest appreciation of Christ and of the Christian mission with "our idea of fraternal affection and sympathy in connection with social pleasure." After the evening service, a large Christmas tree was unveiled loaded with "many golden and glittering treasures, and not a few fantastic toys." Adults as well as children received gifts; an unnamed giver left a cow worth forty-five dollars in Ballou's barn, while another anonymous donor placed thirty copies of Ballou's latest book under the tree for distribution among the members.[6]

These affairs were pleasant ways to reinforce Hopedale's commitment to its goals. The same could be said about its efforts to create a communal cultural life. The Practical Christians had little use for the fine arts, although they were pleased when in 1845 a generous neighbor in Milford paid a portrait artist, Bass Otis, to paint a portrait of Ballou, which was then exhibited in Boston as well as in the Milford area. A town people suspicious of the high culture of the corrupted cities, they were not inclined to the visual arts. On the other hand, Ballou and his associates did believe that artistic works could be used as agencies of moral power to "regulate all the affections, faculties, interests, relations and conduct of rational creatures."[7]

The greatest of these instruments of moral power, they believed, was music, the most harmonious of the arts. Although Hopedale gave some encouragement to instrumental music, its dominant concern was singing, an art form sanctioned not only by religious tradition but by the example of the singing Hutchinson family, who lent their popularity and talents to the abolitionist cause. "Who has ever listened to the simple, pathetic, soul-subduing, heart-purifying strains of our Hutchinsons," asked Ballou, "without confessing the majesty of music—the potency of its sway over all the feelings of our nature? Could we bring every band, every choir, all the masters of this captivating art into the service of Temperance, Freedom and Peace, what would they not accomplish for our world?"[8]

From the beginning the community intended to make the moralizing power of music a central element of its life, voting in May 1842 that every Tuesday evening be "appropriated to improvement in singing." Vocal music enlivened both its festivals and its religious services. When in 1843 the Fraternal Communion gathered to celebrate Ballou's fortieth birthday, its members sang a hymn written by Abby Price for the occasion:

> Sing! Hopedale, sing! your voices raise,
> Let every heart attuned to praise,
> Raise loud the cheerful lay;
> Praise God who gave our brother dear,
> Who spares his life from year to year,
> To cheer us on our way.[9]

Over the next decade, members of the community composed dozens of hymns to celebrate special occasions and especially its mission to free the intemperate, slaveholding, fighting world from its sinful ways:

> This heaven and earth shall be renewed
> By God's regenerating word,
> All nature to be Christ subdued,
> Nor sound of sin or woe be heard.

Most of these hymns were published, first in the *Practical Christian* and then in two collections: *The Hopedale Collection of Hymns and*

Songs for Use of Practical Christians (1850), which included some three dozen of Hopedale's own songs along with others selected from various sources, and the more completely original *Communal Songs and Hymns* (1856). The two collections were an armory of hymns for the temperance, abolitionist, and nonresistance causes.[10]

Ballou, the author of didactic verse as well as prose, wrote the greatest number of hymns, with such titles as "Who Is a Christian?" "Breakfast Hymn," and "Social Reform." Almost as prolific were two women. The talented Abby Price composed songs both for various celebrations and on general themes of reform, ten of which were published in the *Hopedale Collection*. The other woman was Mary Colburn, Mary Jackman until she married the recently widowed Samuel Colburn in 1844. Mrs. Colburn contributed eleven hymns on reform themes to the *Hopedale Collection*, including one entitled "New Social State":

> Then man, transformed in mind,
> His God-like powers shall prove,
> And make this new-created earth
> A paradise of love.

Although she lacked Abby Price's dynamic interest in woman's rights issues, she impressed Ballou as being a woman of "literary genius in poetry and public addresses on reformatory themes."[11]

Many of Hopedale hymns were intended to awaken the outside world to reform themes, but others were designed to remind itself of its special commitment to a Practical Christian life. One of the longest in the 1856 collection was the "Song of Compact," which began:

> We cheerfully agree, all agree,
> To live in unity, unity
> And faithfully fulfill
> The compact we have made.

Another, "Money," acknowledged the importance of the green stuff even in a Practical Christian society but reminded all that it was "made for righteous use" and not for "idol worship."[12] Overall, Hopedale made the song and the hymn a force for communal unity and a reminder of communal obligation.

Music was not the community's only or perhaps even most revealing cultural pride. In general, the members of the community were, as the *Practical Christian* boasted in 1857, "a plain, practical people . . . much like the middle class of New England generally," not one of whom held a university degree. Like most of the small-town middle class, however, they hungered for the cultural benefits often found only in cities during these years of limited communications. Although true Christianity was opposed to the corrupted culture of the corrupted world, Ballou insisted, it was not opposed to "any kind of useful knowledge, per se, or to any kind of mental culture or accomplishment in itself"; rather, true Christians should make "it an imperative duty—a part of their morality—to cultivate by continued exercise the intellectual nature." Like Ballou himself, Practical Christians had little use for university education, which seemed perversely designed to suppress rather than to nurture both good sense and inspired creativity.[13] It was the right and duty, then, of plain people like themselves to find a better way to cultivate the intellectual as well as the moral side of human nature.

Hopedale attempted to balance its control over moral behavior with a commitment to intellectual freedom as part of its larger pledge to protect every member from the "oppression" of ignorance. "Hostility to new opinions is exceedingly unfavorable to the intellectual and spiritual improvement of our race," said William Henry Fish in 1846. "Hence we have assumed the position that every conscientious individual should 'utter all his moral convictions as freely as the winds blow and the waters run.'" As the editor of the *Practical Christian*, Ballou said that it was his policy to go "for the largest liberty of thought and expression, not fundamentally intolerable," meaning that, beyond the "few and plain" truths essential to the community, nothing was sacred and nothing was to be ignored in the search for truth. Such limitations as Fish's reservation of freedom to "conscientious" individuals did not please radical libertarians, but they cast few shadows over thought at Hopedale. When Robert Owen spent two days in the village in late 1845, his opinions were welcomed even though his naive communism and materialism had been rejected by the community.[14]

The *Practical Christian* provided space for members to state their opinions, and at various times this opportunity was expanded by two other periodicals issued by the Hopedale press. In the mid 1840s

Ballou's son, Adin Augustus Ballou, published a young people's paper, the *Mammoth*, on an irregular basis until he grew tired of it in 1848.[15] For a year in 1851–52, a somewhat more mature paper, the *Diamond*, was published as a bimonthly; one of its three editors was George T. Garrison, the eldest son of William Lloyd Garrison, who had been sent by his abolitionist father to the Hopedale school because "it is a great thing to be with those who are virtuous, upright, kind, and loving in all their dealings." The paper was largely a miscellany of stories, bits of information, and various puzzles (a conundrum: "Why is congress like a ledger?" Answer, because "it contains ciphers."), but its young editors did uphold their promise to "fearlessly denounce errors and propagate truth." Although they rejected one reader's demand that they take a stand in favor of boy's rights ("wait till your beard grows"), they did advocate a woman's right to "define her own sphere and be and do all she is capable of doing." The *Diamond* was terminated in March 1852 when its editors completed their education at Hopedale.[16]

Far from attempting to cut itself off from the outside world, Hopedale made a determined effort to keep itself informed of intellectual progress. The *Practical Christian* published in every issue various articles clipped from other periodicals, mostly from reform papers like Garrison's *Liberator* and Horace Greeley's *New York Tribune* but also from a wide variety of more-worldly sources such as the *Scientific American*, the *Boston Traveler*, and the *New York Herald*. To assure itself even greater access to the outside, the community voted in 1846 to create its own postal service to provide for the delivery of outside papers to individual subscribers. By 1855 this village of less than two hundred people was taking a total of 130 issues of various periodicals on a regular basis, not counting the issues of some 60 papers received by the community in exchange for the *Practical Christian*.[17]

Ballou took great pride in the belief that Hopedale demonstrated how nonresistance could enable society to concentrate its spending on education and culture rather than on instruments of violence and coercion. In 1850 he deplored the wealth wasted in war which might have been used to eliminate human ignorance, estimating that the amount of money spent on even a small conflict like the Seminole War in Florida could have purchased three collections of all of the some three million books that the world had published over the previous four centuries.[18] In 1842, while it was still struggling to get started, the community began a small public library, one of the first in the country. By 1855 the Hopedale library, located in the combined school and chapel building, had over six hundred volumes, excluding various public documents sent to it by Senator Charles Sumner and other sympathetic congressmen. Open at least once a week for lending purposes, the library had its established rules, including fines for overdue books.[19]

For purposes of entertainment as well as edification, the community had met to discuss ideas and issues from its earliest days. "In the course of each year, we have had," said Fish, "not only some new, but some strange . . . views presented to us—sometimes by members of the community, sometimes by persons from abroad." In 1846 Hopedale began to institutionalize this practice by providing for monthly "Lyceum and conference meetings," and in 1849 this scheme was expanded by organizing all inhabitants over twelve years of age into a community lyceum that was to meet once a week during the colder months and once a month during the growing season. The officers of the lyceum were instructed "to procure the delivery of at least one instructive scientific or literary lecture every month, to provide suitable questions for public discussion . . . to encourage the writing of brief essays by the members . . . to promote the formation of original classes for the prosecution of useful studies, and in general to execute its order and minister its affairs in such a manner as to render it an efficient instrumentality for mental improvement." Over the following years, members gave lectures, declamations, and readings on such matters as vegetarianism and the industrial advantages of a cooperative community, inspired by the hope of improving their knowledge and reasoning powers.[20]

A shortage of money limited the number of outside lecturers, but in the summer and fall of 1850 the lyceum did get Professor William S. Brown to give a course of lectures on chemistry, probably in response to Ballou's call earlier in the year for a scientific analysis of the soils in the community domain. Brown evoked much interest among the members, some of whom formed a chemistry class during the winter: "Who seeks for science will her treasures gain." Later, it listened to Luther Hills, a phrenologist, lecture on the "causes of cerebral, physiological, mental, and moral deprivation." Hills returned to give two lecturers on physiological abuses, "especially those of a sexual nature," supporting his case with numerous pictures and with "stubborn facts in resistless array." Ballou was convinced that Hills had brought "a measure of physiological and temporal salvation" to at lest some of his listeners.[21] In general, the lyceum seemed to demonstrate the ability of a community like Hopedale to provide itself with intellectual advantages not available in towns many times larger.

The lyceum meetings were only part of a much larger system of intellectual improvement that Hopedale was attempting to create. Ballou was an ardent advocate of education at every stage of life. In 1846 he asked: "If every human being over seven years of age could be enabled and induced to expend habitually four hours per day in positive intellectual and moral exertion, need there remain through the third generation a single ignorant, vulgar, vicious, irreligious person on earth?" He dreamed of a comprehensive system of education that would progressively improve the physical, emotional, intellectual, industrial, social, and religious natures of all people, down to such details as their diets, habits, skills, manners, and sexual relationships.[22]

Ballou placed much responsibility on individual parents. The training of the next generation was to begin even before birth with appropriate care of the mother to prevent debilitating damage to the fetus and was to continue in the family until adulthood. In 1841, before Hopedale was established, he published a long article addressed to parents on the development of their children. After confessing that he had been himself a "sinner in the treatment of my children," he condemned the prevailing tendency to depend for discipline on "whipping, slapping, cuffing, shaking, and pinching," a battering of children's bodies that had no place in a nonresistant community. He emphasized that he was not opposed to discipline but rather that he was advocating a better means that required from parents a "steady hand and general good management." With the promise that he would himself try to practice what he preached, he laid down fifteen rules to manage children, culminating with "train them to think, feel, speak and act for themselves, as answerable to God rather than man."[23]

Outside the family, the community was also to be the good, steady parent of its young. From the beginning children were a major presence at Hopedale; of 163 people listed by the census taker in 1850, 70 were younger than eighteen. While it was struggling to survive during its first year, the community had begun to create its own educational system, in fulfillment of its constitutional promise "to secure to our posterity the blessings of a more salutary, physical, intellectual, and moral education." The first building erected in the village, in the spring of 1842, contained a schoolroom, and less than two years later the community built the combined schoolhouse and chapel with the help of outside donations. Initially, the community had to finance its education on its own while also paying school taxes to the town of Milford (of which it was a part), being unwilling to accept town interference in its educational affairs. Finally, in 1847 Milford agreed to return part of the taxes to the community, while allowing it control over its school.[24]

By then Hopedale was able to provide schooling for all of its children, ages five to eighteen, four hours a day for nearly forty weeks a year, in line with its determination that "no child or youth . . . shall be permitted to grow up without a decent education in the common branches of useful learning." In 1848 the school was placed under the authority of a newly created Board of Education and Mental Improvement and supported by a "perpetual" education tax of 1 percent on the income of members; this tax was later raised to 1½ percent and then in 1852 made dependent on the ability of each member to pay, "he or she being privileged to abate or increase the rate." By 1854 the growth in the number of students to nearly sixty required the creation of two separate classes and the enlargement of the school building.[25]

The physical facilities were hardly better than those of an ordinary one-room village school. The system of instruction, however, was a source of much pride, particularly after 1848 when the Board of Education and Mental Improvement put the school in the charge of Ballou's daughter, Abbie, recently graduated from the state normal school at West Newton. Abbie S. Ballou was a natural teacher who had acquired an understanding of the art and science of teaching. "We admire the system of instruction adopted by Miss Ballou," wrote an observer from Milford in 1848. "We have rarely witnessed so much affability blended with so much dignity. . . . In her recitations, joining herself with the class, addressing them as though she were only an older member of their own body." She was herself only nineteen.[26]

The Milford observer and subsequent visitors were even more impressed by the facility of the children in answering difficult questions, particularly those in arithmetic. In 1854 Ballou was very pleased with the performance of the pupils during their public examination, noting that they multiplied, divided, and squared numbers given to them in rapid succession without difficulty; he made special note of their ability to understand the basic principles of arithmetic: "The principles thus brought within the comprehension of your children, will enable them to solve all kinds of problems that ever occur." The pupils also impressed him with their knowledge of such subjects as grammar, reading, geography, and, one of Ballou's favorites, physiology.[27]

Undoubtedly, public exhibitions did not represent day-to-day realities, as the community itself recognized. There was some expressed concern over absences and the less than perfect order among the pupils. And among the reasons given for the expulsion of Matthew Sutcliffe in 1853 was his persistence in complaining that his children had been "slighted, neglected, degraded, or mistreated either by the Teacher or other scholars."[28] However, the school seems to have been a fair expression of a community concerned with the preparation of its children to be rational as well as useful citizens of the new social world. More than occasionally, the process received reinforcement from the lyceums and from individual members, especially Edmund Soward. The English-born mechanic and father of horticulture at Hopedale had a self-educated man's enthusiasm for knowledge which made him "the *Encyclopedia of reference* to our whole Community." Soward, a widower, took special delight in instructing the young, holding special classes for them during the winter months. On his death in late 1855, he willed his little property to the Hopedale school; in one instance, money from the Soward fund was used to take some of the younger children to Boston to see some "trained seals and mice."[29]

The strongest communal reinforcement for education came from Adin Ballou himself. Although generally satisfied with the school's performance, Ballou wanted much more, a system that would cultivate all children in all aspects so as to assure an intelligent adherence to the requirements of Practical Christianity. This, he complained in 1847, the community had neglected to do, allowing by this neglect for the development of "vicious habits" in the young. He urged that the women meet frequently to consult on ways by which the range of moral and religious influence could be extended.[30] The chief problem was the free time that children had beyond the control of the community. In theory, idle minds and hands could be kept busy in useful work. In 1846 the community appointed a committee "to see that the boys be employed after school hours"; nine years later it appointed another committee to draft some plan to incorporate manual labor into the children's schooling. Except for the infrequently mobilized Industrial Army and more frequent exhortations to parents, however, little was done to resolve the problem, probably because the village simply did not have enough work for its young people to do.[31]

Ballou gave more personal attention to another situation in which he took a particular interest. Perhaps because he was the father of two teenagers, he became concerned with extending the moral and intellectual culture of young people beyond the existing school. In 1848, when he was elected a member of the new Board of Education and Mental Improvement, he began to meet every Monday evening with a group of young adults for the purpose of discussing various issues. When that group proved to be too small and unstable to be perpetuated, he expanded it to include adolescents, giving it a formal organization in 1849 as the Inductive Communion. As its named indicated, this association was intended to complete the preparation for membership in the Practical Christian Communion. It was designed to be a self-regulating "mutual improvement society for the cultivation of the religious and moral sentiments, the intellectual faculties, and true self-respect of our young people." Generally with Ballou in attendance, groups of from five to thirty youths met each Monday evening at the home of a member of the community to discuss readings and to give papers on various subjects. Beginning in July 1851, these papers and other writings were published in a handwritten monthly, the "Inductive Harbinger," with an appointed editor, female or male, for each issue.[32]

Ballou generally guided the discussions with a gentle but strong hand. When he was asked to give his opinion on novels and other forms of fiction, he said that he was "a matter of fact man" who found enough interest in nonfiction without resorting to readings of a doubtful character. Much of the early attention of the group was devoted to historical works because Ballou hoped to teach the right use of history. Over the years, though, the group seems to have become more active in selecting for itself such subjects of contemporary interest as woman's rights, education, and vegetarianism (Ballou confessed that he had not been able to decide on the matter of meat eating but recommended against it when possible).[33]

The writings in the "Inductive Harbinger" were probably a fair reflection of Ballou's influence on the thinking of the young. In the first issue John Gaffney, a twenty-two-year-old laborer from Ireland, stated the position of the new paper: "We will make no compromise with War, Slavery, Intemperance or the thousand ways which man has invented to oppress and live at the expense of his fellow man, but will ever speak the truth." In a subsequent issue young John Mundy rejected the idea that sinful men could be saved by a simple act of conversion: "I think that the redemption of this world is to be expected by obeying the moral and physical laws of our Creator," which demanded a lifetime of self-discipline. Later one writer was enthusiastic about the progress of science and invention, especially in creating improved conditions for moral and intellectual development: "The world was never wiser nor better than it is today." It was, then, the duty of the young to strive even harder to improve themselves—to aim, said another young enthusiast, as high as possible: "I will only stop at perfection." In a still later issue "Lida" defended idealists like herself against the criticism that they were too fanciful and visionary, by arguing that imagination "elevates the mind above that which is sensual and selfish, and quickens it into spiritual life & allies the soul to angels."[34]

Ballou found much satisfaction in this involvement with young minds, but the Inductive Communion was not enough to fulfill his ambitions for education. Aside from the occasional nature of its meetings, the Communion suffered from fluctuating membership. In 1853 Joseph Bailey, one of its leaders, said that only a handful of the founding members remained, most of the rest having "left this place and scattered in various directions. Some . . . have gone astray in the paths of sin and folly."[35] The fact that Bailey, a twenty-seven-year-old English-born worker, himself remained with the group from beginning to end was not particularly exceptional, but the turnover was high enough to underscore the need to provide greater opportunities for the education of young adults within the village.

That Ballou was obliged to send his own children outside to complete their education intensified his interest in the problem. What Hopedale seemed to need was some way to realize his dream of a system that would embrace all, "from the infant group to the highest collegiate class." In 1848 he served on a committee, along with his exassociate George Stacy, that recommended that the town of Milford establish a high school, but the establishment of such a worldly school would not serve Hopedale's needs.[36] The village was too small to support a higher school by itself, but by 1851 Ballou had devised a solution that he hoped would provide the right kind of advanced education not only for Hopedale but for the outside world.

In December the *Practical Christian* published his plan for "the Hopedale Educational Home" to provide every level of education from the primary through the collegiate. This "new and peculiar Educational Institution" was to provide training at reasonable rates for all youth regardless of class, race, or sex:

> One great want of the age is an Educational Institute, in which the sons and daughters of the common people, especially those friendly to the great Reforms and to constructive Progress, may receive a comprehensive and well balanced development of all natural faculties. An Educational *Home* for children and youth is demanded . . . where by day and night, in study, in active exercise, in recreation, in the parlor, in the dining-room, in social intercourse, and in public places, they may be cared for with parental fidelity.

The new school would give students "a high toned moral character . . . a sound mind well cultivated, stored with useful knowledge and capable of inquiring, reasoning, and judging for itself . . . a healthful vigorous body . . . good domestic habits . . . and generous social qualities." It would teach all to be self-sustaining individuals not only by giving them an education in the useful arts but also by providing them with practical work for which they would be paid on the basis of actual results.[37]

Ballou projected a boarding school for two hundred students, some from Hopedale, to be built for twenty-five thousand dollars, mostly from outside sources. He had plans drawn for a large three-story academy building, potentially the most imposing edifice in town. It was an ambitious plan, but he believed that the reform-minded world was ready for it, citing as an example a recent call by Horace Greeley for colleges "which shall graduate not merely Masters of verbal, but Masters of useful arts."[38] By benefiting the outside world, the Educational Home would also benefit Hopedale, making it a center of advanced reform culture, providing it with a new and large business, and extending the education of its own young people. It would be the nonresistant version of the "booster college" common to town-building schemes, especially in the West, which would attract the right people and support from outside. And it would satisfy Ballou's personal need to find a place within the community for his son, Adin Augustus Ballou, who was soon to reach adulthood.

Ballou took great pride in his daughter, Abbie, but the apple of his eye was the son whose birth in 1833 had saved him from the utter despair of having lost his first two sons to disease. The father tried his best to mold Augustus along both rational and spiritual lines. When the boy requested to see a militia muster at nearby Milford, Ballou used it as an opportunity to present his nonresistant views, refusing either to deny or to agree to the request; the boy decided not to go. When he was seventeen, Adin Augustus expressed an ideal for himself that his father undoubtedly approved: "Be an independent man, a free thinker, a mighty actor. Be a wise man, a careful discriminator. Be a good man blending humanity with impetuosity, humility with power. Be independent and hold for the right and let your whole strength go to improve and not to destroy God's creatures."[39] The young man was raised to be a responsible and productive leader in his father's world. At the age of ten he was placed in the Hopedale printshop with the idea of making him a printer and publisher, and when he was twelve he began the periodical *Mammoth*. At fourteen, he became foreman of the printshop, while also issuing the *Mammoth*, attending school, managing the community post office, and learning to play the violin.[40]

In 1849 he was liberated from the burdensome job of foreman in order to prepare himself to attend the state normal school at Bridgewater, but the gentle yet persistent pressures exerted by his father remained. In 1850 he was taken to the graves of "my departed brothers," two boys he had never seen but whose places he must have felt obliged to fill. The next year he was admitted to membership in the community, having resolved, so his father believed, to devote his life to creating the new Practical Christian social order. Although Adin Augustus had many happy moments at Hopedale, he was undoubtedly ready and eager, in the summer of 1850, to begin his training as a teacher at Bridgewater; in little more than a year he so impressed the normal school authorities that he was offered the position of junior assistant principal.

Again, however, there were pressures, since by then Ballou had conceived of the Educational Home, whose principal when it opened was to be Adin Augustus. The young man's feelings are not known, but it is notable that, as his father did when he had faced career anxieties many years before, Augustus had a vision. Early in 1852, as a friend later told Ballou, he was returning to his room when "suddenly a spirit-voice uttered distinctly to his soul the premonition *You are going to be very sick!*" Within hours he became violently ill from influenza, and two weeks later, on 8 February, he died despite the watchful care of his helplessly anxious parents.[41]

The remains of Adin Augustus Ballou, aged eighteen, were buried in the Hopedale cemetery; the tombstone erected by his parents was inscribed with a verse that began "most precious treasure of our hearts." It was a crushing blow for Ballou, who only shortly before had resigned as president of the community in part to concentrate on the Educational Home. Rather than carry out his dream, he wrote and published a memoir of his departed son, expressing the hope to its readers that "if you are parents, may you be blessed with children like Augustus. If you must mourn their early dissolution, may you mourn with as much to comfort you, as they [the Ballous] have who hope in a few fleeting years to be welcomed by such a son and brother to the home of the angels."[42]

Ballou had more than the usual confidence that he would see his son again, since in April 1852 he printed in the *Practical Christian* a lengthy report on a series of communications "purported to come from the spirit of Adin Augustus Ballou, our dear Son, through Elizabeth Alice Reed of Hopedale, Writing Medium." Starting a few days after Augustus's death, the communications presented a hopeful view. In one, Augustus said that he was finally able to meet his two dead brothers, who were doing well; in another, he assured his father that while he saw travails ahead for the people on earth, he could glimpse the dawn of a better day: "Father, be patient. . . . Another century cannot commence, before this great change will be wrought." After describing heaven in notably rational terms, the messages abruptly ceased without explanation, but not before they had convinced Ballou that they were authentic.[43]

The communications not only gave heart to the grieving father but seemed to confirm a new phenomenon that had already begun to add another dimension to his thinking. In the summer of 1851 Hopedale had become aware of modern spiritualism, which had started to sweep the world of progressive religion like a prairie fire. In the fall, six months before Augustus died, Ballou published a series of articles in the *Practical Christian* on spiritualism in which he accepted as "absolute fact" that there had been thousands of indications of "some invisible power or agency not consciously existing in mortal human beings" which had made connections with the spirit world. He himself had "received many excellent communications. . . . My whole moral nature has been purified and elevated by the influences which flowed in upon me." Subsequently, he wrote a book on the subject of spirit manifestations which was first published in Boston in 1853 and then republished in England.[44]

On the surface at least Ballou remained the rationalist he had ever been in spiritual matters. He warned his readers to be skeptical about many alleged phenomena, a skepticism reinforced by some of his followers, including Abby Price, who, after noting the widespread interest in séances at Hopedale, said that the communications were often no better than those "received from the same persons in a natural healthful state." Moreover, Ballou was concerned that spiritualism might evolve into a religion at the expense of Christianity, or at least encourage such "sexual aberrations" as free love.[45]

On the other hand, he was willing to describe himself as "a rational, discriminating, Christian Spiritualist." He was excited by visions of a world of spiritual energy that promised ever-new miracles of progress. When the spiritualist Andrew Jackson Davis proposed a scheme to control and direct the fall of rain so as to benefit arid regions, Ballou republished the idea with the observation that, as wild as it seemed, it was not necessarily impossible: "We have passed the age of impossibility."[46] And so it was that practical men drifted into fantasies of new and miraculous powers.

Ballou took some special hope from the thought that spiritualism might, if rightly guided, aid the cause of Christian reform, particularly by intensifying popular spirituality and by confirming the belief that "Mankind are by nature one family of brothers and sisters." He saw in the writings of some of the spiritualists "many truthful, sublime, and beautiful ideas" that served to confirm his faith in the eventual coming of the millennium, of that glorious time when heaven would invade the earth.[47] Out of his grief, with the help of spiritualism, he wrought a strengthened hope for the triumph of good over evil. Out of it, also, he formed a new resolve to continue his own efforts to work a conversion of the world. For a short time he was inspired to a renewed hope that, indeed, Hopedale would prove to be the place from which an earthly heaven could be made for all humankind.

7

Larger Worlds

Spiritualism added new life to hopes for spiritual revolution and regeneration during the early 1850s. Later, Thomas Low Nichols said that it had "affected the religion, philosophy, and, more or less, the morals of great numbers of the American people." Nichols concluded that the most pronounced effect was to break down old religious loyalties and to set people adrift from the established churches. Whether this was good or bad was a matter of much dispute, but most observers could at least agree that the new phenomenon was a populist one born among the people, outside traditional institutions of religion. "Spiritualism did not radiate from a definite center," said the spiritualist Emma Hardinge, "but sprang with a spontaneous and irresistible life of its own."[1] As such, at least during its early years, it offered the hope for some dramatic leap away from the stodgy, if not corrupted, religions of the past toward a new and larger world of spirit open to all people.

William S. Heywood, Ballou's son-in-law, went so far as to compare spiritualist phenomena with "the wonderful things that purported to have taken place near the commencement of the Christian Era."[2] A new age of intensified religion seemed to be opening. Ballou's Restorationism, with its emphasis on the continuation of moral struggle beyond death, prepared him to accept the idea of a great world of individual spirits eager to communicate with earth on ways of moral improvement. In 1853 he noted approvingly that "regular religious Circles have just been organized at Hopedale, for Spiritual improvement and communication." On May Day of that year his sometime associate John Murray Spear visited Hopedale, where, wrote Abby Price, "he went into a Magnetic state, during which he gave us a good talk about good things."[3] Although Ballou remained skeptical regarding many of the alleged truths revealed by spirits and anxious over the possible impact on Christianity, he was influenced by spiritualism in ways even he did not fully recognize.

Spiritualist belief often produced a fantastic expansion of thought and imagination. Spear, for instance, claimed in 1854 that the spirit world had revealed to him the specifications of a "New Motor" that would provide unlimited power; he later maintained that a mob had destroyed the marvelous new engine before it could operate and that the spirits refused to repeat the specifications.[4] Ballou avoided such contraptions, but spiritualism influenced his cosmological ideas, some of which had become by this time both fantastic and eminently modern. In discussing the fundamental principles of Practical Christianity, he wrote that God had manifested his divine nature "in all earths, heavens and universes" and went on to describe what he called God's "Infinitarium," a universe of innumerable suns and earths only partly revealed by modern telescopes: "If we could be transported with such telescopes to one of these distant earths, probably we should there discover as many others beyond, mere specks in the remote skies." In such a universe of ·innumerable earths, there would be innumerable populations and innumerable heavens occupied by innumerable souls, a universe teeming with spiritual life.[5]

Ballou's earlier Universalist and Restorationist beliefs had prepared him for this cosmology, but there was at least one important difference between the old and the new. Practical Christianity had been shaped to the example provided by the historical Jesus and his Primitive Church, a unique instance of devoted Christian community, but in the Infinitarium there was room for numberless manifestations of God through numberless Christs. Although Christ Jesus remained God's highest manifestation on earth, "our great Prince Messiah," his uniqueness and importance were diminished in the endless expanse of space and time.[6]

This new universe was even more pregnant with progress than the old, to be guided not only by New Testament truths but by "fresh and even more glorious" revelations in the future. In the course of progress, spirit was sure to triumph over a dead church and an evil world. Ballou grew more convinced than ever that there was "a glorious destiny for mankind" for which it was the obligation and the glory of the faithful to labor.[7] Heartened by Hopedale's success, he redoubled his efforts to persuade the world that he had found the way to that glorious future when heaven would be realized on earth.

His principal pulpit continued to be the biweekly *Practical Christian*, the four-page sheet he had begun in 1840 under the motto "We love all, but can flatter none." Year after year, he and his associates dreamed of making it a weekly, but they were unable to get a sufficient number of paying subscribers, although their circulation extended as far west as Illinois.[8] "We are too radical and yet too conservative, too exclusive and yet too liberal," wrote Ballou in 1848. "Too visionary and yet too practical . . . to be acceptable to many people." At times, disappointed hopes drove him to some bitter but not inaccurate observations about the general reading public: "*This public* loves to be *flattered* rather than *corrected*—to be caressed into sin, rather than chastened into righteousness." Even among the small band of loyal readers, there were those who failed to pay their dues, leading him to threaten to evoke "our non-resistant plan of collecting debts," that is, to stop the subscriptions.[9] Year after year, however, he continued his efforts to make the *Practical Christian* a mighty force for righteousness and reform.

The paper and various other Hopedale publications were printed in a little shop attached to Ballou's house. The work could be unhealthy as well as demanding. Soon after Adin Augustus Ballou became foreman of the shop, he began to have recurrent headaches, which he blamed on the noxious fumes from a small charcoal furnace used to keep the ink and type warm. Having purchased the printing business from the community in 1847, the older Ballou realized that he did not have the time to manage it and, in order to relieve his son from the work, sold the business in 1849 to Asaph G. Spaulding, who ran it for several years. Spaulding improved the typographical style of the paper, increased its meager advertising, and generally tried to make the paper self-sustaining. Although he was able to realize a modest profit from printing done for people in the surrounding area, the *Practical Christian* continued to lose money, forcing the community to provide a small annual subsidy.[10]

Ballou continued as editor of the paper. Many of his editorials were labored disquisitions on various religious and moral issues, but he also provided much lively and often acute commentary on the events of the day. In March 1854, for instance, he predicted that the Kansas-Nebraska Bill would raise a conflict over slavery that would not end "till chattel slavery is numbered with the abominations that *were*." Although he once complained that he could not print every bit of "scribbling and babbling" sent to him, he published many letters from not always sympathetic correspondents and responded to those dealing with serious issues. Along with occasional reports on events at Hopedale, he included a potpourri of articles on spiritualism, temperance, physiology, education, and various other matters of interest to the reform-minded reader. The *Practical Christian* was destined to remain only a feeble moral light in the often lurid blaze of American journalism, but those who paid the one dollar a year subscription price got their money's worth in a generally well-printed miscellany enlivened by the influence of a first-rate mind.[11]

The 1850s also raised new hopes for more direct missionary work. In 1841 the Fraternal Communion had established quarterly and annual conferences to coordinate what was expected to be a growing number of Practical Christian communities, but the communion remained little more than Hopedale itself, and in 1847 it was abandoned. With better times in 1848, Ballou, Fish, and Whitney had revived their missionary effort by creating the Practical Christian Ministry with the aim of organizing people into local "Inductive Communions" that would prepare their members to form new communities like Hopedale.[12] The Practical Christian Ministry brought some life back into the quarterly conferences, which were held at various places in Massachusetts in the hope of attracting converts. Although the immediate results were rather meager, they were enough to convince Ballou that, like Hopedale itself, the Practical Christian Ministry was destined to enjoy a sure growth and ultimate success.[13]

That conviction became an enthusiasm in 1854 when a combination of factors, including the rise of spiritualism, persuaded him that Practical Christianity was ready to shift from the faltering steps of childhood to the strides of maturity. Before the end of 1852 he had recovered sufficiently from Adin Augustus's death to resume his missionary work and to publicize Hopedale. The growing prosperity of the orderly little village seemed to demonstrate that it could become an example to a world that, with the reckless times that had begun with the California gold rush, was becoming more corrupt, unequal, and chaotic than ever before. Early in 1853 Ballou published his *Concise Exposition of the Hopedale Community* to illustrate how the community had resolved what he considered the great social problem of the day, that is, how to achieve "moral order, individual freedom, and social cooperation, each in *due degree*, and all in *harmony*."[14]

The *Exposition* was part of a broader campaign to win the world's attention to Practical Christianity. In the summer the Practical Christian Communion announced that its annual meeting to be held at Blackstone (a textile village near the Rhode Island border) would welcome all those who were friendly not only to Practical Christianity but to "Constructive Reform." To emphasize the point further, Ballou announced that he was sending free copies of the *Practical Christian* "for an indefinite length of time to a large number of friends, understood to belong to the Reformatory and Progressive Class." This time, the effort evoked at least a few heartening responses. Several hundred people attended the Blackstone conference, where they were both edified by Ballou and other speakers and entertained by "the choir of the East Blackstone Inductive Communion, with their Seraphine, and numerous voluntary singers from Hopedale."[15]

More heartening still was the growing interest in establishing communities like Hopedale. In December 1852, for instance, A. C. Church, a resident of Luzerne County in eastern Pennsylvania, asked for help in forming a community on the Hopedale model. Although Ballou refused to commit any of Hopedale's still meager resources to Church's plan, the request did help reanimate Ballou's old dream of a grand confederation of Practical Christian associations. "The day is coming," he wrote in the fall of 1853 regarding Church's project, "when such communities will be numbered in the hundreds and thousands." His enthusiasm was brought to a focus in February 1854 when the New York *Independent*, a leading reform journal, published an article, "Christian Colonies in the West," urging the formation of cooperative communities dedicated to building a

Christian civilization on the frontier. It seemed that the world was beginning to awaken to Hopedale and its Christian socialism. It was time for Practical Christians to redouble their own efforts, wrote Ballou, "thereby securing to ourselves and the Future, a Heaven on the Earth. . . . Socialism is yet to be the acknowledged orthodoxy of the world."[16]

Early in 1854 Ballou's longtime associate William Henry Fish began a series of articles in the *Practical Christian* entitled "Combined Industry and Co-operative Life" urging the reorganization of American society on the Hopedale model. Although Fish stressed the essential importance of Christianity, more notable was his emphasis on the virtues of cooperative social and economic organization. The critical weakness in American society, he said, was the pervasive isolation of individuals whether they lived in crowded cities or in rural areas, an isolation that prevented them from combining their physical, economic, and moral energies. If the sparsely populated areas of America could be transformed into "neighborhoods of fraternal cooperation," then the people would be able to combine their labor, talents, and possessions to provide themselves and their children with the benefits of urban life without the corruptions and miseries of cities.[17]

Events soon indicated that Fish's articles were part of a campaign to awakened popular interest in Practical Christian communities. In March Ballou submitted a plan for "a religious and civil confederacy" to the quarterly conference for its consideration. The plan proved to be too detailed for ready acceptance, and the conference adjourned its discussions until May. On 6 May Ballou's son-in-law, William Heywood, published a long article, "The Opening Future— Prospects and Plans," in which he predicted approval: "Then it will be important, and indispensable even, to have Agents and Missionaries . . . go up and down the earth to teach and preach . . . and thus multiply, strengthen, and confirm the disciples of the NEW SOCIAL ORDER." Finally on 1 July Ballou announced that the conference had approved the plan, thereby giving to "Christian Socialism a character, *as a system*, which it has never in form and to the world possessed."[18]

The essence of the plan was a constitution for a worldwide "Practical Christian Republic." In some basic respects, the new constitution resembled that of the earlier Fraternal Communion, particularly in its emphasis on nonresistance, temperance, abolitionism, equality, and sexual purity, but it was notably grander and also more abstract. Beyond the old moral code, it included twenty-four cardinal principles of faith, formal articles of belief that suggest that Ballou had drifted away from the inspiration of the Primitive Church to a more formalistic view of religion.[19] Although he insisted that he was only presenting fundamental truths, the very effort to list articles of faith reflected some remoteness from the first Christians, with their concrete time and place, and from his own earlier religious experiences in the Mill River Valley.

This distance from the specific circumstances that had inspired and sustained Hopedale was also evident in his master plan for a "complete Social Superstructure, from foundations to pinnacle," a social contraption formed from three different kinds of communal organizations: on the one extreme, "rural" communities consisting of separate households and individually owned properties; at the other extreme, common-stock communities practicing the communism that Daniel Lamson had once demanded; and in the broad middle, communities, like Hopedale, holding their larger and more public property on a joint-stock basis while allowing for individual ownership of houses and other small properties.[20] These communities were the building blocks for Ballou's "complete Social Structure." Two or more would combine to form a "communal municipality," and two or more municipalities would constitute a "Communal State," and two or more states would make up a "Communal Nation"—all such nations forming the Practical Christian Republic.[21]

Although this was more a desktop utopia than an organization rooted in real life, Ballou believed it could harmonize the interests of millions of people and create a power strong enough to overcome the selfishness of property. Infused with the governing spirit of Christian nonresistance, the grand confederation of communities would progressively remove "the partition walls which now divide the numberless interests of everyday life" and eventually establish a universal brotherhood of mankind.[22] By their own initiatives, men and women could achieve the Eden that God had intended for them:

You are to solve your own problem, and work out your own destiny. Therefore walk on your own feet; use your hands; eat your own bread; sit under your own vine and fig trees. Make your Republic religiously, morally, intellectually, socially, pecuniarily, peacefully and benevolently independent. . . . So shall your banner of truth, love and peace finally wave in serene majesty over every temple turret of regenerated humanity.[23]

Even in the fullness of his enthusiasm, Ballou was too much the practical man to believe that the world would instantly rush to his door. The rich and the powerful could not be expected to abandon their positions, while the rest would be slow to recognize the promise of paradise. Whatever its successes, Hopedale remained too small a light to attract the world's wearied eyes. Ballou did believe, however, that he could at least begin a people's movement that would ultimately convert the world: "'Despise not the day of small things.' The Coral slowly builds a continent."[24] In order to direct small things to the great end, he gave much thought to publicizing his plan, particularly through a reorganized Practical Christian Communion, which was to "employ all available resources, mental, moral and pecuniary, in well directed efforts to disseminate the Principles and Polity of the Practical Christian Republic." He himself devoted much of his energies in 1854 to preparing what Heywood proclaimed in May to be "the *great* Work of its author's life." The result was *Practical Christian Socialism*, a 656-page volume that, when its printing was completed at Hopedale in November, he advertised for sale at $1.50 a copy either from himself or from Fowler and Wells, the New York publishers of reform works.[25]

Ballou cast the entire work in the form of a "conversational exposition" between Inquirer, who raises the world's objections to Practical Christian socialism and asks various leading questions, and Expositor, who readily answers Inquirer. As Inquirer is all too easy to convince, the dialogue is no more than Ballou's puppet show, but at least it enabled the author to present his ideas in what he hoped would be a popular and readable form. The first 160 pages of the book discuss at length the fundamental principles of the Practical Christian Republic. This is followed by a longer section on the practical characteristics of his social system, more than half of which is devoted to education and to love and sexuality. The long last section attempts to demonstrate the superiority of Practical Christian socialism over other radical social systems both religious and secular from Shakerism to Fourierism.[26] Basically, Ballou believed he had found the way to resolve what for him and many others was becoming the leading social problem of their day, the use and abuse of property. The rapid and often frenzied progress of the 1850s was yielding great wealth but also great deprivation, an inequality in the human condition that a quarter of a century later Henry George would attempt to explain to his deeply troubled times in *Progress and Poverty*.

Ballou's Christian socialism was grounded in the belief that while each person was entitled to the property earned by his own talents and labor, his use of property should be governed by his obligations to other human beings. By their natures, all men are social in that they depend on each other for their welfare; no individual has the capabilities needed for his own happiness. In 1849 Ballou had written:

> The time has arrived when Christian Socialism must be proclaimed and insisted on. Mankind are becoming more and more social in the prominent interests. They are becoming more and more combined in organic social arrangements. Consequently social influences are becoming stronger in the formation of individual moral character. There never was a period in which the constitutional arrangements, laws, customs, usages, and general action of society did so much to make individuals virtuous or vicious, happy or miserable.[27]

The great flaw in existing society was that it encouraged each person to believe that he could use his property simply for his own gratification and aggrandizement regardless of how it affected the welfare of others. The general solution, then, was to establish the social principle that all persons held their property only as "stewards in trust, under God," with an unqualified obligation to use whatever was not required by their own basic needs for the improvement and happiness of other members of the human race. "We must magnify great Christian principles," he wrote in 1850, "which will move the minds of men to consecrate property to its true ends—employing it to reform, enlighten, redeem and bless the suffering classes."[28]

Ballou was aware that the idea of stewardship had failed in the past, but he was confident that his system of Christian socialism would make it effective. In part, the abuse of property would be restrained by the moral requirements of Practical Christianity: "Our strong moral prohibitions relative to intemperance, war, slavery, and other notoriously prolific evil customs will operate as strong safeguards."[29] No saloons, cannons, or chains would waste wealth and destroy human happiness. Moreover, the joint-stock ownership of at least a part of the property would provide for some direct social management in the interests of the whole. And the temptation to abuse property in any form would be effectually controlled by two important provisions in his constitution of the Practical Christian Republic, each of which had been put into practice at Hopedale.

One provision limited the maximum wage or salary paid to any person to no more than that paid on average to "the first class of operatives," that is, skilled workers. Ballou believed that this would prevent the talented and powerful from using their superiorities to exact unjust gains, while it would also allow, below the maximum, for differential rewards based on actual work and contribution. By narrowing the gap between the best and worst paid, Ballou hoped to prevent the extremes of wealth that had destroyed the sense of fraternity and community in every other society. Ballou conceded that his communities sorely needed the talents of "the managing and professional classes," people accustomed to receiving large returns, but he hoped that at least some of them would apply their "skill and prowess" for the common good out of a sense of Christian duty. Although he admitted that many would not, he refused to budge on the maximum:

> If we cannot enlist them by a fair conversion to our principles and policy, we must go without them, though it take a thousand years longer to reach our grand consumation. Of what use would it be to go through the long process of founding a new order of society, if when founded it should be radically like the present order, which impoverishes, degrades, and imbrutes five hundred families in order to enrich, elevate and refine one family?[30]

Ballou was equally insistent on the second provision, which limited what he saw as another source of social extremes—interest on loans, including dividends on investments. He accepted some level of interest as a natural and desirable element in a progressive modern economy; money had contributed to the general advance in wealth and should be rewarded. He believed, however, that the usual interest charged for money enabled the greedy few to exploit the labor of the great and productive many. He therefore insisted that interest rates be limited to the 4 percent already established at Hopedale. Eventually he hoped to eliminate the moneylenders entirely through the creation of a system of "Mutual Banking" in which the people would lend to each other at even lower rates, sufficient only to cover the costs of making the loan: "What a deliverance will it work from the covetousness and growing extortion of the existing Mammonish order!"[31]

If such ideas seemed like provincial crank economics to the big-city financial world, they made sense to this member of the small-town middle class, the way to transform and redeem the only world he truly knew. And for him they had proved they could work. The grand scale of his book left little room for tiny Hopedale, which he called "an infantile and imperfect sample" lacking many features of the ideal community: "It has no Unitary Mansion, Bakery, Refectory, Baths or Laundry." Whatever its deficiencies in details, however, Hopedale was a viable success that had outlived its supposed superiors, "a social Bethlehem, which though least among the Communities of Israel, would ultimately become the most illustrious."[32]

Ballou said that he limited the first printing of *Practical Christian Socialism* to 1,000 copies because he anticipated little initial interest in a book that did not "excite, dazzle, amuse or please the popular masses." He did hope to attract the scattered few who aspired after a higher form of society, and thus to begin a popular movement. In advertising his book, he announced that having helped put Hopedale on a permanent basis, he planned "to advance into the great field of the world as a determined advocate of the *New Order of Society*," employing lectures and writings not only to spread the gospel of Practical Christian socialism but also to encourage the founding of new communities. For five dollars anyone could receive the book, along with other writings on the subject, enlistment in the Practical Christian Republic as an "inductive candidate," and information regarding suitable sites for a community.[33] In combination with the newly reorganized Inductive Communion, Adin Ballou would enlighten the troubled conscience of his times and begin the regeneration of the world.

The contrast between this enthusiastic plan and its actual results was so extreme as to be ludicrous. Ballou's great work was largely ignored, even in the world of reform. One of the few periodicals that bothered to review the book—the *Universalist Quarterly*—distorted its meaning in order the better to condemn it. Eventually, the book did win the praise of John Humphrey Noyes, a rival religious leader and a careful student of attempted new orders of society, who said that "if it were our doom to attempt community-building by paper programme, we should choose Adin Ballou's scheme in preference to any thing we have ever been able to find," but even this rather snide praise came more than a decade after the book had fallen into oblivion.[34]

Ballou's ambitious lecturing campaign also failed. In February 1855 he launched his new career as "an Advocate of the New Order of Society" in and around Hopedale and by June had extended his efforts into western Massachusetts, commencing at the village of Florence a few miles from Northampton. Since that village had developed out of the old Northampton Association with which Hopedale had cooperated during the heyday of Fourierism a decade before, he expected a positive response. Unfortunately, his small audiences there "would probably have been more interested in a puppet show or a mountebank exhibition than in my harangues about doing away with the ignorance, vice, poverty and misery of human society."[35] He was less chagrined when he visited Connecticut in July but only because he expected less, having concluded that the Nutmeg State contained few of "the middle class of liberal religionists with high toned morals" on which he had come to depend. In the fall he spoke at Providence, Philadelphia, and New York City, moving from there to upstate New York. In December he ended his campaign in the familiar territory of northern Rhode Island, where he had been invited to speak by "a zealous Spiritualist and lover of

Practical Christianity."[36] The year that was to actualize the Practical Christian Republic had simply vanished in the void of the world's indifference.

Ballou's disappointment, for a time, was partly palliated by a new enthusiasm that embraced him in 1855. Although he forced himself to leave Hopedale on his lecture tours, he was notably a homebody who in the past had resisted the thought, common among his fellow Yankees, of moving west to find a new life on the frontier. The decision to begin Hopedale on familiar territory among friends had proved to be the right one. But even Ballou was affected by the enthusiasm for western colonization that reached almost tidal proportions in New England by the mid 1850s. As early as 1852 he had begun to take an interest in the West, encouraged by letters from transplanted Yankees asking for support in civilizing the frontier.[37] His personal interest was intensified when in the spring of 1854 he and Ebenezer Draper, along with their wives, had toured as far west as Cincinnati. This first exposure to western society had excited him to dream of a time when every "young man and woman in our Practical Christian Republic" would be afforded the opportunity to take a similar tour.[38] A greater world than that of the Mill River Valley had begun to beckon.

The actual effort to establish a Practical Christian colony in the West, however, was less the work of Ballou than of William Henry Fish, who said in the fall of 1854 that he had long hoped "to have some of God's acres in the far West redeemed from the curses of present civilization." Two months earlier Fish had begun to urge quick action to acquire some western land for a colony, and soon a possible site was suggested by Mary J. Colburn, a member of the Hopedale Community and author of many of its hymns who had recently migrated to the Minnesota Territory: "If you value a fertile soil, healthy climate, and a society that knows how to appreciate the various means of moral and mental improvement, visit Minnesota." There was the usual problem of finding the money needed for colonization. Early in 1855 Fish began an effort to organize support from the people of the Mill Valley, only to discover that his nonresistance principles were not acceptable to many potential supporters. During the summer Ballou made a special visit to the wealthy abolitionist

Gerritt Smith in the hope of persuading him to support the venture; he managed to get five dollars.[39]

The western project, however, had captured the imaginations of at least a few people at Hopedale. In May 1855 the *Practical Christian* published an imaginary account of a future community called Expansia, named so because it had been the first effort to "expand the Practical Christian Republic beyond the original nucleus at Hopedale." By a fictitious 1889 this community had grown to some two thousand people inhabiting five thousand acres, one of nearly fifty communities constituting the ever-expanding Practical Christian Republic.[40] Two months after the publication of this fantasy, Fish announced that some members of Hopedale were planning to visit Minnesota to look for a community domain, and in September the community officially delegated George O. Hatch and Elijah S. Mullikan, two new members, to carry out the mission. By the next month Ballou had drafted a constitution for the new community with the confidence "that the project will be actualized in a few months, or a few years at the farthest."[41]

Unfortunately, bad timing ruined this adventure. Hatch and Mullikan got to Minnesota only to have their effort at settlement defeated by the onset of a harsh winter. They soon returned to Hopedale, unaware that a second small party, including John Lowell Heywood, the brother of Ballou's son-in-law, had followed in search of them. This party also was stopped by the winter, but it decided to remain in the territory. By May 1856 it reported that it had staked a claim to an extensive tract of land on both sides of the Crow River some sixty miles west of Minneapolis. The new pioneers called on those who were committed to Practical Christian socialism to join them in developing a settlement they called Union Grove. In a few years, however, this small colony broke up and most of its members returned to the East, ending forever the western movement of Practical Christian socialism.[42]

By 1856 a great deal more had ended than the dream of the West. In fact, Ballou's entire hope for Practical Christianity had suffered a devastating blow at home from which it never recovered, a failure at least indirectly caused by his own changing interests. It is perhaps the general fate of religious movements born from local conditions to suffer when the leaders who inspired them become preoccupied with larger worlds. The successful Perfectionist community at Oneida, for instance, was to collapse in 1880 after its aging leader, John Humphrey Noyes, had concentrated his attentions on what he called "American Socialism." Ballou had first risked this fate in 1852, when he stepped down as president of the Hopedale Community, and he deepened the risk by developing his outside interests in the Practical Christian Republic and spiritualism. He convinced himself that he and his followers had found a way to create a community that could stand by itself without his continued inspiration and direction; if that were not so, then there could be no hope for the Practical Christian Republic.

Ballou's experiment seemed to work. After 1852 Hopedale had prospered, entering by 1854 into what Ballou later called the "palmiest" period in its history: "It throve in all its departments. . . . Materially, socially, and religiously."[43] Indeed, it was raised to new heights of glory in the mid 1850s—only to collapse abruptly into the dust of a shattered dream.

8

Days of Glory

The 1850s was a time of notably mixed blessings both for the world and for the Hopedale Community. In some respects, this opening of the second half of a progressive century reinforced hopes for the eventual triumph of Practical Christianity. "A new Christian chivalry has sprung up within our century," declared the *Universalist Quarterly* in 1851. "Want, darkness, suffering and oppression are beginning to be studied . . . in the light of the law of brotherhood, the supreme good of spiritual culture, and infinite value of the soul." In other respects, however, the surge of spirituality and morality intensified the passions, especially over the slavery issue, that engendered violence and led eventually to the Civil War. On the great moral and economic tides of the times, Hopedale was to be first raised to high expectations and then dashed to despair.

In May 1854 Ballou began the fifteenth volume of the *Practical Christian* with an editorial on the Sermon on the Mount. The Sermon, he said, was a great epitome of the spirit and principles of Practical Christianity, a code of conduct without the doctrines and dogmas over which Christians had long quarreled, a simple code that if only men had followed it "would have regenerated the entire human race before this time, and rendered the habitable globe a paradise." If Hopedale had only imperfectly realized this promise, it had for Ballou demonstrated how the code could bring harmony and happiness to those who practiced it. In 1855 he said that the village afforded "a peaceful and congenial home for all conscientious persons of whatever religion, sect, class or description," enabling them to meet the needs of both body and mind through rational Christian cooperation. There Christians could invest both money and energy with moral as well as financial safety, since property had been made "pre-eminently safe, useful, beneficent. It is Christianized. So, in good degree, are talent, skill, and productive industry." Seemingly, where property holders were governed by the obligations of Practical Christianity, capitalistic instincts could coexist with brotherhood and love.[1]

The village was not an isolated island of Christian socialism, however, but a tiny vessel attempting to navigate the world's often stormy seas during a time of chaotically uneven prosperity. Having determined to demonstrate that it was possible to combine Christianity with economic security and physical comforts—and to do so in the familiar confines of a settled area, the community paid for its successes with a growing dependence on the outside economy. In the new age of railroads and quickening activity, what in 1840 had been the semiautonomous little world of the Mill River Valley was fast becoming a part of a larger economic world. By the mid 1850s surrounding Worcester County had become a leading manufacturing county in a manufacturing state, ranking first in the number of manufactories and second in the production of cotton cloth, much of the cloth coming from mills in nearby towns such as Blackstone and Uxbridge. Hopedale's own town of Milford had developed into an important boot- and shoe-producing center, employing nearly 3,500 men and women in that line. In this changing world even the Christian village would be affected by what one of its members condemned in the world's progress: "It is rash and irreverent. It rushes with railroad speed over the Holy Land itself . . . crushing beneath it the most Paradisal flowers without remorse."[2]

During the early 1850s the community was able to bask in the sunny side of economic progress. In 1854 Ebenezer Draper, Ballou's successor as president, estimated that over the previous decade the value of its communal and private property had risen from less than $12,000 to more than $90,000; in 1853 alone, it had added more than $17,000 to its holdings, chiefly new houses, shop buildings, and equipment. By 1855 it had nearly six hundred acres of land, fifty houses, a cooperative grocery store, a printing establishment, a sawmill, a gristmill, and "several mechanic shops with water power." And its progress was evident in more than its financial and industrial accounts. "The general appearance of the Village is improving from year to year," wrote William Heywood in the summer. "New dwellings are going up; new streets opening; new sidewalks made; new House Lots taken up and cultivated; fruit and ornamental trees take their place and extend their branches along the public ways." The once rundown farm had become the site of a prospering village with nearly three hundred inhabitants; in 1854 Hopedale's self-financed post office handled nearly seven thousand letters, private and commercial, to and from the official post office at Milford.[3]

The Hopedale experiment was perhaps too undramatic in appearance as well as too complex in reality to win much attention from the great world, but it did attract the interest of some people within its own region. Both the Milford *Journal* and the Woonsocket *Patriot* took note of its successes, and a visitor from Providence wrote a poem celebrating its virtues:

> In your magic bowers would linger,
> In your homes would long abide,
> But it may not be, for tendrils
> Stretching homeward, draw me back.
> I must go once more and journey
> In the old and beaten track.[4]

Other people came to stay. Between 1852 and 1856 the population of the village increased by nearly 50 percent, and the number of members of the community rose by nearly as much, from 75 to approximately 110. In 1853 some 40 people applied for membership, of whom 18 were admitted either as probationers or as regular members; in just two months of the following year, the community voted to admit 14 persons to membership.[5]

The rapid increase of newcomers caused some concern. Early in 1854, after the free-love scandal of the previous year, the Council of Religion, Conciliation and Justice—one of whose duties was to examine applicants for membership—urged the community to demand the highest moral character in every applicant. Better that Hopedale limit its growth than to open itself to the influence of the old social order: "It is acknowledged on all hands that this Community presents far greater attractions for the worldly wise, at the present time than it did ten years hence." Apparently, the majority paid little heed. In 1855 Heywood complained of the laxity of admission standards.[6] Only too late would there be occasion for regret.

During the good years, the new members seemed to fit readily into community life. However little they understood the special character of Practical Christian socialism, they generally came from the same local culture that had nurtured the experiment, men and women with at least some interest in radical reform and progressive religion. Often, they were come-outers from conventional institutions who sought a home. One new member, Jonathan Whipple, had belonged to the "Rogerine Quakers," a religious group peculiar to one locality in Connecticut, while another, Harriet Greene, was a feminist and spiritualist.[7] Justus Soule had first been attracted to the village by an advertisement for a husband placed in the *Phrenological Journal* by Mary Ann Heywood, one of four unmarried sisters; Soule liked what he saw and became both a husband and a member. Still another newcomer, George Gay, had once been a Universalist minister. At Hopedale these people seem on the whole to have found the opportunity to satisfy their special needs and dreams.

Life at Hopedale was not for everyone. No one there was to keep or use any deadly weapon, and all were obligated to "discountenance utterly in any of our children the use of all warlike, savage-like, or ruffian-like toys, playthings, sports and amusements." No one was to drink an alcoholic beverage, gamble, swear, or engage in anything that could be viewed as dissolute behavior. Nor could anyone have a dog, since the normally tolerant Ballou had a strong aversion for what he saw as useless beasts noted only for their "endless fightings, growlings and barkings." Beyond the outright prohibitions were the more subtle restraints of communal expectations. While not prohibited, "idle words and foolish jesting" were discouraged, as were tobacco using and coffee drinking. By the 1850s many of the villagers had become interested in the dietary practices proposed by Sylvester Graham and other members of their progressive reform culture. They were especially inclined toward vegetarianism, limiting meat to a small part of their diet if they ate flesh at all. In "our general practice," wrote William Heywood in 1854, "two or three pounds of choicest beef, free from fat as possible, has been deemed admissible to our larder once in three, four, or six weeks."[8]

With its strong commitments to specified behaviors, Hopedale was not a place for the freewheeling individualist. But it was not an uncomfortable place for those who, under the influence of moral reform, dreamed of a society without drunkeness, brawls, gambling, bickering, petty meanness, and the other seemingly endless causes of the social friction, wasted effort, and personal unhappiness that afflicted the world. In 1856 one sympathetic observer called Hopedale "a great and excellent social-reform institution" in which there was "nothing crazy or visionary, but everything . . . required by nature, reason, and the highest good of mankind."[9] In such a view, the community represented not moral repression but the beginnings of a new moral order that would free humankind to live a higher and happier life in a world without violence, war, slavery, crime, or poverty.

Certainly, a not insignificant part of that life already existed at Hopedale. Along with the exclusion of slavery and violence, there was security from poverty and a guarantee of productive work in a community obliged to use its resources to provide for all of its members. And there was the chance for women as well as men to participate in the decisions that affected their lives. There was schooling for the children and informal education for adults in the weekly lyceum. There were periodic festivals, singings, and musical affairs.[10] Along with security, the village provided opportunities for a satisfying social and cultural life beyond those available to most Americans in either city or countryside.

Of course, even Hopedale, as Ballou had learned, was not protected from the tragedies of life. In July 1853 Ida A. Draper, the five-year-old adopted daughter of Ebenezer Draper, died suddenly from scarlet fever soon after she had given her first recitation at a community festival; she was the Drapers' only child. Before the end of the summer, two other children died suddenly from dysentery, and another drowned in the village millpond. The year ended with the death of twenty-eight-year-old Hannah H. Swazey from "billious cholera." Ballou visited her as she was dying: "She welcomed him with a smile at once ghastly and angelic, as if one about to join some blessed circle in the Spirit-Home. She had just had a delightful vision of God and heaven, and beckoning angels; and said she was ready to ascend to their embrace."[11]

In general, life in the village, as elsewhere, was dominated by the need to earn one's bread by the sweat of physical labor. "We are troubled by no idlers, loafers," reported the *Practical Christian*. "If there be any not sufficiently supplied with manual labor, they are expected to be employed about something else that would make them useful to themselves and to mankind." And the wages paid for labor, while at least adequate, were hardly in the utopian range: In 1854 the combined community and private operations of the village paid out a total of $21,410 to an undisclosed number of workers. Of this amount, $16,410 went to some eighty resident members, an average income of about $200 each. Undoubtedly, pay for skilled workers was greater. During a three-month period in the spring of 1854, for instance, the Cabinet Branch paid out on the average more than $30 a month to each of its four full-time workers, but there were sharp fluctuations in pay, the four averaging less than $18 a month each in November. Two years later annual living costs in the village were estimated to be about $145 for a single man and $200 for a married couple "keeping house in a small tenement with a little garden."[12]

Whatever its present limitations, Hopedale could continue to look to the future it was building for itself. In time, it would attain the "new and glorious Christiandom" that Ballou predicted for it, a godly society solidly grounded in economic success. Part of this success was to be found in the various private businesses allowed in the village since the great changeover of 1847, especially that operated by Ebenezer Draper. Before joining the community, Draper had acquired the rights to the self-acting loom temple developed by his inventor father, Ira Draper. When he had come to Hopedale from Uxbridge, he brought his new business with him and it produced a modest but growing income, the loom temple being much valued for its ability to speed up the weaving process. Because of Draper's devotion to Practical Christianity, his private affairs were closely related to those of the community, much of his income being invested in various village enterprises for communal good.[13]

Soon the Hopedale Community would recognize that it was too dependent on Draper's success, but during the prosperous years of the early 1850s the community itself accomplished substantial economic progress. Part of this involved the expansion of the community's joint-stock enterprises, like its Machine Branch, which employed as many as a dozen operatives in the manufacture of tools, hardware, and other small metal appliances, and also its Transportation Branch, whose teams of horses and wagons were hired for hauling materials in the surrounding area. Although Hopedale had become somewhat more cautious than it had been in the 1840s in promoting new industrial enterprises, it continued to diversify. It created a new Soap and Candle Branch managed by its chemical wizard, Dudley B. Chapman, who by 1855 was advertising a chemical soap of his own invention, called Eureka, for sale to the world. By then it had added a "book bindery and blank book manufactory," a logical complement to its established printing business; the new operation was soon advertising in the *Practical Christian* that, being "supplied with the best modern equipment," it was prepared to provide blank books for diaries, ledgers, and drawing as well as other kinds of paper such as sheet music and ruled paper.[14]

Growth brought complexity. In early 1855 the community voted to erect an "Advertising Bulletin" at a central location in order to "facilitate the daily publication of necessary commercial and business information." To accommodate its expanding business operations, it also established a "Contingent Fund" to provide short-term credit both to its own branches and to private businesses within the village. Even with these improvements, Hopedale remained a petty economy by the world's standards, but it seemed to be making steady progress in realizing what one of its members in 1855 called "the hope of ultimate strength, productiveness, maturity, order, and self-subsisting competency," a competency that would assure adequate care and employment for all its members.[15]

The community also made some notable efforts to strengthen the softest spot in its economy, agriculture. Although in 1852 more than half of its capital assets consisted of land, farming employed less than a quarter of its work force, and most of its nearly six hundred acres was unimproved and unproductive.[16] Its village-oriented members had a natural preference for trade and manufacturing, but at the same time they were governed by the romantic view of agriculture common to their day. Most probably agreed with Ballou when he declared that agriculture was the God-intended way to paradise:

The first man was an agriculturalist, a gardener. The last man will be such. What a pleasant thought is this—that in the far-off future, nearly the entire surface of this earth will be tilled to the perfection of a garden, and teem with perhaps fifty or a hundred times its present population—all wise, holy and happy. So predict the prophets of God. So sing the divinest of bards.[17]

This biblical vision was to be attained by modern means. Ballou urged the community, as part of its "ground culture," to carry out an analysis of its soil to determine what could best be grown and what "chemical changes are necessary to render it productive," no easy task given the poor quality of local soils. Anticipating increased agricultural production, the community borrowed two thousand dollars to construct a large barn for its crops and livestock, a belated replacement for the much repaired farm buildings from the original purchase. Financed through the sale of a new issue of joint stock, the barn was begun in May 1854, but its construction suffered a setback resulting from the community's decision to experiment with gravel walls as a way of cutting costs: after raising the walls to a height of twenty feet, it was concluded that they were too weak and would have to be partly rebuilt with wood, delaying completion of the work until the summer of 1855. The barn was eighty feet long, forty feet wide, and nearly thirty feet high, making it, with its large cupola-ventilator, "the most conspicuous building on the domain."[18]

The great barn bolstered the hopes of the community that its Agricultural Branch could be made more effective and that its extensive farm could be made far more productive than before. No action, however, did much to remedy the basic defects in agriculture, neither improving the fertility of the soil nor converting the members into farmers. The principal result of the efforts to enlarge farm production seems to have been the planting of about twenty-five acres in potatoes and corn—out of some five hundred acres of available community land. In general, there was little to affirm the claim of one member that the principal "business of the people should be the *cultivation of the soil*." Later Ballou said that the community's farm had been a drain on its finances, and he concluded that, rather than trying to work the domain collectively, it would have been better to have divided the land into individual holdings.[19]

While the cultivation of the soil continued to lag in the Agricultural Branch, it continued to flourish in the Horticultural (chiefly market gardening) and Orchardry (fruit raising and nursery stock) branches. Between 1854 and 1855 Horticulture expanded from eight to twelve acres the land devoted to growing vegetables, to meet a large demand in Milford and elsewhere; in 1855 the community opened a store in Milford center for the sale of its produce, while continuing its past practice of making deliveries by market wagon to its regular customers. By the 1850s the Orchardry branch was benefiting from the some two thousand apple trees that had been planted on the community domain over the years, along with a smaller number of other fruit trees. In the spring of 1855 the community was confronted with an invasion of caterpillars, which had stripped the leaves from neighboring orchards: "By constant watching and considerable labor," the invaders were nearly all destroyed in Hopedale. The most profitable part of Orchardry was the nursery, which did an extensive business in the sale of fruit and ornamental trees, grapevines, berry bushes, and various kinds of shrubs and flowering plants to the outside world.[20]

The vitality of such ventures reflected the existence of strong entrepreneurial instincts at Hopedale. In 1854 the village welcomed a new and important venture that promised to partly fulfill Ballou's long-deferred dream of a great Educational Home. The death of Adin Augustus Ballou early in 1852 had disrupted that dream, but his father kept it alive with the encouragement of some of his associates; a quarterly conference called the school "an enterprise which the world greatly needs as promotive to its individual and social redemption." Although Ballou had discussed it at length in his *Practical Christian Socialism*, he was too busy with his missionary work to start the school himself, but he probably paved the way for its establishment by Mr. and Mrs. Morgan Bloom, newcomers who had not even seen Hopedale until 1853. It was with the community's sanction that in October 1854 the Blooms—previously associated with the Five Points Mission in New York City—opened their Hopedale Juvenile Home School, a boarding and day school for boys and girls between five and seventeen.[21]

In their advertising the Blooms emphasized the moral order and healthful environment of the village. It would, they promised, complement their efforts to give each child "a healthy body, a well toned mind, and a loving heart," preparing him or her "to detect and combat evil, and discern and desire to follow good and truth." At the school the young Christians would become well equipped to deal with the ways of world, since they would learn not only habits of productive labor but the value of money and the art of keeping accounts; all students were expected to do some work, for which they would be credited on the school's accounts.[22]

The Juvenile Home School was a rather bare shadow of Ballou's ambitious Educational Home; it opened in one of the larger houses in the village rather than in the great academy building of which he had dreamed two years before. Moreover, the Blooms had trouble attracting boarding students—at forty dollars per quarter—perhaps because they were strangers to New England. In 1855 they attempted to expand their enrollment by adding an adult department to their renamed Hopedale Juvenile and Collegiate Home School, striving to make it "a well ordered HOME, in which youth . . . middle-aged, and elderly people should compose the family, and unite in instructing each other." This experiment apparently did not help, however, since in April 1856 they sold the school to William and Abbie Heywood; the Blooms' last reported activity at Hopedale was an attempt to run a boardinghouse for summer vacationers.[23]

The sale opened the way for what proved to be the more successful Hopedale Home School, a venture especially consoling to Ballou because it was the accomplishment of his daughter and son-in-law. William was principal and teacher of ancient languages, higher mathematics, philosophy, chemistry, and English literature, while Abbie served as associate principal and teacher of French, phonography, history, botany, physiology, painting, drawing, and penmanship. With the assistance of a few part-time teachers, the two attempted to provide a "thoroughly Reformatory and Progressive" academy and precollegiate education for older youth, especially for those who favored "the better tendencies and movements of the age." Although they maintained the Blooms' emphasis on moral and physical culture, the Heywoods gave particular emphasis to the development of disciplined reason and intellectual self-reliance. They announced that they conducted their classes "in the spirit of inquiry rather than dogmatism," in accordance with the method Abbie had learned in normal school:

> Oral teaching is mingled freely with that derived from text-books. *Mere* book-knowledge is of comparatively little value. An accumulation of facts . . . does not constitute the wealth of the intellect. . . . Hence the importance of the analytical method of instruction, which investigates the reasons and uses of things, unfolding "the why and whereof" of every operation and assertion. This method is rigidly adhered to, in order to the revealment and elucidation of great principles and general truths.[24]

Until the Civil War disrupted its enrollments, the Heywoods' Home School seemed well on its way to becoming a successful educational enterprise. Beginning with 28 full-time students in 1856, it increased its enrollment to over 50 by 1858. In the two years from 1857 to 1859 the Heywoods educated at least 167 different students on a coeducational basis. Most were boarders, the children of progressive parents from as far away as Boston who were willing to pay sixty dollars per term; but more than 25 of Hopedale's own children were able, for nine dollars a term, to get at least some academy education without leaving home. Beyond its contributions to Hopedale's income and culture, the Home School promised to satisfy the provision in Ballou's Constitution of the Practical Christian Republic for an education that would "develop harmoniously the physical, intellectual, moral and social faculties of the young," inducing not simply sound morals and good habits but a sound mind "capable of inquiring, reasoning and judging for itself" and a healthful, vigorous body.[25]

The school helped round out what seemed by the mid 1850s to be the successful establishment of a godly community suited to modern conditions. On the surface at least, Hopedale was able to combine a strong commitment to brotherly love and practical morality with a notable amount of personal energy and entrepreneurship. In its economy, it had worked out a balance between socialism and individualism, especially in its property relationships. On the socialistic side, its collective joint stock owned the basic resources in land and waterpower, along with the school, the great barn, and various shop buildings; every member could acquire a claim on the 4 percent dividend guaranteed to stockholders by purchasing one or more of the fifty-dollar shares in the collective. On the individualistic side, it was possible for members to acquire considerable amounts of their own private property. As early as 1850 the census taker indicated that of twenty-seven people clearly identified with the community, at least fifteen were property owners. Of these, Ballou was credited with the $35,000 in joint stock held by the community, but fourteen others had individual holdings of between $800 and $2,000, much of it in the tools of their trade; most of the rest probably had some property.[26]

The decision to allow and indeed to encourage private ventures like Draper's production of loom temples and the Heywoods' Home School contributed significantly to Hopedale's overall development. In 1856 a correspondent for William Lloyd Garrison's *Liberator*, in presenting the village as a working example of the nonresistance paradise, made note of a significant reason for its economic success: "A few men of capital and business talent generously devote them to establish business and furnish employment." Ballou was thinking of this entrepreneurship when he praised the community for having found a way to harmonize individual freedom and social obligation: "All may thrive together as individuals, without degrading or impoverishing any."[27] And so socialism, with its stress on collective welfare, was able to benefit from the energy of capitalism.

As Ballou was well aware, the lion did not lie down easily with the lamb, but he believed that the requirement limiting ownership in the village to those who had agreed to abide by the Standard of Practical Christianity virtually guaranteed that the more energetic and successful would use their talents and property for the welfare of all. With economic power safely confined to members of the Practical Christian community, property could grow in extent and power without threatening peace and brotherhood. For a time, it seemed as if this were true as Hopedale entered the mid 1850s. "It throve in all departments," Ballou later recalled, "materially, socially, and religiously."[28] Its foundations seemed secure.

It soon became apparent, however, that there were several cracks in those foundations, including two that were particularly serious. One was a weakening of religious zeal and of commitment to the godly mission of the community, a natural consequence of prosperous times. That crack might have widened for years before it became fatal if not for a second flaw, one that in 1855 was imperceptible to the common eye. This involved not the heart and inspiring word but the calculating brain and the account book—and a new, dominating figure who would soon give Hopedale a very different direction from that which Ballou had planned.

9

Days of Dust

The weakening of commitment to the Hopedale experiment expressed itself most seriously in challenges to the system of joint-stock property that had been the practical basis of the experiment from the beginning. What had begun as a way of accumulating the money needed to buy the original farm had evolved into the collectivist heart of the village economy. "The Joint Stock capital," reported the *Practical Christian* in 1855, "is now owned almost entirely by resident stockholders, and is variously parceled out among the several Industrial Branches so far as best to subserve the general welfare, and to afford the largest amount of subsidiary employment to the resident operatives."[1] In theory, at least, joint ownership gave the members of the community control over their economic and social life.

In practice, however, most members seem to have acquired few if any shares, giving them little interest, pecuniary or otherwise, in the joint stock and creating an inequality of ownership potentially dangerous in a community devoted to all. Undoubtedly, that inequality provoked at least a few to outright hostility to the joint-stock idea. In March 1855, for instance, one critic urged the community to "go up higher" on the grounds that a joint-stock community still allowed room for individualism and selfishness, when in a truly godly society the members should be "to each other like the sons and daughters of a well-ordered Christian family," willing to share and to sacrifice for the good of all members. This inclination toward religious communism was apparently shared by few, but it eventually evoked an editorial from Ballou condemning what he called the "communistic error" of assuming that all property should be held in common. Perhaps remembering the days of Daniel Lamson, he warned against efforts to "hurry people into socialistic intimacies."[2] Although he had allowed for common-stock communities in his Practical Christian Republic, Ballou doubted that Hopedale was ready or would perhaps ever be ready to advance into the dangerous ground of communism.

A more serious threat to the joint stock came from the opposite direction, from the entrepreneurial instincts of individual members. This included Ballou himself in an odd sort of way. In December 1855 the community approved a plan devised by him for "the establishment of distinct subordinate communes" which in its implications involved a radical decentralization of communal activity. Hopedale had already allowed for the formation of private business associations, but each "commune" in Ballou's scheme was a whole new subcommunity authorized not only to carry on a business or businesses but "to prescribe its own territorial localities, limits, and inhabitancies" and to establish various ways "for promoting the improvement and happiness of its own population."[3] This decision opened the way for the formation in early 1856 of "Commune No. 1," a joint-stock association, by Ballou and nine associates (including his wife, Lucy). Over the next two months, the associates met each week to decide, after opening prayers and hymns, on the details of their new organization.[4]

They discussed such matters as a communal boardinghouse and the nature of their "entertainments," but their main concern was with developing an economic base for the commune. What was especially interesting was their decision to manufacture and sell a "self-acting nipper block," a tackle block that had been developed earlier by Jonathan Whipple, one of the newer members of the community and a member of the commune. In January the commune acquired the rights to the block and began to advertise it as a great labor saver, since "in raising burdens of every description in every situation, it holds fast all that is gained from pull to pull." Probably, the commune had been formed primarily to manufacture the block, the profits from which were to be distributed among its members on the basis of the 4 percent limited dividend sanctioned by Practical Christian socialism.[5]

This whole affair was rather strange. Although Ballou later implied otherwise, he was obviously a leading force behind the creation of the commune. In his history of Hopedale, written in the 1870s, he said that he had intended his plan to strengthen the community and, at the same time, to allow for greater variety and freedom of action on the basis of "congenial companionship in business affairs and in other cherished interests common to those associated together." Yet the very completeness of the commune organization set it apart from the rest of the community. At the least, it reflected a declining sense of unity in the village as a whole. Even though Hopedale's population was still less than three hundred people, its economic progress seems to have created some of the divisive tendencies of the old society. The willingness of Ballou, the resident inspiration, to serve as chief "Intendant" of Commune No. 1 highlighted this tendency, even more so because the new subcommunity included the printing business and with it the *Practical Christian.*[6]

The weakening of communal unity was underscored when the community, at the same meeting that sanctioned the communes, established a "Judicatory of Commerce," an appointed body with broad authority over wages, prices, and debts within the village. The new act allowed every member "to set up and carry on any laudable business separate from the general Joint Stock" but with the important stipulation that the books and accounts of every business be open for inspection by the Judicatory. After January 1856 no separate business by a member was to be conducted outside the new requirements, a provision that presumably applied to those businesses that had already been established.[7] In preference to direct communal operation of the economy through its joint stock, Hopedale had begun to move toward something like private enterprise under a set of public controls.

Perhaps, as Ballou hoped, this new scheme would have encouraged variety and individual ambition while also assuring that property would serve the good of all. Essentially, it made all business in the village subject to the Constitution of the Practical Christian Republic, including those provisions that limited profits to 4 percent, wages to no more than those of a first-class operative, and prices to the "fair cost value" of the products.[8] Perhaps, Hopedale might have demonstrated that Christian socialism could work in an increasingly complex world. If it did anything, however, this new experi-

ment added to an accumulation of forces that in 1856 suddenly reduced the dreams for a paradise of Christian socialism to dust.

Like most upheavals, this one had its beginnings in previous
years. An innocent cause was Ballou's good friend and successor as
president, Ebenezer D. Draper. There is no question that Draper, one
of the original founders, was deeply devoted both to the community
and to Practical Christianity, but that became part of the problem.
Having decided to devote much of the profits from his loom-temple
business to the good of the community, he apparently purchased
most of the joint stock issued by the community to finance the construction of its school, barn, and other improvements, in the process
making himself the community's largest stockholder and creditor; in
1850 the census listed him as a temple maker with only $1,200 in
property, but this did not include his share of the $35,000 in com-
munity assets credited to Ballou.[9]

Draper's experience and income gave him a reputation as a businessman that was not entirely deserved. An inherited patent was
the basis for his success, and it is noteworthy that when he later
ventured out to do business in the great world he failed. Certainly,
he did not bring a particularly businesslike government to Hopedale
either as its treasurer or as its president, and neither did his successor as treasurer, Lemuel Munyan, whom Ballou later described as fi-
nancially "not a favorite of success."[10] The annual financial reports
of the two men were models of accounting simplicity. On the one
side of the ledger, they added up the physical assets of the community and the money owed to it; on the other side, they added up the
joint stock and other forms of indebtedness; the difference between
the two sums meant either gain or loss.

The key determinant of yearly success or failure was the amount
of money available to pay the 4 percent dividend on the joint stock.
It was only when the balance on the positive side was large enough
to meet the full dividend that Draper and his associates believed
they had experienced financial success. In his report for 1854, for instance, he reported community assets of $60,441 and liabilities of
$59,090, leaving a surplus of $1,351; with the addition of certain
other sums, he concluded that the community had made net profits
more than sufficient to pay the $1,821 due for dividends on the
$39,350 worth of joint stock in the community.[11]

In the same report, however, Draper took an anxious look at the financial crisis that had recently begun to afflict the outside world with bankruptcies and unemployment, using it to underscore "the necessity of looking *at home* to see if we cannot improve our condition by more labor, more economy, and by more knowledge of the things in which the financial success of an individual and a Community consists."

It is notable that in this call for a community belt-tightening, Draper chose to mention particularly the financial success of *individuals*, one sign of changing times. When in September the *Practical Christian* listed the virtues of the community, it included a reference to Hopedale as "a suitable sphere of individual enterprise and responsibility, in which each one may by due self-exertion elevate himself to the highest point of his capability." [12] Although individual enterprise had always had some place in Practical Christian socialism, the idea of personal elevation through "self-exertion" seemed out of place in a community dedicated to cooperative effort and fraternal love.

The meaning of such references began to come clear when Draper made his next annual report to the community in January 1856. After noting that Treasurer Munyan was not yet ready to report on the financial affairs of the community, the president gave his attention to information that had been collected, for the first time, on the individual financial standing of the members. It revealed how much individual possession and enterprise had grown in the village. Draper reported that private property had a total value of $146,000, while the debts of individuals amounted to $53,000, a tidy balance of nearly $93,000. [13]

Intentionally or not, the timing and manner of this report intensified the shock generated in February when Munyan finally reported on the community's financial state. The treasurer estimated the total assets of the joint stock as $65,275, an 8 percent increase over the previous year, but he also reported a more than 10 percent increase in liabilities to $65,420. Although the deficit was a modest $145, it was immediately noted that this did not include the $1,652 needed to pay the 4 percent dividend on the joint stock, nor did it include any allowance for the depreciation of community assets, an accounting item that had previously been ignored. Further investigation disclosed some new problems, particularly that Dudley Chapman, the soap wizard, had over the previous several years secretly contracted debts for which the community was liable.[14]

However one read the community's balance sheet, it was not good, but neither was it a sign of financial ruin. Part of the deficit could be attributed to the troubles experienced by the outside economy in 1854–55 and part to the spending made for improvements, notably for the community school and for the great new barn. There seemed nothing that the members could not resolve. They arranged, for instance, to pay Chapman's debts, in exchange for which he agreed to repay the community in installments at no interest. They also decided to levy a special tax on their property and income in order to pay the 4 percent dividend, money that would remain largely in the village, since most of the stock was owned by residents.[15] Basically, the community seemed well on its way to resolving the crisis and to continuing the progress it had been making since its beginning. There seemed no reason why it could not have continued for an indefinite time.

By March, however, a powerful reason why it might not do so had suddenly presented itself in the form of Ebenezer Draper's brother, George, one of the newest members. The brothers Draper constituted the contrasting stuff of a Victorian moral drama. Although George shared Ebenezer's interest in abolitionism and temperance, he was formed by a different experience that allowed little room for ideals of nonresistance or dreams of brotherhood. Ballou later described him as "a natural born man of the world," given to moneymaking and impatient of high ideals. In the 1830s he had been employed by the Uxbridge cotton mills, whose bankruptcy in 1837 may have been a significant influence on the formation of Hopedale. While Ebenezer Draper and others from Uxbridge became involved in Practical Christianity, George struggled to rise in the world of business, eventually becoming superintendant of the Otis Company textile mills at Ware, Massachusetts. On the way up, he had patented some improvements in the loom temple invented by his father and manufactured by his brother. In 1853 he decided to go into partnership with Ebenezer in the temple business at Hopedale, and the next year he was admitted as a member of the community; his wife, however, refused membership since she had no use for Practical

Christian socialism. Less than a year after his admission, he began to expand his business by forming a partnership with Warren Dutcher of Vermont, the inventor of an improved temple, whom he persuaded to come to Hopedale; it may have been the formation of this company that inspired the scheme to manufacture the Whipple tackle block.[16]

Plainly, George Draper had big plans, but they were not for Ballou's Practical Christian Republic. What he originally intended is not clear, but his essential inclination became evident with Hopedale's financial crisis in early 1856. By then, Ballou later estimated, he and his brother had acquired about three-quarters of the whole joint stock. By then, too, he surely understood the basic character and implications of community ownership. In September 1855 the *Practical Christian* published an account of the community that he undoubtedly read with great interest, especially where it mentioned that because of the nonresistant aversion to government, the joint stock had not been legally incorporated and so was simply a general partnership founded on "conscience, honor, and discretionary precaution."[17] For an ambitious, sharp-minded businessman like George Draper, this character presented both an opportunity and a threat.

On the positive side, the joint stock afforded him a chance to acquire control of a village whose productive assets exceeded the value of the stock; Hopedale was a developing town with waterpower, facilities, and skilled labor useful in the manufacturing business. The essence of Draper's business genius was a strong acquisitory instinct combined with a shrewd ability to determine the potential value of capital assets. On the negative side, the general partnership left stockholders like himself liable for any and all debts of the community, a danger given concrete form by the financial revelations of early 1856. Moreover, community policies that would inevitably affect business were determined by a majority vote of members in their meetings.[18] The fear that community concerns would intrude on his interests was deepened by the decision to establish the Judicatory of Commerce with its powers to examine accounts and to influence wages and prices of any business operation in the village.

The only reason for accepting this situation had to be a deep commitment to Practical Christian socialism, but there was no such restraint on Draper's calculating mind. Ballou had envisioned a society in which everyone would be content with rewards for their talents within the limits acceptable to a small-town middle class, but the idea of limiting income to the wages of a first-class operative and dividends to 4 percent was intolerable to Draper.

How does nonresistance deal with such a Napoleon? The question became threateningly real when George persuaded his brother to join him in a coup against the community. After watching the members struggle to devise a solution to the financial crisis, the Drapers suddenly announced at the end of February that they were withdrawing their investment from the joint stock. As they owned three-quarters of the stock, their withdrawal meant the dissolution of the joint-stock association. In theory, the community had means to defend itself, particularly a provision in its bylaws limiting stock redemptions to no more than 4 percent of its joint stock per year.[19] If only because nonresistance denied such a provision any legal basis, however, the Drapers had the commanding position, one further strengthened by the argument that the community would eventually fail anyway; the contrast between private success and communal failure reported earlier by Draper and Munyan had had its effect. And so the community surrendered rather than attempting to resist even by nonresistant means.

This Napoleon, at least, was an honorable man. Ballou was able to persuade the Drapers to assume the debts of the community in exchange for its productive assets at a fair appraised value; the community was permitted to retain about ten thousand dollars in property, chiefly in the form of the Hopedale school, public square, cemetery, and the unsold portions of the village site. Although the agreement evoked considerable controversy, it was approved on 8 March 1856 by the members, fifteen to one. Notable, though, was the fact that five of the ayes were cast by George, Ebenezer, and Anna T. Draper, and by Ebenezer's brother-in-law, Almon Thwing, and his wife, while fourteen of the thirty members attending this meeting abstained. To implement the bargain, the community's constitution was amended in several places; eliminated were the restriction of property ownership in the village to members only and the pledge to provide everyone with "adequate employment, edu-

cational advantages and protection from the evils of poverty, ignorance and vice."[20] And so a revolution against Christian socialism
in favor of private enterprise was accomplished with the reluctant support of Ballou and the acquiescence of a majority of the
members.

The results were soon apparent. Less than a month later the
Drapers consolidated their control of the manufacturing facilities of
the village by forming the Hopedale Machine Company with two
other members of the community, Joseph B. Bancroft and William
Stimson. This company and the Dutcher Temple Company formed
earlier became the basis for George Draper's fortune.[21] Although
Ebenezer Draper was a partner in both companies, he apparently
agree to let his brother have most of the manufacturing assets of the
old community in exchange for possession of most of its lands. By
1858 he had laid out the old domain into large house lots and small
farms of from two to twenty acres, advertising that the domain was
now "opened for settlement" to "persons of liberal and reformatory
ideas and tendencies, sympathizing with the fundamental principles and objects of the Hopedale Community." In part because the
presence of the Home School increased the sale value of his property,
Ebenezer lent the school more than four thousand dollars, which
was still owed to him at the end of 1860.[22]

Conspicuously absent from this scene, however, was Commune
No. 1, whose members had been notably aloof from the proceedings
leading to dissolution; other than Ballou, only one of its members
was even at the meeting that voted to dissolve the joint stock. It
may have been their interest in this subcommunity that persuaded
Ballou and the others to acquiesce so readily in the termination of
the larger experiment. For a brief time after dissolution, the commune continued to exist under the sanction of the revised constitution, but if its members expected to continue their new association they were soon disappointed. They were unable to make money
from the printing business, and the Whipple tackle block, on which
they had staked their future, proved to have flaws that limited its
sale. On 6 April, a few days after they had tried to boost their spirits
by engaging in a "charade" on the theme of Whipple's invention,
they held their last recorded meeting as a commune.[23]

The Practical Christian community itself survived as a shrunken presence within the village it had created. Gone were its savings bank, Industrial Army, Fire Insurance Company, Council of Religion, and industrial branches. By the end of 1857 its joint stock had shriveled from $41,300 in 1855 to only $7,600; presumably, most of the $33,700 in liquidated stock belonged to the Drapers. During the same period its assets declined by $40,671 to less than $15,000; three years later they were little more than $3,000, much of this later decrease resulting from the sale of village house lots to pay debts owed by the community. As its property shrank, so did its membership; at least nineteen persons formally resigned, including Dudley Chapman, who, three years after the disclosure of his part in the financial crisis, finally concluded that his presence in the community was "an offense and a stumbling block." Chapman continued his soap business in the village, however, and in 1862 paid off the last of the $2,154 he owed the community for assuming his debts six years before.[24]

By far the most important departing member was the last of Ballou's original ministerial colleagues, William Henry Fish. Fish, who had been doing missionary work in upstate New York, decided not to return to Hopedale when he learned of the change. In May 1856 he dismissed the effort to establish socialism in any form as premature, since few people seemed as yet to be sufficiently developed in wisdom and goodness "to live and labor together." The millennium of Christian brotherhood, Fish said, would have to wait until that distant time when man's "slowly unfolding and slowly progressing nature" had finally prepared him for the fraternal life. Although he had planned to make Hopedale his last resting place, Fish now determined to cast his lot with the great outside world.[25] For him and for others, the Hopedale Community, once the rising star of Bethlehem, had become a dying ember in an ever more worldly Hopedale village.

The community might have survived as more than an ember if Adin Ballou had tried harder to sustain it. Whatever his private bitterness toward the Drapers, Hopedale's founder and resident inspiration made no effort to rally his followers against them. Instead, he allowed the brothers to convince him that he had no choice but to salvage what he could from impending ruin. After he had arranged for them to take over the debts of the community, he accepted dissolution with the conviction that at least he had protected his followers from indebtedness.[26] His close friendship with Ebenezer, the last and most generous of his original supporters, was probably the key influence on his behavior, even though it was his successor's casual financial management that had contributed to the financial crisis.

In any case, Ballou was slow to recognize the full extent of the disaster. Six months after the change he confessed that he had been "deeply pained, mortified and discouraged for many months," and at the end of the year he wrote privately that he had abandoned his hopes for cooperative association: "Few people are near enough right in heart, head, and habit to live in close social intimacy." Only later, however, would he recognize that what in his *Autobiography* (1890) he called the "revolution of 1856" marked the beginning of the end for Practical Christianity. Moreover, in these earlier years he was often preoccupied with his own affairs. As late as 1859 he continued to advertise that he was prepared to sell a modified version of the Whipple tackle block, the last remnant of the failed Commune No. 1; the defects in the original had led to more costs than sales, forcing him to improve it at "great cost and pain." And he became more preoccupied with the *Practical Christian*, taking on full responsibility for the newspaper in the spring of 1856 when William Heywood became principal of the Home School.[27] Under the circumstances, he was probably not disposed to condemn the Draper brothers for their pursuit of individual gain.

It was understandable, then, that his first public reaction to the change was to abandon his earlier hopes for cooperative ownership of property even in the joint-stock form. Associated property would be desirable and workable if human nature were ready for it, but not even reformers had proved that they could unite in meaningful association. Realistically, most of the world belonged to individual property. In May 1856 he wrote that capital had become the dominant power in the material realm: "Those who hold the property of the world are becoming more and more its governors. We cannot set this power at nought and defy it, if we would." It was foolish to preach indifference to property, he said, if only because the preacher himself was fed and clothed by property owners.[28]

Ballou was not yet ready to abandon his hopes for the Practical

Christian Republic, however. In November 1856, when he first publicly expressed his feelings about the change, he said that he had first been humiliated and crushed by it but that further reflection convinced him that the Hopedale Community had attempted too much. He was willing, therefore, to work with simpler, less completely organized forms of association and with individuals in the hope of eventually raising them to a higher plane. With characteristic optimism, he tried to convince himself that dissolution had freed true Practical Christians from local distractions to carry on a more comprehensive campaign to spread their principles.[29]

Ballou even retained some of his old dream for Christian socialism, envisioning the formation of societies whose wealthier members would voluntarily limit the personal use of their property to their basic needs, reserving the surplus for the benefit of the less fortunate; when the rich and able could be persuaded to avoid extravagant consumption, there would be enough wealth available to eliminate all forms of poverty. In the summer of 1857 he published a lengthy editorial urging the members of the Practical Christian Republic, at Hopedale and elsewhere, to commit themselves to the grand goal of guaranteeing to

> every orderly citizen of this Republic a comfortable home, suitable employment, adequate subsistence, congenial associates, a good education, proper stimulants to personal righteousness, sympathetic aid in distress, and due protection in the exercise of all natural rights. . . . Good homes in good neighborhoods for all who try to be worthy of them; this is the way to regenerate human society, and render the earth a manifold Eden.[30]

Without the complexities of overorganized communities, these benefits could be assured through a simple commitment to the stewardship of property required in Ballou's model republic.

The times offered some support for Ballou's hopes. The mid 1850s brought an upsurge of religious feeling and reform that peaked in the months after the Panic of 1857. Moreover, Ballou could find some particular hope in spiritualism. Several months after the failure of the Hopedale Community, he visited Southold, Long Island, where he encountered Thomas Lake Harris, who was later to establish religious communities first in western New York and then in

California. Ballou was profoundly impressed by this "Spiritual Medium, Poet and Lecturer," remembering years later that Harris had had a vision that "was sublimely grand and holy, and agreed so closely with my highest aspirations, that I could but accept it as substantially true." He returned to Hopedale with renewed confidence in the future.[31] Perhaps the days of miracles had not passed.

In 1858 he gave some support to the Harmonial Township Association, organized by New Englanders with the aim of acquiring tracts of land to provide "a home for all settlers on reasonable terms, free from the trickery of monopoly and speculation." And he continued to hope that he could at least begin to convert the world to Practical Christianity, that he could, as he said later, "be a modern John the Baptist, preparing the way for a better future and making ready for the coming of the divine kingdom."[32] Perhaps the unstable and disappointing times would renew and complete the spiritual revolution that had molded him in the 1830s. Indeed, the later 1850s were preparing a profound revolution that would significantly alter his world. It was not a revolution that would benefit Practical Christianity, however. In fact, the coming upheaval was to extinguish even the tiny flame that had been left burning at Hopedale.

10

Island in the Storm

The loss of the Hopedale properties to the Drapers destroyed the economic basis of Practical Christianity, reducing it to little more than a small sect of diminishing importance even in the world it had originally created. At Hopedale, though, the full impact of the change was drawn out over a long period. On the surface, much continued as before. Morally, the village remained free from the blight of saloons and crime, an island of peace where persons could find, promised Morgan L. Bloom in 1857, refuge from "the tumult of the world, untrammeled by the artificial restraints of fashion." In this peaceful atmosphere, the village continued to develop slowly as a place of pleasant homes on tree-lined streets.[1]

Some of the essential social elements of the old community also remained. As in the past, it was ethnically homogeneous, more than three-quarters of its population claiming birth in New England, the majority in Massachusetts, while less than 10 percent were foreign born. And occupationally, it continued to be a society of skills. Of some eighty-six villagers whose occupations were reported in the national census of 1860, at least forty-two were machinists, molders, carpenters, and other skilled workers, while another dozen were businessmen, professionals, and clerks. Educationally, Hopedale could boast that it had only one illiterate in its adult population.

Although many of the inhabitants in 1860 were newcomers, there also remained numerous residents from 1850, the year of the previous census. For these individuals, the imperfect information provided by the two censuses indicates various and generally modest changes during the 1850s. Stephen Albee, whom Ballou described as being a skillful painter and glazer, had doubled his reported property to $1,600 and increased his family from two to three children; living with him as a housekeeper was Charlotte Gay, a single woman who had frequently served the community as a nurse and seamstress. William Henry Humphrey, a carpenter and window maker, had increased his holdings from $1,600 to $4,500; and Fenner Inman, who had risen from laborer to lumber dealer, had acquired $2,000 in property. On the other hand, Joseph Bailey, one of the stalwarts of Ballou's Inductive Communion, reported no property in either census but had made other gains, rising from laborer to cabinetmaker while marrying and having two children. There were various other changes in job status: Delano Patrick had moved from carpenter to farmer, Henry Lillie (one of the few remaining original members of 1842) from machinist to carpenter, and Alonzo Cook from carpenter to painter (Cook was later to become a paint dealer in Milford Center); while Daniel H. Carter went from carpenter to day laborer, William Heywood rose from carpenter to cleric schoolmaster.

By 1860 there was some evident economic inequality, especially given that 40 percent of the recorded $50,000 in property owned by villagers belonged to the two Draper brothers. Ebenezer Draper had increased his holdings from $1,200 to $11,600, while George (not a resident in 1850) reported $8,500, along with a wife, five children, and Jane Johnson, a black servant. In contrast, there was one small boardinghouse crowded with fourteen adults, mostly laborers without property. On the other hand, the Draper properties, at least in their reported value, were not so much more than the $3,000 reported for Ballou or the $6,500 owned by his son-in-law, school proprietor William Heywood, or the $3,500 held by Heywood's brother, John. Among the twenty-eight people listed as family heads, seventeen owned at least $1,000 in property, while many of the others had lesser amounts.[2] On the surface at least, differences in wealth remained within tolerable limits.

And there was no dearth of either opportunity or energy. George Draper's Hopedale Machine Company and the Dutcher Temple Company had begun to outgrow their beginnings, while numerous small businesses continued: Ballou struggled to sell his improved version of the Whipple tackle block in order at least to pay off the debts acquired to produce it; William Walker Cook, one of the original Uxbridge members and a horticulturist, advertised his nursery stock and locally produced flower seeds for sale through a mail-order catalog; Samuel S. Brown, who had made himself something of an expert on strawberries, offered strawberry plants at two dollars per hundred; Dudley Chapman claimed that he had "the woman's friend" for sale in the form of a newly concocted soap suited to hard water; and Emily Gay, Hopedale's self-taught "intuitive physician," announced that she had ink and, later, homeopathic medicines for sale. And there was Richard Walker, an ardent spiritualist and "heavy thinker on important subjects," who was becoming locally well known as an inventor of improvements in textile machinery; before he joined the community in 1853, Walker had patented the first power loom for knitting underwear. The *Practical Christian* probably understated the situation when in 1857 it said of the villagers that "in respect to business enterprise, and the laudable ambition to acquire property for good use, they have their full share."

Ebenezer Draper added a new note of enterprise when he tried to dispose of the lands he had acquired from the dissolution of the joint stock. Dividing up the old domain into tracts of from two to twenty acres, he advertised them for sale in the *Liberator* and similar papers to "persons of liberal and reformatory ideas and tendencies" sympathetic to the fundamental principles of the community. Besides the land itself, he emphasized that Hopedale's manufacturing facilities and waterpower made it a favorable location for skilled workers "either to commence or continue business," and he used the presence of the Home School to appeal to persons of "literary inclinations." His sale was endorsed by Ballou, who declared in the *Practical Christian* that since the original hopes for "unitary social arrangements" had been disappointed, "the next best thing is to see so good a neighborhood built up as circumstances will allow." Few if any of the reform-minded seem to have bought Draper's lands, but his boosterism made some contribution to village development. By 1861 Hopedale was large enough to warrant a federal post office to replace its defunct penny post.[3]

If the new times perhaps brought too much attention to business at Hopedale, there also remained much of reform culture and progressive religion. As in the past, the village made 1 August, the anniversary of the abolition of slavery in the British West Indies, a day for a major celebration of freedom. In 1856 over a thousand people from the vicinity gathered at a "sweet pine grove" south of the village to listen to speeches by Ballou and various other local abolitionists, including George Stacy, and to sing "stirring Anti-Slavery songs." The gathering also approved thirteen antislavery resolutions that concluded with a renewal of dedication to the great goal: "Slavery nowhere but Liberty everywhere, throughout our nation and throughout the world." In 1857 another large crowd, which included William Lloyd Garrison, again gathered at Hopedale to celebrate the cause of freedom, in part with songs composed for the occasion by members of the community. That the commitment to freedom was more than mere theory is indicated by the census of 1860, where one of Hopedale's two black residents, Henry Johnson, was boldly identified as an "Alabama fugitive."[4]

The year 1857 saw two other meetings that expressed the concerns of the community. The first involved the Inductive Communion, Ballou's informal educational gatherings for young people. Soon after the dissolution of the community, Ballou had withdrawn as the teacher of the Communion with the expressed hope that it would be continued by its members, but it seems to have quickly lost momentum; its last recorded meeting was in July 1856. Nearly a year later, in June 1857, Hopedale gave a festival in its honor. Beginning in the afternoon with the playing of Harrison's Grand March by the village band, the affair featured an address by Ballou, the singing of songs, and the reading of various compositions by members of the Communion; after a picnic in the pine grove, the celebrants gathered for an evening session in the chapel, where they listened to several skits that "excited much laughter." At another gathering later in the year, the villagers crowded into the chapel to attend "a fest of spiritual elements," listening to communications from the spirit world spoken by a young medium from Michigan. Although some listeners were skeptical, one of Hopedale's numerous spiritualists saw in the gathering another sign that mankind was beginning to recognize the "superior mission of the New Spiritual Philosophy."[5]

Events like these helped preserve Hopedale's sense of uniqueness in the world. One member of the old community, Harriet N. Greene, declared that the people of the village were indeed a rather peculiar people, peculiar in that they disavowed violence in any form and opened their doors to the fugitive slave; peculiar too in that there was no poverty, unemployment, drunkeness, or wasted lives in their midst. For Greene and probably for most members, Ballou remained the undisputed inspiration in their world: "To us, Hopedale is dearer than any other spot, and we would ever be worthy of a place in the memory of one who, years ago, laid his reputation, talents, and entire labors, upon the unpopular altar of the social emancipation and regeneration of mankind."[6]

Hopedale also continued to be a local moral and cultural center. It remained the headquarters for the quarterly conference of Practical Christians in the Mill River Valley and elsewhere. As the home of the Hopedale press, it also retained some local publishing importance. In 1857 the press issued William Henry Fish's *Orthodoxy versus Spiritualism and Liberalism* (an attack on conventional religion and "the conservative and stationary money power of the land") with the observation that it was "a racy, suggestive, well written publication" that would likely sell more than the three hundred copies requested by its author. Also, the quarterly conference continued to handle the sale of other works previously published by the press, basically three of Ballou's books, the Hopedale collection of hymns, Fish's *Memoir of Butler Wilmarth*, and nine tracts by Ballou on various subjects, the last at prices ranging from two to six cents a copy.[7]

Above all, the village remained the home of the *Practical Christian*, which in May 1857 celebrated the completion of its seventeenth year of continuous publication. Shortly before, Ballou had again taken over all the editorial and publishing responsibilities. In the hope of attracting new subscribers, he added a MONITORIAL COMPENDIUM, "a microcosmical review of what is going on in the various spheres of human interests," but he could not make the paper self-sustaining: "Even reformers and progressives in many cases give it the cold shoulder; because it is too fast or too slow, or too homely for them. It is too much tinctured with the radical, sober, calm, undashing, practical Christianity of the Sermon on the Mount." Nor did his subscribers provide reliable support; in 1858 he was forced to publish a list of 341 people who owed him between $1 and $5.68 on their $1-a-year subscriptions with the threat that if this did not work, he might give up the paper.[8] With the help of annual subsidies from the shrinking old community, however, he struggled on, and the *Practical Christian* remained his most influential podium for the various causes to which he had committed himself over the previous decades. So long as the *Practical Christian* stayed alive, so long would there be hope for the eventual triumph of radical religion and moral reform.

In the late 1850s that hope found a fresh though not always reliable voice in Bryan J. Butts, who spoke for the new age of spiritual ferment. A native New Yorker, Butts joined the community in 1852 when he was twenty-six and soon became a leading figure in the Inductive Communion, where he was remembered for his spindly body, long hair, deep voice, and very solemn face. However complete his devotion to Ballou's ideals, it was a devotion shaped by the romanticism and spiritualism of his times. Butts later described himself as "a Socialist and Progressivist of the most unfettered individualistic type." Although he had been trained for the ministry, there seems to have been less of Christianity and more of spiritualism in his religion. In a long and ornate lecture that he gave before the Hopedale lyceum in 1853, for instance, he declared that a new and promising element was entering civilization:

> Spiritual light has been hastening long, very long, to reach the dull cold air of our planet. A few hearts to-day are throbbing with its divine heat. . . . The naturalist has found that the waters of the sea are moved by the moon's attractions; but for the spiritualist there awaited a sublimer discovery—that the sea of humanity is moved by the attraction of Spiritual Spheres.[9]

Butts's radical individualism left him even more completely apolitical than Ballou, isolating him from any responsible role in the community or any other organization. He was remote from movements, a solitary spokesman who placed his faith in the power of rhetoric and ideas. In 1856 he composed a long, turgid drama, "The Medley of Reform," involving a convention of reformers who debate the merits of socialism, spiritualism, and especially nonresistance; the climax of the play is a successful nonresistance defense of a fugitive slave from would-be captors followed by much singing about the triumph of freedom. Butts was soon advertising that he would read his play "to such Lyceums, or Societies as may wish to hear."

He also offered to recite two of his poems, "The Angel and the Bigot" and "The Angel and the Slaver," but there seem to have been few if any engagements. As late as November 1858, though, he continued to advertise that he would recite revised and improved versions of the poems to interested groups in New England "FREE TO ALL— after the gospel method—'without money and without price.'"[10]

Butts's resort to the stage ended in late 1858 when he married another member of the community, Harriet Greene, with whom he had been boarding. Greene, one of whose aunts was a Quaker preacher and another a writer, had come to Hopedale in 1852. When they were married by Ballou, Butts and the feminist Greene, who was six years his senior, issued a "protest" against existing forms of marriage, particularly the expectation that the woman adopt the surname of her husband: "We protest against any such annihilation of her personality, and request that the public and all private friends call us by our original names." Less than four months later Butts and Greene announced that they were about to issue a new monthly, the *Radical Spiritualist*, in which they intended "to apply the principles of Spiritualism to the great moral and political questions of the times." As a token of their determination to labor especially for the forgotten ones in society, they announced that their journal would be given free to the "Outcast, Oppressed, and Unfortunate," everyone else paying fifty cents a year.[11]

The couple succeeded in sustaining their periodical over the next six years under four different titles: the *Radical Spiritualist* and then the *Spiritual Reformer* until 1862, after which it was first the *Progressive Age* and then the *Modern Age*. Whatever the title, it was an eclectic journal expressive of Butts's creed as he summed it up in 1860:

> Spiritualism, Natural Science, Socialism, Individualism, Phonetic Reform, Non-Resistance, Anti-Slavery, Temperance, Anti-Tobacco, Vegetarianism, Anti-Voting, Anti-Oath Taking, Woman's Rights, True Freedom in Love, Sexual Reform, Dual Marriage Outside of the Institution.[12]

Although Ballou and other older members probably had their doubts about this creed, the new monthly did at least help sustain Hopedale's image of itself as a lighthouse of progressive ideas and liberal religion. Its presence kept alive the hope that the village might still ignite some great spiritual revolution that would eventually transform the world. Even before the monthly was renamed the *Progessive Age*, however, the world had taken a very different turn.

Ballou had long expected that the spiritual revolution that had begun in the 1830s would eventually move society in Hopedale's direction, but by the mid 1850s the moral world was developing a tendency that threatened the very essence of Practical Christianity. Although abolitionism, temperance, and the other moral concerns of progressive religion were important to Ballou, Christian nonresistance was the bedrock of his faith and of the Hopedale experiment. His entire dream of the millennium, of a time when sin had disappeared, depended on humanity's acceptance of the divine principle that only good was to be returned for evil. By the mid 1850s, however, mounting moral concerns over slavery were becoming ever more entangled with the temptation to use force in some form.[13]

Part of that temptation involved the resort to politics and government against the apparent political aggressions of the slaveholding South. The Fugitive Slave Act and especially the Kansas-Nebraska Act of 1854 convinced many northerners of the need for some kind of political defense, opening the way for the dramatic rise of the Republican party as a major political force by 1856. The appearance of this antislavery organization presented a dilemma for abolitionists in general and for nonresistants in particular. On the one hand, it threatened to entangle these moral reformers in the corrupting world of politics against which they had rebelled. On the other hand, the new party was potentially a powerful moral force for the elimination of slavery and other sins from American society.[14]

Even Ballou was occasionally tempted by political thoughts, and he respected a few political figures, notably Charles Sumner, who as a senator paid some attention to Hopedale, sending it government documents and "a specimen of *Russia* wheat" to plant on an experimental basis; Ballou praised the senator for his "faithful testimony against injustice, oppression and wrong." Sumner was the exception, however, and in the end Ballou dismissed politics as no more than "a worldy game of chance, full of trick and uncertainty, suited to cunning minds rather than wise and good ones." He said that under existing governmental arrangements, no nonresistant should vote, even for building a schoolhouse, since some form of legal coercion would be used to accomplish the goal. Before the presidential election of 1856, he urged his followers to avoid any association with the Republican party on the grounds that a vote for "Freedom and Fremont" would actually be a commitment to a system of government that sanctioned slavery: "The Constitution acknowledges slavery and gives it sanction and power. To support the Constitution is to support Slavery. Political action implies fealty to the Constitution without doubt."[15]

Ballou grew even more concerned about the tendency toward violence, which grew ever stronger during the late 1850s, most disturbingly even among some of his fellow progressive reformers, a tendency driven especially by the conflict that had broken out over slavery in Kansas. At a convention of "The Friends of Peace and Universal Brotherhood" held at nearby Worcester in 1858, for instance, Thomas Wentworth Higginson expressed his general faith in the principle of returning good for evil, only to argue that in exceptional cases it was a right and a duty "to take the sword and the rifle, and march to the battle-field." Even among Garrisonian abolitionists, the idea of a righteous war to destroy the wickedness of slavery was growing. Ballou urged his readers to consider history—in which every war had been a righteous one to at least one side: war had produced "the destruction of at least 14,000,000,000 of the human race; enough to people eighteen such planets as the Earth," and yet wickedness and violence remained as strong as ever.[16] Only devotion to the principles of nonresistance could break the bloody cycle while also eliminating slavery.

Over the next years Ballou became increasingly alienated from abolitionism because of the growth of the "war principle." In September 1859 he declared that while the Practical Christians had aligned themselves with Garrisonian abolitionists in the past, the cause of nonresistance was superior to the cause of antislavery. Once the two had been in harmony, but now, under the motto "peacefully if we can, forcibly if we must," abolitionists were accepting an evil even worse than slavery: to use force to eliminate slavery was "like attempting to cast out Satan with Satan." Ballou wondered whether he could continue to stand on the antislavery platform "because of the increasing egotism, extremism, exaggerationism, antagonism, and contemptuous personality, which we are obliged to witness." In contrast to this, he proclaimed himself to be a "Practical Christian Anti-Slavery man—loving all, hating none."[17]

The prospect of a loving world vanished the next month, however, when John Brown launched his raid on Harpers Ferry. For Ballou, Brown was a natural product of the rising war spirit: "We have no faith in the utility of murder, and least of all when resorted to in the name of philanthropy." When the abolitionists of southern Worcester County met after the raid, Ballou tried to win support for his position only to have the meeting pass, by a nearly unanimous vote, resolutions praising Brown as a hero who had chosen "to break the rod of the oppressor by the same means by which our revolutionary fathers secured our national independence."[18] There was to be no millennium of peace and brotherhood.

Less than three weeks after this defeat, Ballou announced that he planned to give up his long struggle as editor of the *Practical Christian* at the close of the present volume in April 1860. In his "editorial farewell" published in the last issue, he adopted a generally positive tone, condemning no one and expressing satisfaction with his paper: "Its work was to sow seed for the coming age—to generate a higher public sentiment—to prepare the way for a wiser, holier and better condition for mankind." Although not much had been accomplished, he continued to believe that the seeds he had planted would ultimately bear fruit, taking some comfort in the thought that he had formed "a small nucleus of minds" committed to Practical Christianity.[19]

The termination of the *Practical Christian* was a painful closing of Ballou's pulpit to the world, but he found at least a little hope in the new preparations that were being made in Hopedale. He sold his press and printing equipment to Bryan Butts and Harriet Greene for use in publishing their monthly, assuring some future for the cause of radical religion. More significant was a reorganization of Practical Christianity itself. In January 1860 he and his dwindling band of followers established the Practical Christian Church of Hopedale with the avowed intention of promoting "our own progress in Christian life as well as the extension of Practical Christianity." The new church soon formed a promulgation society headed by Ballou for the dissemination of its beliefs. And in November it was able to move into a new two-story meetinghouse capable of seating five hundred people built on the village square with money contributed by the Drapers and others.[20]

None of this could conceal the fact that the Hopedale Community was a diminishing entity even in its own village. Although the old community organization was retained, this was done largely to maintain the cemetery and streets and to uphold the provisions prohibiting the un-Christian use of village property.[21] In January 1861 Ballou urged the continuation of the community not only for these reasons but also as a form of defiance to a changing world. Termination would proclaim that the social principles of Practical Christianity no longer had any meaning, and it would weaken the ability of its members to protect themselves against "the influx of strangers" who might in the future turn Hopedale "against the original Community faith and morals." Even in the village, "we may yet be pointed at with the finger of scorn as fogies and fossils, clinging tenaciously to a superannuated Christ and a dead past." Should that day ever come, "then, with our organization remaining still intact, we may purchase us a new location, pack up our archives, take our sacred fire, and bid adieu to this valley—carrying with us all of Hopedale, that represented its primal past."[22] So much for the local future.

More generally, by early 1861 the Hopedale Community had become a tiny island of peace about to be swallowed up in a raging storm. In December 1860 Ballou had deciphered the times when in a discourse on Christian nonresistance given at Hopedale he took note of the secession of South Carolina. More than three months before the attack on Fort Sumter, he predicted a civil war. Since South Carolina and other seceded states could be expected to demand possession of the forts and other property of the nation, he thought that a "sanguinary contest between North and South" was inevitable. He also considered the possibility that a general war would "necessitate the abolition of slavery by the process of arms," but even then he wanted none of it, since the result might not be the abolition of which he dreamed: "There is uncertainty and crooked purpose in war."[23] A war even in the cause of freedom could not but further corrupt the soul of Man.

The outbreak of the war confronted the Hopedale Community with the choice of abandoning its nonresistant soul or of standing ineffectually against the tide. The majority of the members of the community—although not all—chose to stand by its principles. In July 1861 they passed a series of resolves establishing their old principles as a creed to which each person had to subscribe to remain a member; of fifty responses, eleven chose to purge themselves from the membership rolls by refusing to sign the pledge. Two months later the remaining members proclaimed their loyalty to both the Union and the cause of antislavery but pronounced themselves nonparticipants dedicated to a higher power and greater cause:

> We deem it our mission under Jesus Christ to bear such testimonies and to lead such lives as will tend to regenerate mankind, elevate them to the true Christian plane of personal and national righteousness, conform all human governments to the divine, abolish all dernier resorts to carnal weapons, supersede all deadly forces by beneficent ones, and thus consumate the reign of universal love and peace.[24]

As a testimonial to their faith, the community voted not only to send the declaration to the outside press but to print a thousand copies of it for distribution. They recognized, though, that it was a mere straw against the wind, and nothing in the next few years eased their sense of isolation from the times. In 1862 three members of the community volunteered to work with the freed slaves in the Union-conquered areas around Port Royal, South Carolina, only to be rejected on the grounds that their nonresistance principles would antagonize the soldiers and take from the ex-slaves what "little manhood" they had. And when several members had earlier signed a petition calling for the use of the war power to emancipate the slaves, only to be rebuked by their brethren for turning to the god of war, the community resolved by a unanimous vote to be in the future on guard "against all solicitations" of that sort, thereby denying itself any connection with the Emancipation Proclamation.[25]

While their beliefs excluded them from the nobler side of the war, their young men might still be drafted into its bloody side. During the summer of 1862 Ballou and William Heywood were appointed to petition the government for an exemption of members "from all enrollments and service, placing them in the same footing as the Quakers and the Shakers." They were not successful. In the summer of 1863 John Heywood received notice that he was drafted into the Union army, a threat that divided the community. Should Heywood defy the order and go to jail, a martyr to a just cause, or should he pay the three-hundred-dollar commutation money allowed under the conscription law? It was finally decided to pay the money under protest.[26]

Throughout, the loyal band was forced to see the erosion of the remaining commitment to nonresistance. Outside Hopedale the drama of the conflict had raised an enthusiasm for war even among moral reformers. In 1863, for instance, Emerson wrote in his journal that "war, I know is not an unmitigated evil; it is a potent alternative, tonic, magnetiser, reinforces manly power a hundred & a thousand times." Earlier, this sensitive barometer of his times had favored the nonresistance cause. Closer to home, George Thompson Garrison, the oldest son of William Lloyd Garrison, enlisted in the Union army; a decade earlier, he had been educated at Hopedale and had helped edit its youth newspaper, the *Diamond*.

Even in the village itself, the war god appeared. Less than two months after Fort Sumter, George Draper resigned his membership in the community on the grounds that nonresistance was impractical under existing circumstances; with him went several other members, a disheartening loss to the already depleted community. Over the next years several young men from the village fought in the war, including Draper's son William, whose education in the Hopedale school did nothing to dissuade him from volunteering in September 1861; William rose rapidly in the ranks, retiring as a brevet brigadier general in October 1864 after being wounded in the Battle of the Wilderness—a military hero returned to the village of peace.[27]

Economically, too, the war was eventually good for the Draper family and bad for the old community. During the first year of the conflict, local business suffered, especially because of disruptions in the New England textile industry; in August 1862 one of Hopedale's two machine shops was almost without work, and the next month was even worse. By 1864, though, government orders for military clothing had helped revive the textile mills, which in turn stimulated local business. "Wealth rolled in upon its leading citizens,"

Ballou later recalled. "Money-making, political engineering and advancement and martial patriotism absorbed the thought and energy of the populace," while the old community "grew weaker in membership and in moral power from year to year." The war also deprived the Hopedale Home School of most of its students, forcing it to close in 1863, permanently ending what little remained of Ballou's hope of making Hopedale a center of Practical Christian education; the Heywoods, his helpful daughter and son-in-law, soon left the village for other places and employments.[28] By 1865 Hopedale had become the province of George Draper rather than Adin Ballou. In the early months of the war, Ballou had prophesied better days to come for nonresistance, but by now little remained of the old spirit, in the village or anywhere else.

Late in 1865 Ballou joined with a few other radical advocates of peace in a call to all those who believed in universal brotherhood to meet in Boston to "organize a new, uncompromising, vigorous, and well-ordered Movement against the War System on the basis of Total Abstinence from all resorts to Deadly Force among mankind." A feeble convention was held in Boston in March 1866 to organize the Universal Peace Union, but nothing even like the small Non-Resistant Society of prewar years developed to carry on the radical peace tradition. Five years later, Ballou noted sadly that in the world "at this moment they have more brain, muscle, science, destructive enginery, [and] pecuniary capital invested in the war system than ever before."[29] Perhaps it was fortunate that he was not permitted to see the next century.

11

Twilight

The Civil War drastically reoriented the reform culture that had originated and sustained Practical Christianity, but even under the new conditions some of the tradition of moral commitment and religious radicalism survived at Hopedale. Throughout the conflict, the community sustained some of its old strivings for moral and mental culture. In 1861 Ballou had initiated a series of weekly "inductive conferences" as a means of moral and religious improvement. To guide this conference and the hundreds more that he hoped would be initiated elsewhere, he published in 1862 an elaborate *Monitorial Guide* that detailed fifty-two weekly exercises that he believed would prepare the members of the inductive conferences to be citizens of his Practical Christian Republic. "Advanced minds delight in method, order, system, harmony, and the fitness of things," he explained. "Chaos, confusion, incoherence, discord and uncouthness belong to crude and low development."[1]

During the chaos and incoherence of war, his followers intensified their strivings for self-improvement. Besides the inductive conferences and their normal religious meetings, they held temperance festivals and educational lectures. In the winter of 1861–62, for instance, the young people of the community gave a series of lectures on such subjects as "Women" and "Moral Beauty." And their interest in physical improvement found a new outlet in 1864 when Amelia Chapman, a daughter of the chemical wizard, began a brief "School of Light Gymnastics" where some of them learned to keep their bodies in trim. They also continued their music through the Hopedale Musical Society and the Hopedale choir, which gave several concerts in and around the village; in late 1865 a new and harsher note was added when William F. Draper and other returning war veterans formed a brass band.[2]

The community also retained its old holidays. Until the issuance of the Emancipation Proclamation in 1863, it continued on 1 August to celebrate with music, speeches, and "pic-nics" the abolition of slavery in the British West Indies, as abolitionists had done for more than two decades. Above all, it clung to its Christmas celebration, perhaps the more tenaciously because of the war. In 1863, after religious services, the community met in Hopedale's Social Hall, where in front of a mammoth Christmas tree presents were distributed among the members; from the ceiling were lowered boxes "laden with all manner of indescribable gifts" and bearing such messages as "Remember the Poor" and "Little Things for Little Folks." Significantly, the gifts were publicly reported as having a value of between $1,500 and $2,000. The dollar sign reappeared at a later Christmas, when it was reported that some gifts were worth as much as $200—amid old customs, a sign of changing times, as was the appearance of General Draper and his brass band at the 1865 celebration.[3]

The community was generous with others as well as itself. In early 1863, for instance, the Hopedale sewing circle began to make articles of clothing for the freed slaves around Port Royal, and in October 1864 some of the residents organized the Hopedale Freedman's Relief Society with Ebenezer Draper as president. Early in 1865 the society sent Sarah P. Lillie, a daughter of one of the original members of the community, to South Carolina as a teacher for the freedmen, and in 1866 it raised nearly five hundred dollars to support another Hopedale teacher, Ellen M. Patrick, the daughter of Delano Patrick, to help educate black people in the Charleston area.[4]

More than a glimmer of social radicalism survived in the village, at least among a small group of "progressives" headed by Bryan Butts and Harriet Greene. In late 1860 they had formed the Hopedale Progressive Group to hold weekly meetings for "free Social, Spiritual and Scientific communication" with the aim of "improvement—not amusement." Over the next several years the group helped support the Butts-Greene monthly, renamed the *Progressive Age* in 1862. It also began to take an interest in the plight of northern labor, particularly the lot of poor working women. By the end of the war, it was supporting the efforts of one of its members, Ira Steward, to promote the interests of labor. As secretary of the Boston Labor Reform Association, Steward, a machinist, helped originate the movement for an eight-hour workday, a movement that the Hopedale radicals supported with meetings at nearby Milford. Steward's radical concerns led him in 1878 to help found the International Workingmen's Association, one of the first Marxian organizations in the United States.[5]

After the war the title of the Butts-Greene monthly was changed to the *Modern Age,* and the progressive group was reconstituted as the Hopedale Social Science Association. At least occasionally, the *Modern Age* adopted an anticapitalist stance. In 1865, for instance, one of its articles, written perhaps by Butts, declared that capital had usurped a corrupting power, "the power of capital is the power of *matter* over mind," and warned that there could be no peace until labor learned how to control capital. Butts also reprinted his charge, first made at the Boston peace convention, that the Civil War was partly the work of "the State Street monopoly and the Fifth Avenue aristocracy which despises the claims of northern labor." At the convention and elsewhere, he declared that it was useless to cry for peace without eliminating the gap that separated the classes. As a practical measure, the progressives called for the eight-hour workday to free workers from excessive toil and to give them the time to think and to make decisions for themselves. On "the battlefield of today," such matters had to be decided in favor of labor if there was to be social peace.[6]

In general, according to the Hopedale progressives, there would be harmony in society only when the strong recognized the rights of the weak. The *Modern Age* gave special support to the feminist movement. It advocated shorter working hours, more equitable pay, and greater opportunity for women. It also urged that women be given the right to vote, and in early 1866 published a petition in favor of "universal suffrage" which it hoped would be sent to Washington, D.C., from every town and hamlet in the country. The commitment to women's issues was given a boost in late 1865 when the monthly inherited the subscribers of the defunct *Woman's Journal,* leading Greene to begin a "Woman's Journal" column, which replaced her monthly "Home Letters" on affairs at Hopedale.

Both Harriet Greene and Bryan Butts were driven by the moral ethic of Hopedale's reform culture. Regarding social evils, Greene summed up this ethic when she wrote: "'Work! Work for the elevation of mankind!' is the language that ever comes from the bending heaven to every listening ear." The reformer, wrote Butts, "is the moral giant in an age of dwarfs." But eventually the work of sustaining the *Modern Age* while writing and lecturing on reform subjects proved to be too much, and in June 1866 the two announced that they were suspending publication: "The demand for rest—mental and physical—is imperative." They promised to resume the following year, but they did not, breaking a string of reform periodicals that extended back thirty-five years to Ballou's *Independent Messenger*.[7]

The Hopedale Social Science Association survived only a little longer, but for a time it was active enough to express some of the newness of the changing times. The association had been organized with the intention of investigating "the operating causes and scientific remedies for the evils and inharmonies of our social state." Its general faith was summed up in the first article Butts chose to publish in his new journal. While conceding free will to individuals, the author argued that human acts "collectively conform to laws scarcely less rigorous than that of gravitation," since individual differences were neutralized in the mass in favor of a uniform behavior. The salvation of society, then, depended on an understanding of the laws governing its collective behavior. Although Butts and the others did not entirely ignore moralistic reform, they held that reform itself had to be reformed along the lines of the new social science and the material influences on human behavior. Typically, when Butts chose to argue against war, he condemned it not only as immoral but as disruptive of "those laws of material production by which is secured the greatest accumulation with the least waste."[8] The salvation of the world lay more in scientific knowledge than in moral commitment.

Ballou appeared at least once before the local Social Science Association, but it is doubtful whether he shared its general outlook. He revealed his attitude toward the new mentality in 1867 when he gave a long lecture at Hopedale on the subject "Human Progress in Respect to Religion." In some ways, he was impressed by the new times: "Our age is eminently an age of movement and revolution, both ideally and actually. It is one of great mental energy—great discoveries, inventions, and enterprise." As in the past, he found some hope in the prospect that change would weaken the grip of corrupting conventions, but now he expressed particular concern over the direction influential thinkers and "professed progressionists" were taking, one that was leading "large numbers of people to dispense with the specialties and personal responsibilities of religion."

What troubled him most was the erosion of belief in moral responsibility to a higher authority: "Without an active conscientiousness, man will be merely an intelligent animal. Without an acknowledged God, a divine authority, he could feel no higher obligation than to himself." He especially regretted the indifference among progressives to the moral philosophy of Jesus, for him unexcelled by any other philosophy. Under the influence of the dominating war spirit, even those who dedicated themselves to social justice lacked the self-sacrificing commitment to brotherhood associated with nonresistance. The result was "egotism, antagonism, and discordancy," which would forever defeat even the highest aspirations for humanity. In part, he attributed the problem to spiritualism, many of whose votaries had become, as he said later, "undisguisedly anti-Christian," but he blamed them less than he did the guardians of the Christian religion who had rendered their faith odious to the progressing world by their indifference to "social justice, and what may be called civil, legal, and commercial righteousness," a betrayal of true Christianity.[9]

Ballou made one last great effort to educate the world in the essential truths of Christianity and its place in the world. Between 1869 and 1872 he gave a long series of lectures at Hopedale which were eventually published in three volumes under the title *Primitive Christianity and Its Corruptions*. The religion taught and exemplified by Jesus, he said, had been radically corrupted during the first centuries of its existence and remained so to his own times: many people believe "*that* is Christianity which passes for Christianity. . . . But intelligent and thorough investigators know better, and it is time that the common people should be better informed."[10] Over the three years of his lectures, Ballou ranged over every aspect of Christianity, including its theology and ecclesiastical arrangements, but he gave special attention to its practical social implications.

In one lecture, for instance, he again considered one of the great questions of the age, the relationship of property to human welfare. Although he described himself as "a decided Associationist," he said that Jesus had not condemned private property, leaving it open whether men would own their property individually or collectively. What was important was that property owners accept their divine obligation to use their wealth for moral and social good. Excessive wealth, he warned, was morally dangerous to the possessor and oppressive to the poor; better, then, that the rich donate their unneeded wealth to the welfare of the poor. As a proper basis for the disposition of property, he proposed a rule reminiscent of the better days of Hopedale:

> Never to appropriate to one's self, family, dependent, or personal favorites for exclusive use or consumption, more property in the aggregate than would be each individual's average equitable share if all mankind were ordering their lives by the teaching and example of the Man of Nazareth.[11]

It was a rather tedious way to apply the Sermon on the Mount, but Ballou deeply believed that this one simple rule could redeem the world from poverty, misery, and crime.

Primitive Christianity and Its Corruptions was not only a mellowed summary of Practical Christianity but also a melancholy farewell. By 1870 the last hope for the survival of the old community had vanished. As early as 1861 the annual meeting had considered the question "shall we abandon the community organization," but it was decided to continue, in part as a protest against the war. In 1868, however, confronted with a dwindling membership and a growing population of strangers in the village, the Hopedale Community abandoned what little authority it had and voted to extinguish itself, establishing in its place the Hopedale Parish, a liberal christian society loosely affiliated with Unitarianism. The community was survived for a few years by its Board of Trustees, but the trustees were maintained only to supervise the disposition of such bits of property as the books of the old library, which were "loaned" to the local Mechanics Library in 1871.[12]

What had once been a miniature Christian commonwealth intended to usher in the future millennium had become a part of history. One by one, its remaining members disappeared. In 1865 Dudley Chapman made one last appearance on the village scene as the manufacturer of "Abraham's Union Burning Gas," which he advertised as a highly advantageous substitute for kerosene, but in the same year his wife died and the wizard of practical chemistry moved back to his native Connecticut. In 1870 Anna Thwing Draper, Ebenezer's wife and a pillar of the old community, died of breast cancer at age fifty-five, and soon after her husband moved to Boston, where he failed in his last business venture. By 1876 only fourteen members of the community remained at Hopedale. Ballou served as pastor of the Hopedale Parish until 1880, when he retired on a pension contributed chiefly by the Draper family. His last significant communal act was in 1886 when he supported—reluctantly some said—a petition by the Draper family to incorporate Hopedale as a town separate from Milford. This separation from outside authority completed the family's control over the village, finalizing the conquest begun thirty years before.

By then radicalism, old or new, had vanished from the town. After the termination of the *Modern Age* in 1866, Butts had struggled on into the 1870s, printing his wife's moralistic tales for the young and advertising that he was (1) holding a small private school where young men and women could learn the printing trade, (2) offering a course in "vocal gymnastics, cure for stammering, lung disease, etc.," and (3) willing to assist both authors and publishers in the preparation of manuscripts for publication. Harriet Greene died at Hopedale in 1881, ending more than three decades of active feminism in the village, and Butts had departed for other places by the mid 1880s.[13]

In the early 1870s Ballou turned his attention to writing the history of the expired community both to enshrine its memory and to preserve its experience for the use of future generations. Although the book occasionally omitted or slanted some facts, it was decent, truthful history without spite toward anyone and with pride in his followers and their achievement. They were not, he wrote, foolish visionaries but "a busy, thrifty self-sufficing class of people" who had transformed a dream into an economic success. From first to last, they had paid their debts, a better record than most American business enterprises, and all who had participated in the community had gained materially as well as morally.[14]

Yet it had failed. Why? Having determined to answer that question, Ballou had to deal with the Drapers. They had, he conceded, precipitated the crisis, but he denied the charges of critics that they were guilty of treachery or even of any notable act of selfishness; he could not "count them sinners above others in the money-making, money-seeking world." At the time he had deplored their action, but in the end he had been moved to accept it by his commitment to the "inherent and indefeasible rights" of all members to determine their own actions and the use of their property; then as always, the right of private judgment and individual responsibility remained the cornerstone of his social faith.[15]

Ballou might have judged the Drapers for the way they exercised their rights, but this he refused to do. Instead, he blended their failings into the more essential failings of people in general. The community, he said, would eventually have broken down anyway, because its members lacked the Christlike mind and heart needed for them to live together "on terms of equality, fraternal co-operation, and mutual good feelings." It was not that they were notably weak—on the contrary they were as well equipped in character as any group—but that not even they had been able to escape the general culture of their times, one that left people in general "too egotistical, angular, opinionated, mercenary, combative, belligerent" for any communal life. They could meet as neighbors and associates; they could not live as brothers and sisters. And there was, in retrospect, no chance that they would have been raised to a higher moral and spiritual plane in the future, because the "prevailing currents of society" at mid century were in "the direction of wealth, of political preferment, of fashionable display, of easy-going morality and religion."[16]

Why was society seemingly conspiring against the better side of man's nature? For his explanation, Ballou returned to his starting point, to his unswerving conviction that the fault lay in a corrupted

Christianity that had left its followers with "no lofty, sublime, inspiring ideal of the reign of righteous brotherhood, love, peace, and
joy *on the earth*." While they preached the joys of Christian heaven,
the churches had accepted a subservience to a world of violence and
war, of inequality and exploitation:

> One may laud Christ to the skies . . . , but must not follow him
> too closely or apply his teachings too rigidly in matters pertaining
> to the acquisition and use of property, method of trade, the wage
> system, the relations between capital and labor, treatment of the
> criminal and perishing classes, caste distinctions, and concerns of
> kindred nature.[17]

If the corrupted world was served by a corrupted church, what then?
By the 1870s the spiritual revolution of forty years before had largely
exhausted itself, and the hope of regenerating Christianity through
such individual action as had produced Hopedale had faded before
the new forces of industrial society. What then?

Ballou could do no more than look to some distant future, when
a divinely ordained progress would finally have prepared humanity
for the golden day. Only then would people be ready to understand
the meaning of Hopedale. It was apparently for this reason that he
did not publish his *History of the Hopedale Community*, leaving it
in manuscript with instructions for its publication after his death.
When the world was prepared for change, then would the book have
its effect: "The great question involved in our Hopedale experiment
is not yet settled; only postponed to a wiser and better time." Ultimately, Hopedale would give confidence and direction to those who
dared to make Christianity the church of Christlike practice. In the
concluding sentences of his book, Ballou reaffirmed his expectation
that the good time would come:

> Then will unrighteousness be done away, unkindness, hatred,
> wrath and war will be unknown, and every unhallowed usage,
> custom, institution be abolished; the reign of justice, love, broth-
> erhood, peace, will be established, men will dwell together as one
> great family in harmony and happiness, and God even in this
> world will "be all in all."[18]

Ballou completed his manuscript in August 1876 and closed the
book on the subject of Practical Christianity. Although he was to

write three books in the future, they dealt with different matters: the history of the town of Milford, the genealogy of the Ballou family, and his general autobiography. Despite his disappointments, these were not unpleasant years. He could take much pride and comfort in living in the midst of a practical success, the one his faith had initiated on the banks of the Mill River, "along whose intervale," he wrote in 1875, "the pleasant village of Hopedale is extending its bright array of machine-shops and homes." By then the village had grown to nearly a hundred homes and over six hundred people, a "beautiful and cheerful" place that grew more prosperous year by year. Ballou took special pride in its industrial vitality, calling it "a seminary of inventors, and may now, without extravagance be called a miniature university of ingenious patent-lore."[19] If most of the physical village belonged to George Draper, its birth belonged to Adin Ballou.

Despite his many writings, Ballou was largely ignored even in his native region. Long before, he had been dismissed by Emerson and his coterie of intellectuals as someone of no importance; while Concord had memorialized Brook Farm and even the ridiculous Fruitlands, it said nothing about Hopedale. In 1889 Ballou received some distant recognition when Leo Tolstoy, the Russian novelist and reformer, proclaimed him "one of the first true apostles of the 'New Time'" and had two of his tracts on nonresistance translated into Russian. Even this was bittersweet, however, since Tolstoy criticized him for compromising nonresistance by allowing for the physical restraint of violent drunkards and madmen; the apostle of Practical Christianity was not pleased to be told that the true Christian should be willing to be killed rather than to limit anyone's freedom.[20]

On the whole, though, Ballou was content to believe that his true recognition would come after his death. By 1889 he was eighty-six, nearing the end of a long lifetime. In 1887 both George and Ebenezer Draper died, each from a kidney disease. Ballou may have taken some secret satisfaction from the death of George Draper, but the loss of his old nemesis and benefactor was one more sign of the passing of his age.[21]

By July 1890 Ballou's hand had grown too weak for him to continue writing his autobiography. The last words in his own hand dealt with the annual four-hundred-dollar pension from the Draper family and with his earnings from his ministrations at weddings and funerals. He cited this success in achieving a competence as evidence of "the good providence of my heavenly father." It fulfilled not only the assurances of Christ but "the promise repeatedly made to me in moments of deep despondency and gloom by the voice of the Spirit speaking to my inner consciousness and saying 'I will never leave nor forsake thee.'" He was prepared to meet his maker.

On 5 August the old man reached back to his past one last time, asking his daughter, Abbie, to read to him some of his favorite passages from the Bible and also his own account of the "profoundly impressive" vision that the spiritualist Thomas Lake Harris had revealed to him in 1856. Within hours of that reading, he had himself passed to the world of the spirits to rejoin his three sons.[22]

There were plenty of eulogies at his funeral, but the one that caught the most attention was from his own pen. Having presided over obsequies for hundreds of others during his long career, it had occurred to him to prepare a sermon about himself to serve as his last testament. Most of the long sermon expressed his lifelong dedication to the practice as well as the preaching of Christ's ideals: "With me, his thoughts were God's thoughts, his will God's will." Again, he took note of the failure at Hopedale, but he expressed the hope that eventually his cherished ideals would be "realized in their highest excellence on earth by devoted disciples." He spoke with even greater confidence than before:

> I have left the world under a very strong impression from Heaven that a regenerate Christlike form of the church will erelong be devoted to prosecute this work, and now leave you a solemn prophecy that the coming century will witness a glorious practical consummation of the cardinal principles in behalf of which God made it my high privilege to bear testimony.[23]

By the year of his death only a handful of the two hundred people who had participated in the Hopedale experiment remained alive; Lucy Ballou, his helpmate for half a century, died less than two years later, leaving only two of the original members of the community, William Henry Fish and William W. Cook, still living. Ballou might have found some comfort in the efforts of a new generation to carry on the cause. The years after 1890 saw the emergence of small but promising movements for both Christian socialism and peace. His son-in-law carried the cause of peace into the twentieth century. While serving as a minister in Dorchester, Heywood spoke out against the growing militarism of his times and, in 1910, republished Ballou's book *Christian Non-Resistance* in support of a revitalized Universal Peace Union.[24]

This new age of hope, however, gave way after 1914 to an age of war. When Ballou's daughter, Abbie Heywood, died in June 1918, a minister at Hopedale observed that she had "lived to see what her father could not, with all his prophetic power have dreamed—a planet writhing in the agonies of a warfare such as no great Milton could have described."[25] In these new times the nineteenth-century hopes for moral progress died, perhaps never to be reborn. After night, there came a very different day.

12

A Different Day

While Ballou's Hopedale dwindled away, George Draper's Hopedale grew in wealth and numbers. In 1868 Ebenezer Draper sold his interests in the village to his brother and moved to Boston and eventual bankruptcy. In contrast, George stayed at home in the familiar territory of the Blackstone textile region and prospered. After liquidating the unprofitable businesses of the old community, he concentrated on manufacturing tools and small machinery. Soon after the breakup of the community in 1856, he and his partners in the Hopedale Machine Company advertised that "they have in their shop at Hopedale a supply of first-rate Machinists' tools" which they were using to build machines for use in Milford's extensive boot and shoe industry as well as to make loom temples and such other textile appliances as "Perry's Patent Parallel Shuttle Motions for Looms," one of many patented innovations that Draper was to bring under his control. By the mid 1870s he had commanding interests in three local firms: the Hopedale Machine Company, the Dutcher Temple Company, and George Draper & Sons. The Draper firms employed over three hundred men and produced half a million dollars in machines, machine parts, and tools for sale in Europe as well as in the United States and Latin America.[1]

Draper was an aggressive promoter and accumulator of technological innovations. Beginning in 1867, he acquired control over various inventions relating to a new high-speed spindle. Since the new spindle drastically reduced the costs of cotton spinning, it revolutionized the industry, creating a great market for Draper's expanding organization; in the 1880s alone, textile firms bought more than six million of the new spindles, most produced either at Hopedale or, under contract to Draper, by a firm in nearby Whitinsville. By the early 1880s the small community machine shop where Draper had begun business had given way to a sprawling three-story brick factory building that loomed large over the village.[2]

In 1886, when Hopedale was incorporated as a town, Draper's dominance was such as to lead one critic to say that if it were not for an accident of history the place would have been called "Draperville." By then Draper and his three sons had controlling interests in the now incorporated Hopedale Machine and the Dutcher Temple companies, two manufacturing firms begun in the mid 1850s as small partnerships, and exclusive possession of George Draper & Sons, which acted as general business agent for the producing companies. These three firms had nearly $200,000 in property at Hopedale, while in addition the Drapers privately owned some $150,000 in personal property and real estate; the total was more than half the total assessed value of all the property in town, and the proportion was destined to grow larger over the next decades.

Among the few others with notable wealth was a longtime resident of Hopedale and ally of the Drapers, Joseph B. Bancroft. Originally a machinist listed in the 1850 census schedules as having $1,500 in property, Bancroft in 1886 had over $15,000 in taxable holdings, not particularly impressive until it is recognized that this figure did not include his 285 shares in the machine company and his fourteen valuable patents on textile machinery. In contrast, in the same year Ballou, the founder, had total property valued at $3,000, no more than he reported in 1860.[3]

Hopedale's evolution into a company town was slow and subtle, allowing for the survival of what Ballou called in 1881 "some of its original moral and social character." Ballou himself continued to live in his modest white frame house with its attached printing office on a half-acre lot at the corner of Peace and Hopedale streets. There, passersby could see him working in his ample garden or at his desk in the south window of the house. Along with its conspicuous orderliness and the absence of poverty and drunkenness, Hopedale retained much of its old interest in moral and mental culture. Soon after it became a town, its school committee established the "Hopedale High School," setting space aside in its school building to educate some 30 students at that level, a major achievement for a small town of 926 inhabitants. It also taxed itself for the support of a public library, noting that the old community had established one of the first such libraries in America, an action that had contributed to "the constant use of books and periodicals in our town at the present." There were at least three reading clubs involving some thirty families who pooled their resources to subscribe to a variety of newspapers and magazines, continuing habits from the communal past.[4]

On the other hand, signs of the new times were also there to see. In place of the diversity of enterprises, individual and communal, that had enlived the community in its glory days, there was outside of the Draper firms and a few farms only one independent business, a grocery and dry goods store conducted by Henry L. Patrick, the son of a community member, Delano Patrick. And in contrast to the voting and officeholding of women in the Hopedale Community, both political life in the town and management in the company were the exclusive preserves of men.

Moreover, evident class differences had appeared. At the one extreme, there was a growing number of propertyless workingmen: In 1886, of the some 356 taxpayers in town, slightly more than half paid only a poll tax, having no taxable property; most of these lived in houses rented to them by the Drapers. At the other extreme, wealth was becoming more conspicuous. Although George Draper and his partners had built large houses, they chose to reside close by their shops and their old neighbors; in 1886 Draper's house was valued at four thousand dollars, while Ballou's was assessed at one thousand dollars. Draper's sons, though, had by this time begun to build mansions in a new and fashionable section of town set apart from rest. William F. Draper, the general, had initiated this trend in 1872 when he erected a lavish three-story mansion with a dominating tower, a conspicuous monument to wealth in a place once dedicated to equality and brotherhood.[5]

The Drapers' wealth stemmed primarily from their entrepreneurship and business creativity rather than from anything like exploitation of their workers. Indeed, as Hopedale became a company town, it also became for a second time a model social experiment, in welfare capitalism rather than Christian socialism. From the beginning, the profitability of the Draper firms had allowed them to pay reasonable wages and to provide decent housing at low rents to their workers. The family, which shared at least some of Hopedale's emphasis on mental and moral culture, took an interest in creating conditions that would enable workers and their children to improve themselves, supporting the town's school and library and in 1887 cutting the workweek in their shops to fifty-five hours, more than a decade before Massachusetts made that number a statewide requirement; ten hours a day with a half day on Saturday was then thought to allow adequate time for self-improvement and recreation. Again, Hopedale had found a way to avoid the social evils commonly associated with industrial society.[6]

The Drapers, as hardheaded businessmen, explained that they were motivated not by philanthropy but by pragmatism, primarily by the aim of assuring their firms a dependable supply of skilled, reliable workers. Their policies also reflected some of the advanced social thinking of their times. Whereas the early years of Hopedale had focused on profound moral concerns, the post–Civil War years brought special concern over the relationship between capital and labor, a concern highlighted by often violent strikes and other disruptions of the industrial order. Although the industrial towns of the Blackstone region remained generally quiet, they were not entirely remote from the problem. In 1886, for instance, Thomas Edwin Brown, a Baptist minister at nearby Providence, called attention to what he called the primary social facts of the day, "a world never before so rich, yet in every land a vast army of the discontented," an army potentially threatening to the whole society. To fend off social catastrophe, Brown urged businessmen to accept their responsibility both to God and to humanity for the righteous use of their wealth to benefit workers and others.[7]

The masters of Hopedale had their own local sources of social consciousness. Adin Ballou, who long before the Civil War had considered the problem, continued to urge the rich to be responsible stewards of their wealth on the principle, as he put it in 1870, "that all property, being supplied to mankind originally by divine Providence, should be subject to divine law—the supreme moral law of justice, charity, and brotherhood." On his death, he left a sizable sum of money to be used to disseminate his views on such matters as the application of Christianity to the relations between capital and labor; out of it came the Adin Ballou Lectureship in Practical Christian Sociology at the Meadville [Unitarian] Theological Seminary.[8]

George Draper rejected Christian socialism, but even he could not entirely escape the influence of Practical Christianity. Moreover, his principal partner and heir, his eldest son, William, had spent his formative years in Ballou's Hopedale, as a teenager getting his formal education in Abbie Ballou's school and then in the Home School and attending the Sunday religious meetings and the Tuesday evening lyceums. For a time, William F. Draper worked in the machine shop managed by his uncle Ebenezer before he completed his industrial education in the mills of nearby Uxbridge. Although he had broken with the community over the Civil War, the general retained an interest in its successor, the Hopedale Parish, serving at various times as its treasurer, trustee, and Sunday-school superintendent.[9]

The most creative and forceful influence behind the Hopedale solution to the labor question, however, was probably none of the Drapers but one of their partners, Joseph Bancroft, eventually vice president and then president of the Draper firm. Although he did not settle in the village until 1847, Bancroft had deep roots in the old community. He was part of the Uxbridge group so vital to Hopedale's early success, being married to one of three Thwing sisters, the other two being the wives of George and Ebenezer Draper. In 1851 the Bancrofts lost a set of new-born triplets, a devastating loss even though they eventually had seven other children. Bancroft worked with Ebenezer in the little machine shop at Hopedale and later became the superintendent of industrial operations for the Hopedale Machine Company, working directly with its small labor force, which included his brother William, also a skilled machinist.[10]

In 1856, for reasons unknown, he broke with his in-laws and future partners by casting the lone vote against the dissolution of the community, an act that may have won Ballou's special trust. Later he and his oldest son, Eben (head accountant for the Draper firm), both served as officers in the Hopedale Parish. Bancroft's daughter Lilla recalled that after the Civil War Ballou would often visit the Bancroft house "to see what 'Brother Bancroft' thought of this or that scheme for the improvement of village life." Whether because of Ballou's direct influence or not, Bancroft was remembered as having a strong interest in providing good living conditions for workers, on the principle, as his daughter recalled, that "give a man a comfortable house, with his own front door, flowers in the yard, a good meal on the table, and he will not wander far afield." Eventually, he provided the money to build one of Hopedale's most distinguished buildings, the Bancroft Memorial Library.[11]

After George Draper's death in 1887, his model company town entered into a new and higher phase, thanks in no small part to the business skills and ingenuity of his sons, particularly William, who had from the late 1860s been a major force in the company's progress. In 1892 the firm succeeded, after years of costly effort, in perfecting the automatic Northrup loom, which reduced manpower requirements in the weaving process by half while improving the quality of the cloth. Over the next decades the great majority of textile mills replaced their looms with the new automatics, making Hopedale the nation's leading producer of textile machinery. In 1901 William Draper estimated that his firm was making some two thousand looms a month, and he expected to make many more, since most textile mills would have to buy the new looms to remain competitive. Under the spur of expanding production, the town's population grew from 1,176 in 1890 to 2,188 in 1910, most of the increase consisting of skilled workingmen and their families.[12]

By then the Draper family had acquired a fortune in the millions and the influence that went with it. General William F. Draper had served as a United States congressmen and as ambassador to Italy in the 1890s, and in the next decade his younger brother Eben became the head of the state Republican party and governor of Massachusetts; most of the day-to-day management of the firm was left to Joseph Bancroft. At the same time, the Draper firm expanded its welfare programs. Although it took full advantage of the intense competition among textile mills, it was itself largely protected from competition both by discriminatory tariff duties against foreign machine builders and by its control over a network of patents giving it exclusive production rights. With its assured profits, it could commit itself to a long-range plan of benefits, often with the cooperation of the Hopedale town government.

The firm provided recreational facilities, health benefits, and general job security, the last by a policy of reducing working hours for all during the few times of slowdown. Having from the beginning furnished good cheap housing for workers, it intensified its housing programs, employing various architects to provide differing designs of its standard house, the double house or duplex, which was preferred to apartments because, while it didn't take up as much room as a single house, it fulfilled Bancroft's dream of giving workers comfortable homes with their own front doors and access to their own yards. In the 1890s the firm began the development of Bancroft Place, a small suburb with curving streets and larger and better appointed houses, establishing a trend that stressed improved site planning as well as home design. Throughout the town, the company provided a building maintenance program that kept its houses in good condition. By 1910 all its houses had water, gas, electricity, and indoor plumbing; and Hopedale had won international recognition for its model housing for workers: an English housing expert, after investigating various company towns, declared it to be "America's best."[13]

Housing was only part of a broader ambition of the Draper firm to create a good physical and aesthetic environment for its employees. Over the years both family and company had purchased surrounding lands, increasing the original domain acquired from the old community from 600 to over 3,500 acres and giving them a strong basis for environmental control. In the 1870s the company had begun to develop an infrastructure to support an expanding town population, laying gas and water lines and improving its streets. To protect public health, it provided an efficient system of garbage collection and trash removal and, as a matter of special pride, it constructed a sewerage system that by the late 1890s was connected to every house in town. Taking advantage of its power, the company prohibited fences between properties, thereby avoiding unsightly dividers and creating a unified parklike appearance along the streets.[14]

These accomplishments owed much to the support of the town of Hopedale and at least something to the distant influence of the Hopedale Community. During its glory days the community had developed a tradition of tree planting and gardening that survived in the new company town. In 1886 the new town included among its ordinances a prohibition that "no person shall tie or fasten any horse to any shade or ornamental tree in any street in town, or wrongfully injure or abuse such trees in any other matter." In the same year the company helped initiate a village improvement society, and eight years later it began to give prizes to encourage tree and shrub planting, flower growing, and similar improvements in the town's appearance. These policies may have been devised by Joseph Bancroft, who in 1853 had been an officer of the Hopedale Industrial Army when it accomplished such communal improvements as the replanting of forest trees along the streets of the village.[15]

Before the turn of the century the Draper firm also committed itself to an ambitious park-development program around its principal millpond. Over the years it had tried to squeeze the maximum benefit out of the waterpower privilege it had acquired from the community by deepening and expanding the pond, creating a small lake that invited efforts to improve its shoreline. The company took an interest in the matter in part because it wanted to prevent any development along the lake that might threaten its waterpower, but it also heeded the desire of the townspeople for some place, besides the community cemetery, to enjoy tranquility and solitude. In the late 1890s it employed Warren Henry Manning, a landscape architect who had worked for Frederick Law Olmsted in the development of Boston's regional park system, to prepare a plan for the area around the millpond. Manning's plan won the support of the town government, which appointed a park commission to implement it.[16]

Over the next decade, Hopedale spent $2,500 a year to develop a park of a thousand acres (nearly one-third of the town's acreage) around the lake, employing a trained forester to create a diversified woodland setting. The pine groves inherited from the community were groomed, with the largest becoming a picnic ground, and extensive areas were planted or replanted with a variety of trees and shrubs. Particular care was taken to plant picturesque trees along the edge of the lake, with the result that there was "never a place where the white birch and its slim reflection fail to add delight to the men canoeing by." In the forest, more than four miles of winding trails were opened and steps were taken to entice birds, rabbits, and squirrels to inhabit the woods, where they were protected from hunters. By 1914 an observer could tell the world that Hopedale had obtained "a park whose path plunges from her very threshold into cool deep woods, whose lake surface is fit for fishing, boating, swimming, and skating in winter, whose brooks are crossed with artistic bridges, whose gorgeous and varied forest looks as though it originated there."[17]

While most of the lake area was developed as a wilderness refuge, other portions were incorporated into town life. On one part of the shoreline a short distance from the factory, sand was dumped to make a beach with a bathhouse, and nearby a "play ground" was completed with ball fields and tennis courts; the area became the site for an annual field day featuring games and athletic events. On the opposite side of the pond, early in the twentieth century, the company developed a small peninsula for residential use, employing another landscape architect, Arthur A. Shurcliff, to prepare the design. This Lake Point development had ten two-family houses, most of which were placed facing the water, both to give their inhabitants a lake view and to prevent the unsightly accumulation of backyard trash near the shore; a service road was built behind the houses and a public loop road was opened along the shoreline in front. With its careful design and placement of houses and its respect for topography, Lake Point was a minimodel of suburban planning.[18]

In its development Hopedale at least partly realized some important nineteenth-century dreams of the good society. In its general character it came close to achieving the goal that Adin Ballou had set in 1857 for his Practical Christian Republic, where every orderly citizen would be assured employment, education, protection, and a comfortable domestic life: "Good homes in good neighborhoods for all who try to be worthy of them." With its tree-lined streets and expanding system of parks, it seemed also to have achieved the popular dream of "a factory in a garden" by placing its dominating manufacturing plant in a softening and protective natural setting, depriving industrialism of its unnatural and destructive influences. Above all, it seemed to have resolved the most formidable problem of its day, harmonizing the interests of labor and capital by way of a profitable paternalism. Early in the new century Hopedale acquired a wide reputation as the industrial "garden spot" of Massachusetts, a shining example of welfare capitalism that was providing good jobs and a good environment for nearly three thousand workers.[19]

In creating their paradise the Drapers, perhaps partly by design, expunged many of the physical traces of the old community, including its meetinghouse, which was replaced by a Gothic church dedicated to the memory of George Draper and his wife; carefully preserved from earlier days, though, was the little machine shop built by the community in the 1840s where the Draper business had gotten its start. At the turn of the century, with Draper support, the town did celebrate the memory of its founder. General William Draper contributed the money for a statue of Ballou as he was "in mid-life, with a light mustache and beard, all his powers in full vigor," and the statue was dedicated with much ceremony, the Draper shops being closed for the event. Even this, however, had its negative side, since at the general's suggestion the statue was placed in a memorial park prepared from Ballou's own yard, forcing the removal of his house to another site.[20]

When the past was not expunged, it was rewritten to suit the new order. Beginning in the 1880s a number of admirers of the Draper success eagerly presented the old community in a contrasting light. In 1887, for instance, ex-Governor Long said that the village had been saved from total bankruptcy only by hardheaded American business: "Enlightened and liberal selfishness became, as it usually does, a beneficence to which a weak communism was as the dull and cheerless gleam of a decaying punk to the inspiring blaze of the morning sun." At the time an indignant Ballou was able to object to this characterization and to say that without the devoted labors of the community likely there would have been no town, but his words had little effect on people who wanted to believe otherwise. Later a writer declared that Hopedale had once been a "futile communistic experiment" that had failed to produce enough for its own needs and was rapidly running into unmanageable debts when it was taken over: "The only wonder is that there were men available who were willing and able to shoulder the burden."[21]

Not satisfied with demonstrating the inadequacies of the cooperative economy, some observers also scorned the attitudes of the founders. In 1891 one attacked the community for "the absence of that instinct to love dumb beasts" (referring to the prohibition on dogs) and for the "dry, barren, prosaic and somewhat repellent character" of its general mentality. Lacking the "poet's frenzy," the members "never dreamed of putting together the perfect parts of a thing to make a beautiful whole for the admiration of posterity." Perhaps the unkindest cut of all was dealt in 1898 when a writer declared, regarding Ballou, that it was too bad that "our Practical Christian Apostle" had little understanding of "scientific sociology," since it would have saved him from "a fatuous experiment" that wasted his life in "the pursuit of a chimera." Of the several authors who took note of Hopedale, only one, James Church Alvord, stopped to consider that the collective tradition established by the old community might have played a role in the town's later success.[22]

The town was by no means indifferent to its past. In 1910, for instance, it published *Hopedale Reminiscences*, a collection of papers given in that year before the Hopedale Ladies Sewing Society, itself a reminder of the past. Nearly all of the papers were written by people who remembered the village from the 1850s. Although one of the ten authors had moved to California, four still resided in Hopedale, while the rest lived elsewhere in Massachusetts. Some took note of the vision that had inspired the community: Ellen Patrick, the daughter of Delano Patrick and Hopedale's teacher of ex-slaves in the South at the end of the Civil War, said that the old dream remained alive: "The new demand for social justice, with the Socialist vision of the future, is the same Community dream given a worldwide sweep." And Abbie Ballou Heywood concluded the collection by saying that the community was "one of the grandest experiments attempted for the good of mankind."[23] On the whole, however, the contributors remembered only the bits and pieces of life they had known as children, especially the oddities of what they had come to see as a distant past to which there could be no return.

Eventually, the Draper Company and its town were themselves caught by changing times. Before World War I the firm continued to prosper from its sales of Northrup looms. Between 1899 and 1914 it sold more than 285,000 looms, either to reequip established mills in New England or to equip new mills in the South, more than 100,000 in the years 1909 through 1913 alone. Although some of the profits from these sales continued to finance town improvements, the firm's expansion and the expanding interests of the Draper family resulted in the weakening of local ties, a development that had important implications for the future.[24]

In a 1909 article in *New England Magazine* G. Sherman Johnson presented Hopedale as evidence that the growth of great corporations was good for America, but he drew the line between corporations like the Draper firm that were rooted in towns where they operated and "alien" corporations that had little interest in the welfare of places they controlled. By this time, though, the situation had already begun to change at Hopedale. General Draper must have found considerable satisfaction in watching the development of the village from the tower of his mansion at the corner of Adin and Hopedale streets, but in the 1890s he acquired significant outside interests far beyond the Blackstone region, first as a member of Congress and then as ambassador to Italy. Eventually, his separation was made complete when in 1906 he was ousted by his brothers as head of the company, supposedly because in their view he was spending too much money on research and development. This coup led him to sell most of his stock in the company and retire to Washington, D.C. When he died there in 1910 at age sixty-eight, no reference was made to Hopedale in his death notice.[25]

Joseph B. Bancroft was persuaded to take his place as president, but Bancroft died in 1909. Essentially, the new head of Draper operations was the general's much younger brother Eben. Eben S. Draper had been born at Hopedale in 1857, but he was born too late to have had much exposure to the old community or its world. Whereas William had gotten his education locally, Eben completed his at MIT. Even more remote than his brother from the reformism of the pre–Civil War years, he was conservative in his social and political views, especially on labor questions. By the time he took control of the company, he had become a prominent Republican political figure in Massachusetts, first as the state's lieutenant governor between 1906 and 1908 and then as its governor from 1909 to 1911, when he was defeated for reelection, in part by the opposition of organized labor. Eben Draper brought no drastic changes in policy at Hopedale, but his outlook and outside involvements undoubtedly contributed to the rise of dissatisfaction among Draper Company workers.[26]

Although there was much to be pleased with at Hopedale, there was also reason for uneasiness and resentment. Because the managerial positions were monopolized by the Drapers and their allies, the great majority of employees had no opportunity for advancement in the firm, and there was little chance for them to acquire a personal stake in the town, since most of the land and houses were owned by the company and there was virtually no business beyond the company's own. Although numerous workers had been with the firm for twenty years or more, the rapid expansion of the work force added many others with little attachment to either the company or the town. Moreover, as the general pointed out in 1901, the increase to over three thousand workers meant that he employed "more hands than there are inhabitants in town," many living in neighboring towns like Milford from which they either walked to work or commuted by trolley line.

In 1901 Draper could boast that the company had never had any "labor difficulty" involving more than twenty men and that although he thought the company's foundry workers were organized, the great majority had not been unionized. Eventually, however, enough dissatisfaction developed to lead to a long strike initiated against the Drapers in early 1913 by the Industrial Workers of the World (the IWW): the serpent had appeared in the industrial Eden.

Under Eben Draper, the company refused to yield, and the strike became an open conflict that attracted national notice. In April 1913 the *New York Times* reported that at Milford strike sympathizers stoned trolley cars carrying nonstrikers to the Draper shops; when a rioter was arrested and jailed, an angry crowd gathered at the jail. The next month came reports that in Hopedale itself IWW strike leaders were arrested—for loitering—and another angry crowd gathered at the Town Hall until the arrested men were released on bail. Three weeks later, the *Times* described a fight that had taken place between strike sympathizers and the police along the trolley line to Hopedale. After four months, the strike was broken and affairs returned to normal. Over the next years the company raised wages and cut its workweek from fifty-five to forty-eight hours, chiefly in response to the conditions that developed during World War I.[27]

The strike shattered Hopedale's well-worn halo, however, and the following years did little to repair the damage. Eventually, the few remaining threads connecting the town with its past eroded way. In 1914 Eben Draper died unexpectedly at age fifty-six in South Carolina returning from a trip to Cuba. He left an estate valued at nearly $7,000,000; out of some $234,000 in public bequests, $20,000 went to the Hopedale Unitarian Parish and $4,000 to the town cemetery. The last of the three brothers, George A. Draper (two years older than Eben), died in early 1923, leaving an estate of over $10,000,000, of which $79,000 was bequeathed to the town.[28]

A new generation of Drapers took control. The most prominent was Eben S. Draper, Jr., who achieved some notoriety in 1926 when a French court awarded his wife a divorce on the grounds of desertion; less than five months later he was remarried in New Jersey to a Seattle woman. Like his father, Draper became an influential Republican politician, trying unsuccessfully both in 1928 and 1930 to win his party's nomination to the United States Senate; in each try, he ran as a "wet" opposed to national prohibition.[29] It was a long way from the days of Ballou's Practical Christian Republic.

By now the economic fortunes of both the company and the town hinged far less on such matters than on changes in the nation's textile industry. Before World War I the company had prospered in part because, having reequipped the New England mills, it was able to sell many of its automatic looms to the rapidly expanding textile industry of the South. After the war, though, competition from the southern mills using cheap labor devastated the industry in New England, many of the casualties being the small mills of the Blackstone region that had contributed substantially to Hopedale's rise.[30] The dominance of the Draper firm in the textile machinery field enabled it to survive first these travails and then the Great Depression of the 1930s, but its golden days were in the past.

Various defense contracts during and after World War II helped to revitalize the company temporarily, and by 1960 it was employing more than 4,000 workers at what had become a massive plant in Hopedale. By then the population of the town had reached 2,904 people, whose median family income was some 10 percent higher than in either Milford or Boston; but sadder times lay ahead, largely because of the decline of the American textile industry. In the 1960s the company divested itself of most of its town properties and was acquired by an outside owner, virtually severing its special links to the town. During the 1970s the Hopedale plant continued to produce automatic looms, principally for export to Asia, but it failed to make adequate profits, and in 1980 it was shut down by the parent company. The following year a *New York Times* reporter called Hopedale the "Cadillac of company-owned towns," but he published a photograph of the abandoned plant that indicated all too plainly that this particular Cadillac was a thing of the past.[31]

And so ended a tie between business and the town that extended back nearly 140 years. Now, to the south of the small shop building where it had begun sleeps the great empty factory edifice. Further to the south, backed by the trees of the still-pretty town, stands the upright statue of Adin Ballou—portrayed as he had been in vigorous and hopeful mid-life—gazing out over the Mill River toward the far western horizon, toward some distant future, perhaps, when finally the reign of justice, brotherhood, and peace will be established over all the earth.

Notes

Chapter 1

1. Lewis G. Wilson, ed., "The Christian Doctrine of Non-Resistance. By Count Leo Tolstoi and Rev. Adin Ballou," 4.

2. Adin Ballou, *Autobiography, 1803–1890*, vii. Ballou's autobiography, based on an extensive and now apparently lost diary, is notable both for its objectivity and for the absence of any profound introspection.

3. Ibid., 1–13.

4. Ibid., 12–14; Peter J. Coleman, *The Transformation of Rhode Island, 1790–1860*, 21, 77, 87, 93; Sheila Steinberg and Cathleen McGuigan, *Rhode Island: An Historical Guide*, 62–68; obituary clipping for Eliza Ballou Garfield, in Adin Ballou, "Funeral Register, 1823–1889," 38.

5. Gary Kulik, Roger Parks, and Thomas Z. Penn, eds., *The New England Mill Village, 1790–1860*, 519; Ballou, *Autobiography*, 24–25.

6. Ballou, *Autobiography*, 40–45, 54–55. Ballou was, despite his busy life, a wide reader on various subjects. See *Catalogue of the Private Library of the Late Adin Ballou*.

7. Ballou, *Autobiography*, 29–37.

8. Ibid., 45–46.

9. Ibid., 55–69.

10. Ibid., 80–83; *Practical Christian*, 17 Feb. 1844; Russell E. Miller, *The Larger Hope*, 104–10; Ernest Cassara, *Hosea Ballou*, 22–31, 148–49.

11. Ballou, *Autobiography*, 85–100, and *The Furious Priest Reproved*, 3–5, 11–12.

12. Ballou, *Autobiography*, 103–10; *Universalist Quarterly* 11 (1838–39): 80.

13. John Coleman Adams, "The Universalists," 307–8; Horace Greeley, *Recollections of a Busy Life*, 71–72.

14. Ballou, *Autobiography*, and *The Inestimable Value of Souls*, 6–11, 15.

15. Ballou, *Autobiography*, 171–78.

16. Ibid., 154, 164.

17. Ibid., 159.

18. Ibid., 173–78; Ballou, *Inestimable Value*, 14–15, 21.

19. Ballou, *Autobiography*, 181–86; *Independent Messenger*, 1 Jan. 1831.

20. Ballou, *Autobiography*, 186–87, 197–98, 213.

21. Ibid., 193–95, 305–6.

22. Ibid., 231–35.

23. *Independent Messenger*, 8 Apr. 1831; Ballou, *Autobiography*, 276–77, 292–95; Ian R. Tyrrell, *Sobering Up*, 77–79.

24. Adin Ballou, *An Oration Delivered Before the Citizens of Blackstone*, 10–15, and *Autobiography*, 277–82; Richard Rollins, "Adin Ballou and the Perfectionist Dilemma," 468–69.

25. Adin Ballou, *Christian Non-Resistance*, 1–25, 102–8.

26. Ballou, *Autobiography*, 306–7, 316; Lewis Perry, *Radical Abolitionism*, 131–33. Ballou's speech was published by the *Non-Resistant*, 16 Nov. 1839. Edmund Quincy called it "the best explanation of the true principles and most effecting reply to the most common objections that we have seen" and noted that it was being printed in pamphlet form. Ibid., 7 Dec. 1839.

27. Ballou, *Christian Non-Resistance*, 5, 101–2; *Practical Christian*, 13 June 1846.

28. *Practical Christian*, 15 Dec. 1840, 11 May 1844, and esp. "The Superiority of Moral Power Over Political Power," 15 Mar. 1845.

29. Ballou, *Oration Before the Citizens of Blackstone*, 9, and *Christian Non-Resistance*, 209, 211; *Practical Christian*, 1 Dec. 1840, 30 Sept. 1843; William O. Reichert, "The Philosophical Anarchism of Adin Ballou," 357–74; Rollins, "Adin Ballou," 472–73.

30. Ballou, *Christian Non-Resistance*, 211, 223, 228; *Practical Christian*, 9 July 1842, 30 Sept. 1843, 23 Apr. 1853.

31. Ballou, *Autobiography*, 292–93.

32. Ibid., 296. A study of temperance in the town of Worcester indicates that its advocates were disproportionately drawn from the more ambitious and talented in the manufacturing, artisan, and farming population. Tyrrell, *Sobering Up*, 96–104.

33. Adin Ballou, *History of the Town of Milford*, 671–72, 720–21, 989, 1070, and *An Address . . . at the Funeral of Mrs. Anna T. Draper*.

34. Ballou, *Milford*, 1026; *Practical Christian*, 1, 15 Oct. 1840, 11 May 1844.

35. *Practical Christian*, 1 Jan., 1 Mar. 1841; Ballou, *Autobiography*, 203–4, 255, 314.

36. Ballou, *Milford*, 746–47; *Practical Christian*, 1 July, 15 Oct., 1 Nov. 1840; 1 Feb. 1841; 26 Oct. 1844.

37. Ballou, *Autobiography*, 223; *Practical Christian*, 1 Apr. 1840, 20 Aug. 1842. The Standard of Practical Christianity has been published in various places, including Adin Ballou, *History of the Hopedale Community* (hereafter *Hopedale*), 3–8.

38. Ballou, *Hopedale*, 28, and *Autobiography*, 327–28.

39. *Practical Christian*, 1 Apr. 1840; 1 Oct. 1842; 3 Feb., 18 May 1844.

40. William Goodell, *Come-Outerism*, 1–6, 14–31; *Practical Christian*, 1. Aug., 1 Sept. 1840.

41. *Practical Christian*, 15 Sept. 1840, 1 Jan. 1841; Ballou, *Autobiography*, 321.

42. *Non-Resistant*, 16 Nov. 1837; Ballou, *Autobiography*, 321–23.

43. *Practical Christian*, 15 Sept. 1840.

44. Ballou, *Autobiography*, 321.

Chapter 2

1. *Practical Christian*, 7 Feb. 1846; Horace Greeley, "The Idea of Social Reform," 146–47.

2. Ralph Waldo Emerson, *Journals and Miscellaneous Notebooks* 7:114; Henry Wadsworth Longfellow, *Letters* 2:257; William Henry Fish, *Memoir of Butler Wilmarth, M. D.*, 89. Later, in the fall of 1842, Ballou rejected an invitation by George Ripley for the Practical Christians to join Brook Farm, because it was not founded on the Standard. Ballou, *Autobiography*, 326–27; John T. Codman, *Brook Farm*, 143.

3. Elizabeth P. Peabody, "A Glimpse of Christ's Idea of Society," 226–27; Emerson, *Journals* 7:255, 281, 348.

4. *Practical Christian*, 15 Sept. 1840, 16 Oct. 1841, 3 Feb. 1844, 12 May 1849.

5. Ibid., 1 Oct. 1842, 3 Feb. 1844. Also two articles by William Henry Fish, ibid., 28 June 1845, 24 June 1846.

6. Ballou, *Autobiography*, 321–22, 340; *Practical Christian*, 15 Sept. 1840; 30 Oct., 13 Nov. 1841.

7. Ballou, *Autobiography*, 321; *Practical Christian*, 15 Feb., 1 Mar. 1841; *Liberator* 11 (1841): 38.

8. Emerson, *Journals* 7:513–14.

9. Ballou, *Hopedale*, 11.

10. Probably the best study of Owen's New Harmony experiment remains Arthur Bestor, *Backwoods Utopias*, esp. 160–201. The literature on Shakerism is voluminous, but nothing replaces Edward D. Andrews, *The People Called Shakers*.

11. Fish, *Butler Wilmarth*, 88.

12. *Practical Christian*, 15 Sept. 1840; 15 Feb., 30 Oct. 1841.

13. Ibid., 15 Feb., 30 Oct., 13 Nov. 1841; 27 May 1843.

14. Ibid., 15 Feb., 30 Oct. 1841; 10 June 1843.

15. Ibid., 27 Nov. 1841, 27 May 1843.

16. Ballou, *Autobiography*, 327, 342; *Practical Christian*, 18 Sept. 1841; Hopedale Community, "Records of the Proceedings of Fraternal Community No. 1. Book 1. Commencing January 28, 1841" (henceforth "Records"), 1, 19–20.

17. *Practical Christian*, 15 Sept. 1840; 15 Feb., 18 Sept. 1841; Ballou, *Autobiography*, 329–30.

18. Adin Ballou, "Valedictory Address," *Practical Christian*, 25 June 1842, and "The Pilgrims of Hopedale," ibid., 11 May 1844.

19. *Practical Christian*, 30 Oct. 1841.

20. Ibid., 11 June 1842, 4 Feb. 1843; Ballou, *Autobiography*, 341ff.

21. John Humphrey Noyes, *History of American Socialisms*, 130. The term *official servant* applied to all elected officers but not to appointed managers.

22. Ballou, *Hopedale*, 70–71; *Practical Christian*, 13 Nov. 1841, 22 June 1850.

23. Ballou, *Autobiography*, 567–72, and *Address at the Funeral of Mrs. Draper*, 8–9.

24. *Practical Christian*, 11 June 1842; Hopedale, "Records," 32.

25. *Practical Christian*, 23 Apr., 7 May 1853 (Borden death notices); Ballou, *Hopedale*, 77–78; Hopedale, "Records," 32.

26. *Practical Christian*, 21 Aug. 1841; Ballou, *Hopedale*, 90–93.

27. Ballou, *Hopedale*, 79, 93–95, and *Autobiography*, 345.

28. Ballou, *Hopedale*, 93–96; *Practical Christian*, 27 May 1843, 22 June 1844.

29. Ballou, *Autobiography*, 346–47, and *Hopedale*, 87–105; *Practical Christian*, 29 Oct. 1842, 27 May 1843, 27 Dec. 1845.

30. *Practical Christian*, 4 Feb., 27 May, 10 June 1843; Ballou, *Autobiography*, 342.

31. Hopedale, "Records," 39; *Practical Christian*, 24 June 1843, 10 June 1848; Ballou, *Hopedale*, 101–2.

32. Hopedale, "Records," 35; *Practical Christian*, 24 Feb. 1855.

33. Ballou, *Hopedale*, 78, 109, 205, 339; *Practical Christian*, 4 Feb. 1843.

34. Hopedale, "Records," 12–14; *Practical Christian*, 11 June 1842, 10 Jan. 1845; Ballou, *Hopedale*, 81–84.

35. *Practical Christian*, 30 Sept. 1843; Ballou, *Hopedale*, 109–10.

36. Hopedale Community, "Proceedings of the Trustees and Executive Council of Fraternal Community No. 1. Book 1. Commenced Jan. 29, 1841" (henceforth "Proceedings"), 14–16, 19–20, 32.

37. *Practical Christian*, 1 Feb. 1845; *Liberator* 14 (1844): 174.

38. *Practical Christian*, 30 Oct. 1841; 29 Oct. 1842; 4 Feb., 27 May, and 10 June 1843.

39. Ibid., 30 Oct. 1841, 4 Feb. 1843; Ballou, *Hopedale*, 113–14.

40. Ballou, *Hopedale*, 127, 133–34.

Chapter 3

1. *Practical Christian*, 1 Apr., 15 Sept. 1841; 27 May 1843.

2. Ibid., 7, 21 Feb. 1846.

3. Ibid., 12 May 1849.

4. Ibid., 15 June 1843 and 29 Nov. 1845; Ballou, *Hopedale*, 116–17 and

145–46. For Ballou's most complete appraisal of Owenism, see his *Practical Christian Socialism*, 497–519. For Fourierist and other secular communities during this period, see Edward K. Spann, *Brotherly Tomorrows: Movements for a Cooperative Society in America, 1820–1920*, chaps. 4–7. Richard Henry Dana, Jr., gives a brief account of the property meeting in his *Journal* 1:162.

5. Ballou, *Practical Christian Socialism*, 474–98; *Practical Christian*, 8 Dec. 1849; *Liberator* 14 (1843–44): 3; *Christian Examiner* 36 (1844): 144; *Present* 1 (1843): 273–83.

6. Ballou, *Hopedale*, 131–33; *Practical Christian*, 8, 22 June, 3 Aug., 28 Sept. 1844.

7. Brook Farm's experience with Fourierism is amply documented in Henry W. Sams, *Autobiography of Brook Farm*, 84–174.

8. The *Practical Christian* published the new regulations and Ballou's exposition of them, "The True Social State," in its 18 Jan. 1845 issue. The regulations can also be found in Ballou, *Hopedale*, 134–37.

9. *Practical Christian*, 18 Jan. 1845.

10 Ibid.

11. Ballou, *Autobiography*, 363, and *Hopedale*, 148–50; *Liberator* 16 (1846): 169, 192.

12. *Practical Christian*, 19 Nov., 13, 27 Dec. 1845.

13. Ibid., 13 Dec. 1845.

14. Ibid., 27 Dec. 1845, 10 Jan. 1846.

15. Ibid., 24 Jan. 1846.

16. Ibid.; Hopedale Community, "Proceedings," 3 Mar., 14 Apr. 1845; 2, 15 Mar., 2, 25 May, 17 Aug. 1846; 4 Jan., 8 Feb., 21 Mar. 1847.

17. Advertisement in *Practical Christian*, 24 Jan. 1846.

18. Ballou, *Hopedale*, 114; Hopedale Community, "Proceedings," 15 Jan. 1845; obituary of Edmund Soward, *Practical Christian*, 27 Jan. 1855.

19. Hopedale Community, "Proceedings," 1 Apr., 22 Sept. 1845; 15, 16, 30 Mar., 13 Apr., 27 Oct. 1846; 19, 27 Apr. 1847.

20. *Practical Christian*, 27 Dec. 1845; Hopedale Community, "Proceedings," 27 July, 21 Dec. 1846; 25 Jan. 1847.

21. *Practical Christian*, 30 Oct. 1841; George Ripley, "Hopedale Fraternal Community," *Harbinger*, 4 (1847): 143–44.

22. *Practical Christian*, 17 Oct., 14 Nov. 1846; 23 Jan. 1847.

23. Ibid., 5, 19 Sept. 1846.

24. Ibid., 12 Dec. 1846, 23 Jan. 1847.

25. Ibid., 23 Jan. 1847; Hopedale Community, "Proceedings," 28 Dec. 1846; 17 Jan., 1 Feb., 21 Mar. 1847.

26. *Practical Christian*, 23 Jan. 1847.

27. Ibid.

28. Ballou, *Hopedale*, 163–64; Hopedale Community, "Proceedings," 6 Sept. 1846; 1 Feb., 5, 14 Apr. 1847.

29. Hopedale Community, "Proceedings," 17 May 1847; *Practical Chris-

tian, 12 June, 22 July, 6, 20 Aug. 1847; *Liberator* 17 (1847): 136; Ballou, *Hopedale*, 169.

30. *Practical Christian*, 12 June 1847.

31. Hopedale Community, "Records," 17 July 1847.

32. The new constitution can be found in ibid., in the *Practical Christian*, 7 Aug. 1847; and in Ballou, *Hopedale*, 165–68.

33. Ballou, *Hopedale*, 167, 171–72; *Practical Christian*, 7 Aug. 1847.

34. Ballou, *Hopedale*, 167, 183; Hopedale Community, "Records," 29 Oct. 1849. In other ways, too, the community continued to take an interest in its industries. At varying times it had charge of the machine, box, transportation, boot and shoe, and other businesses; in 1850 it also provided small loans to its machine, carpentry, box, and transportation businesses. Ibid., 17, 20 Oct., 20 Dec. 1849; Apr. 1850; 25 Jan. 1851.

35. Ballou, *Hopedale*, 165, 167.

36. *Practical Christian*, 2 Oct. 1847; 29 Apr. 1848; 6, 20 July 1850; 12 Mar. 1853; *Harbinger*, 7 (1848): 6–7.

37. *Practical Christian*, 12 May 1849.

Chapter 4

1. Adin Ballou, *A Concise Exposition of the Hopedale Community*, 1–8, and *Milford*, 16–17; also, *Diamond* 2 (1851–52): 58–59.

2. Hopedale Community, "Records," 5 June 1846; *Practical Christian*, 23 Jan. 1847, 8 July 1848, 16 May 1857; Jonathan Prude, *The Coming of Industrial Order*, 200–203.

3. U.S. Census Office, population schedules, Seventh Census, 1850, Worcester County, Mass., Milford.

4. Ibid., 22 Nov. 1851.

5. Ibid., 8 June 1850, 21 May 1853; *Diamond* 2 (1851–52): 66; Ballou, *Hopedale*, 19.

6. Hopedale Community, "Proceedings," 23 Jan., 15 Mar., 25 May, 17 Aug. 1846; 20 Oct. 1849, and "Records," 20 Feb. 1846ff; Ballou, *Hopedale*, 190, and *Concise Exposition of Hopedale*, 8; *Hopedale Reminiscences*, 18.

7. *Practical Christian*, 13 June 1846, also 1 July 1840.

8. Hopedale Community, "'Records," Feb. 1844.

9. Hopedale Community, "Proceedings," 18 Mar. 1844.

10. *Practical Christian*, 26 Apr. 1853, also 10 Apr. 1852.

11. *Diamond* 2 (1851–52): 58; Hopedale Community, "Proceedings," 8 Feb., 30 Mar. 1846; *Practical Christian*, 24 Feb. 1855.

12. Hopedale Community, "Proceedings," 18 Mar. 1844; 8 Apr. 1845; 30 Mar., 21 Sept. 1846; Ballou, *Hopedale*, 130, 143–45.

13. *Practical Christian*, 30 June 1855; "Address on Agriculture," ibid., 11 May 1850.

14. Ibid., 11 Oct. 1851, 13 Mar. 1852, 1 Jan. 1853; Ballou, *Concise Exposition of Hopedale*, 2–3.

15. Ballou, *Hopedale*, 142, 191.

16. *Practical Christian*, 18 June 1853, 2 June 1855; Ballou, *Hopedale*, 192.

17. *Practical Christian*, 15 Mar. 1851; Hopedale Community, "The Hopedale Industrial Army: Record of Its By-Law, Rules, Regulations and Proceedings," 6–7.

18. *Practical Christian*, 6 July 1850; Hopedale Community, "Industrial Army Record," 27.

19. Ibid., 9, 11–13, 23, 25, 60.

20. Ibid., 10–16, 20–22, 28–37, 40–45, 50–52.

21. Hopedale Community, "Record Book of the Hopedale Community. No. 2. Commencing June 17, A.D. 1851," 17, 24 June 1851, and *Constitution, By-Laws, Rules, and Regulations* (1853), 25–26, 29.

22. Hopedale Community, "Records," 25 Jan., 8 Feb. 1848; the nature of this health "insurance" was not indicated.

23. Fish, *Butler Wilmarth*, 252–54; Adin Ballou, *Memoir of Adin Augustus Ballou*, 61.

24. Susan E. Cayleff, *Wash and Be Healed: The Water-Cure Movement and Women's Health*, 1–25.

25. *Practical Christian*, 23 Nov. 1844; 24 Jan., 17 Oct., 26 Dec. 1846.

26. Fish, *Butler Wilmarth*, 19–25, 31, 60–62, 78–104.

27. Ibid., 110–21; *Practical Christian*, 15 May, 26 June 1847.

28. Fish, *Butler Wilmarth*, 38–42, 160; *Practical Christian*, 4 Sept. 1847.

29. Fish, *Butler Wilmarth*, 135–36; Hopedale Community, "Records," Apr. 1850; *Practical Christian*, 11 May 1850.

30. Fish, *Butler Wilmarth*, 138–41, 158–60; *Practical Christian*, 29 Mar. 1851, 21 May 1853; Hopedale Community, "Industrial Army Record," 40–41.

31. Fish, *Butler Wilmarth*, 141–73; *Practical Christian*, 21 May 1853.

32. *Milford Journal*, 23 Feb. 1856.

33. *Practical Christian*, 22 Nov. 1851; Ballou, *Concise Exposition of Hopedale*, 2.

34. Ballou, *Milford*, 632, 818–19, 1031–32; *Practical Christian*, 4 Apr. 1855; obituary clipping for W. W. Humphrey, in Ballou, "Funeral Register, Book 1," 16.

35. *Practical Christian*, 31 Jan. 1852, 6 May 1854.

36. Ibid., 22 Nov. 1851.

Chapter 5

1. *Practical Christian*, 31 Jan. 1852; Ballou, *Hopedale*, 226–34.

2. Ballou, *Hopedale*, 228–32.

3. *Practical Christian*, 1 Apr. 1848; 26 Oct., 7 Dec. 1850; Ballou, *Concise Exposition of Hopedale*, 4.

4. *Practical Christian*, 4 Mar. 1848; 22 June, 9 Nov. 1850.

5. Ibid., 9 Nov. 1850, 3 Jan. 1852.

6. Ibid., 31 Oct. 1846, 24 July 1847, 22 Oct. 1853.

7. Ibid., 8 June 1850, 9 Apr. 1853; Ballou, *Christian Non-Resistance*, 228.

8. *Practical Christian*, 8 May 1846.

9. Peter Brock, *Radical Pacifists in Antebellum America*, 133–38; *Liberator* 18 (1848): 20; *Practical Christian*, 25 May 1850.

10. *Liberator* 14 (1844): 95.

11. *Practical Christian*, 20, 21 July 1850; 15 July, 12 Aug. 1854; *Liberator* 24 (1854): 114, 127; *Milford Journal*, 12 July 1854, 4 Aug. 1855.

12. *Practical Christian*, 26 Oct. 1844, 6 Mar. 1847; Hopedale Community, "Proceedings," 23 Jan., 2 Mar. 1846.

13. Adin Ballou, "Record of Marriages . . . 1823–1889"; *Practical Christian*, 9, 23 Apr. 1853.

14. Ballou, *Concise Exposition of Hopedale*, 5; *Practical Christian*, 15 Mar., 22 Nov. 1851.

15. *Liberator*, 23 Jan. 1842; Hopedale Community, "Records," May 1842. Ellen Dubois notes this acceptance of a sexual division of labor among Garrisonian abolitionists in general and argues that it prevented a full understanding of the problem of sexual inequality. *Feminism and Suffrage*, 35–38. With respect to understanding and practice, Hopedale seems to have been more advanced than Garrisonians outside the community.

16. *Practical Christian*, 23 Jan. 1847; Hopedale Community, "Minutes of the Hopedale Sewing Circle and Tract Society," 19 Feb. 1848, 27 Feb. 1850.

17. Hopedale Community, "Sewing Circle," 22 Mar., 2 Apr., 23 Sept. 1848; 28 Feb. 1851; 7 Feb. 1853; 1 Feb. 1854.

18. Ibid., 24 Apr. 1851, 2 Sept. 1852; *Progressive Age* 6 (1864–65): 5.

19. For annual lists of community offices, see Ballou, *Hopedale*.

20. Ballou, *Milford*, 979–80; *Practical Christian*, 7 Feb. 1846; 1 Mar., 25 Oct. 1851; Mari Jo Buhle and Paul Buhle, *The Concise History of Women's Suffrage*, 112–13.

21. *Practical Christian*, 1 and 27 Mar. 1852; Dolores Hayden, *The Grand Domestic Revolution*, 51ff.

22. Ibid., 20 Dec. 1851; 15 Jan., 12, 26 Feb., 18 June, 3 Dec. 1853; Ballou, *Autobiography*, 463.

23. *Practical Christian*, 15 Nov. 1840, 19 July 1851, 22 Apr. 1854, 19 May 1855; *Hopedale Reminiscences*, 29.

24. From the Declaration, the epitomized version of the Standard of Practical Christianity published as part of every Hopedale constitution; see Ballou, *Hopedale*, 28, 166, 368.

25. *Practical Christian*, 31 Oct. 1846.

26. Ibid., 18 Sept. 1847, 4 Oct. 1856.

27. Ibid., 13 Oct. 1849; Ballou, *Christian Non-Resistance*, 191.

28. *Practical Christian*, 29 Mar., 22 Nov., 20 Dec. 1851.

29. Ibid., 9 Dec. 1848, 2 Aug. 1850, 5 July 1851, 13 Mar. 1852, 11 Feb. 1854; Hopedale Community, "Records," 20 Dec. 1849; 29 Mar., 10 July 1850.

30. *Practical Christian*, 21 June 1851, 27 Mar. 1852.

31. Hopedale Community, "Proceedings," 13 Sept. 1846.

32. Hopedale Community, "Records," 26 Oct. 1848, Apr. 1849.

33. Ballou, *Hopedale*, 202, 384–85.

34. *Hopedale Reminiscences*, 26–28 (this volume, which records the memories chiefly of women who had grown up in the village in the 1850s, tends to exaggerate the degree of moral control in the community); *Practical Christian*, 11 Feb. 1854.

35. Ballou, *Hopedale*, 203–4; Hopedale Community, "Records," 21 Mar. 1850.

36. Hopedale Community, "Records," 22 Apr. 1853; *Practical Christian*, 11 Feb. 1854; U.S. Census 1850, Milford, house #647. Besides his own family, Sutcliffe's house had three families of workers and a young Irish woman, probably a domestic.

37. Ballou, *Practical Christian Socialism*, 185, 358–59, 381–407.

38. Ibid., 361–64; *Practical Christian*, 23 Sept. 1854. Ballou developed his views regarding free love in a debate with Austin Kent of Hopkinton, N.Y., in the *Practical Christian* beginning in Sept. 1854.

39. Ibid., 2, 30 July 1853; Ballou, *Hopedale*, 246–48.

40. *Practical Christian*, 25 Oct. 1851; 9 Apr., 2, 30 July 1853; Ballou, *Milford*, 979–80. Only a few months before she left Hopedale, Price had praised the Raritan Bay Union for its "Unitary domestic operations" but also criticized its founders for failing to prevent "the Slaveholder, or the Warrior, or the user of Intoxicating Beverages, from taking stock and voting in their organization." *Practical Christian*, 9 Apr. 1853.

41. The resolutions and regulations were published in Hopedale Community, *Constitution, By-Laws, Rules, and Regulations* (1853) 33–37; also, *Practical Christian*, 16 July 1853.

42. *Practical Christian*, 15 July 1854. The resolutions and regulations, in a somewhat modified form, were still in effect in 1861.

43. Ibid., 11 Feb., 15 July 1854.

44. Ibid., 27 Mar. 1852; *Hopedale Reminiscences*, 28–29.

45. Hopedale Community, *Communal Songs and Hymns*, 12; Ballou, *Hopedale*, 369, and *Concise Exposition of Hopedale*, 4.

Chapter 6

1. *Practical Christian*, 8 June, 6 July, 12 Oct. 1850.

2. Ibid., 20 July, 9 Nov. 1850; 22 Nov. 1851; Ballou, *Autobiography*, 350.

3. *Practical Christian,* 29 Apr. 1843; Ballou, *Hopedale,* 180, and esp. *Practical Christian Socialism,* 348–57; also *Practical Christianity in Relation to Education and Amusements,* which reprints the previously cited pages.

4. Ballou, *Hopedale,* 181–82; *Mammoth,* 14 Apr. 1847; *Practical Christian,* 6 July 1850.

5. *Mammoth,* 13 Dec. 1845; *Practical Christian,* 16 July 1853.

6. *Practical Christian,* 14 Jan., 30 Dec. 1854; 13 Jan. 1855.

7. Ibid., 11 July 1846; Adin Ballou, *Practical Christianity in Relation to the Superiority of Moral Power over Political Power,* 1, 7, and *Primitive Christianity and Its Corruptions* 2:275–76.

8. Ballou, *Superiority of Moral Power,* 7. For an example of the Hutchinson family's connection with the world of reform, see *Liberator* 14 (1844): 120.

9. Hopedale Community, "Records," May 1842; *Practical Christian,* 29 Apr. 1843.

10. Both of the collections were published at Hopedale. The quotation is from the *Practical Christian,* 23 Dec. 1848.

11. Adin Ballou, ed., *The Hopedale Collection of Hymns and Songs for Use of Practical Christians,* hymn no. 251, and *Milford,* 666.

12. Hopedale Community, *Communal Songs and Hymns,* 3–5.

13. *Practical Christian,* 16 May 1857; Ballou, *Primitive Christianity,* 250.

14. *Practical Christian,* 29 Nov. 1845; 16 May, 12 Dec. 1846.

15. Ballou, *Adin Augustus Ballou,* 29–57; *Practical Christian,* 10 July 1847.

16. William Lloyd Garrison, *Letters, vol. IV: 1850–1860,* ed. Louis Ruchames, 48–49; *Diamond,* 15 Nov., 15 June, 15 Aug. 1851; 15 Feb., 1 Mar. 1852.

17. Hopedale Community, "Proceedings," 22 Feb. 1846; *Practical Christian,* 5 May 1855.

18. *Practical Christian,* 6 July 1850.

19. Ibid., 3 June 1854, 19 May 1855; *First Annual Report of the Hopedale Public Library,* 4–5.

20. *Practical Christian,* 18 Jan. 1845, 3 June 1854, 10 Feb. 1855; Hopedale Community, "Records," 6 Mar. 1849; *Diamond,* 15 Nov. 1851.

21. *Practical Christian,* 22 June, 7 Nov. 1850; 8 Oct. 1853; 28 June 1856.

22. *Practical Christian,* 16 May 1846; Ballou, *Practical Christian Socialism,* 186, 279–337.

23. Ibid., 279–84; *Practical Christian,* 1 Apr. 1841.

24. U.S. Census 1850, Milford; Hopedale Community, "Records," Aug. 1843; *Practical Christian,* 27 Aug. 1847.

25. Hopedale Community, "Records," 12 Jan. 1848, and "Record Book No. 2," 7, 18 Mar. 1852, 3 Apr. 1853; *Practical Christian,* 27 Jan. 1855, 3 June

1856; also, Hopedale Community, *Constitution, By-Laws, Rules, and Regulations* (1853), 22.

26. Ballou, *Autobiography*, 179; *Practical Christian*, 30 Sept. 1848.

27. *Practical Christian*, 25 Feb., 29 July 1854.

28. Ibid., 9 Feb. 1856; Hopedale Community, "Record Book No. 2," 22 Apr. 1853.

29. *Practical Christian*, 30 Sept. 1848, 27 Jan. 1855; *Hopedale Reminiscences*, 30.

30. *Practical Christian*, 23 Jan. 1847.

31. Hopedale Community, "Records," 14 Jan., 1 Apr., 6 May 1846, and "Record Book No. 2," 7, 11 Mar. 1855.

32. *Practical Christian*, 23 Jan. 1847, 26 Mar. 1853, 11 July 1857; Susan E. Whitney, *The Inductive Communion.* "The Inductive Harbinger" (1851–58).

33. "A Record of the Hopedale Inductive Communion, July 1851 . . . ," minutes of meetings, 1, 8, 22 Mar., 5 Apr., 27 Sept. 1852; 14 Mar. 1853; 31 Mar. 1856.

34. "Inductive Harbinger," Aug., Nov. 1851; May, Nov. 1852; 21 Mar. 1853; 5 June 1854.

35. *Practical Christian*, 26 Mar. 1853.

36. *Report of a Select Committee on the Subject of a High School in Milford, Mass.*, 3–7.

37. *Practical Christian*, 6, 20 Dec. 1851.

38. Ibid., 3 Jan., 27 Mar. 1852.

39. Ballou, *Adin Augustus Ballou*, 25–26; "Inductive Harbinger," 17 Nov. 1851.

40. Ballou, *Adin Augustus Ballou*, 28–47, 64.

41. Ibid., 123, 126, 142, and passim. Writing to his own son, Dr. Butler Wilmarth said that Augustus had died from "an over-action of the brain" and speculated that the young man "probably was praised and put ahead— exerted himself to discharge his duties, and sunk a martyr to over-exertion of the young faculties of his mind." Fish, *Butler Wilmarth*, 221–22.

42. Ballou, *Adin Augustus Ballou*, 191–92.

43. *Practical Christian*, 24 Apr. 1852. The purported messages are reprinted in Adin Ballou, *An Exposition of Views Respecting the Principal Facts, Causes and Peculiarities Involved in Spirit Manifestations*, chap. 13.

44. *Practical Christian*, 2 Aug., 27 Sept., 11, 25 Oct., 8, 22 Nov., 6 Dec. 1851; Frank Podmore, *Modern Spiritualism* 1:219–20.

45. *Practical Christian*, Sept. 13, 27, 1851; 15 Jan., 7 May 1853; 26 Aug. 1854; Podmore, *Modern Spiritualism* 1:292.

46. *Practical Christian*, 26 Mar., 16, 30 July 1853; 5 May 1855. William Henry Fish gave a similar qualified, rational acceptance of spiritualism. Ibid., 16, 30 July , 15 Aug. 1853; also, Fish, *Orthodoxy versus Spiritualism and Liberalism*.

47. *Practical Christian*, 8 Nov., 6 Dec. 1853; 17 Jan. 1852; 15 Jan. 1853.

Chapter 7

1. Thomas Low Nichols, *Forty Years of American Life*, 245; Emma Hardinge, *Modern American Spiritualism*, 12–13, 55;
2. R. Laurence Moore, "Spiritualism." *Practical Christian*, 21 May 1853.
3. Ballou, *Spirit Manifestations*, x, 228; *Practical Christian*, 7, 21 May 1853; Perry, *Radical Abolitionists*, 217–21.
4. Geoffrey K. Nelson, *Spiritualism and Society*, 21–22.
5. Ballou, *Practical Christian Socialism*, 38–42.
6. Ibid., 37–38, 43, 45–50, 63.
7. Adin Ballou, *Address Delivered Before the Thwing Family Annual Meeting*, 7–8.
8. *Practical Christian*, 28 Oct. 1848, 8 June 1850, 4 June 1853.
9. Ibid., 28 Oct. 1848, 12 May 1849.
10. Ballou, *Hopedale*, 307–8, and *Adin Augustus Ballou*, 55. At the end of 1852 Spaulding reported that his net earnings for the previous thirty-one months totaled $476.74 and asked the community to assume the newspaper's $115 debt. Hopedale Community, "Record Book No. 2," 31 Dec. 1852.
11. *Practical Christian*, 7 May 1853; 25 Mar. 1854; 21 Apr., 5 May 1855.
12. Ballou, *Hopedale*, 27, 121–22, 170–71, 186–87; *Practical Christian*, 8 Jan., 9 Dec. 1848.
13. *Practical Christian*, 8 June, 14 Sept., 26 Oct. 1850; 30 Aug. 1851.
14. Ballou, *Autobiography*, 386–88, and *Concise Exposition of Hopedale*, 4.
15. *Practical Christian*, 15 Aug., 10 Sept., 17 Dec. 1853.
16. Ibid., 29 Jan., 26 Feb., 29 Nov. 1853; 25 Mar. 1854; 13 Jan. 1855; Ballou, *Hopedale*, 258–61.
17. *Practical Christian*, 11, 25 Feb., 11 Mar., 8 Apr. 1854.
18. Ibid., 11 Mar., 6 May, 3 June, 1 July 1854.
19. The "Constitution of the Practical Christian Republic" is printed as Appendix B in Ballou's *Hopedale*, 398–410; see esp. "Article II. Principles." The constitution is discussed section by section in Ballou's *Practical Christian Socialism*. Ballou probably decided on a statement of principles in reaction against spiritualists like Andrew Jackson Davis who called for a religion "without creeds." *Practical Christian*, 2 July 1853.
20. Ballou, *Practical Christian Socialism*, iii, 206–42, and *Hopedale*, 402–3.
21. Ballou, *Hopedale*, 403, and *Practical Christian Socialism*, 236–38.
22. Ballou, *Practical Christian Socialism*, 52, 175–76; *Practical Christian*, 1 July 1854, 20 Sept. 1856.

23. Ballou, *Practical Christian Socialism*, 654.

24. Ibid., vii; *Practical Christian*, 1 July 1854.

25. *Practical Christian*, 6 May, 18 Nov., 2 Dec. 1854.

26. Ballou, *Practical Christian Socialism*, 600ff.

27. "Epistle of the Practical Christian Communion," *Practical Christian*, 29 Sept. 1849.

28. Ballou, *Practical Christian Socialism*, 25–28, 186–87; *Practical Christian*, 6, 20 July 1850.

29. Ballou, *Practical Christian Socialism*, 244–45.

30. Ibid., 183–84, 246–51.

31. Ibid., 252–59.

32. Ibid., 227.

33. Ibid., vii; *Practical Christian*, 18 Nov. 1854.

34. *Universalist Quarterly* 13 (1855): 210–13; Noyes, *American Socialisms*, 129.

35. *Practical Christian*, 10 Feb., 30 June 1855.

36. Ibid., 28 July, 3 Nov., 15 Dec. 1855.

37. Ibid., 24 Apr. 1852; 1, 19 July 1854.

38. Ibid., 23 Sept., 4 Nov. 1854.

39. Ibid., 10 Feb., 10, 24 Mar., 4 Apr., 11 Aug. 1855; Ballou, *Autobiography*, 399–400.

40. *Practical Christian*, 5 May 1855.

41. Ibid., 22 Sept., 6 Oct. 1855; Ballou, *Hopedale*, 276–77.

42. *Practical Christian*, 26 Jan., 8 Mar., 31 May, 29 Nov. 1856; 7 Mar. 1857; Ballou, *Hopedale*, 279–80, 295–96.

43. Ballou, *Hopedale*, 253.

Chapter 8

1. *Universalist Quarterly* 8 (1851): 20; *Practical Christian*, 6 May 1854.

2. Francis DeWitt, *Statistical Information Relating to Certain Branches of Industry in Massachusetts*, 511–12, 570; U.S. Census 1860, *Manufactures*, 251. Southern Massachusetts in general experienced fundamental changes in the 1850s, especially in the form of the enlargement of industrial operations, commercialization, population movements, and the growth of large towns. Prude, *Coming of Industrial Order*, 191–204; *Practical Christian*, 22 Sept. 1855.

3. Ballou, *Hopedale*, 250–51; *Practical Christian*, 20 May 1854; 27 Jan., 5 May, 22 Sept. 1855.

4. *Practical Christian*, 4 Nov. 1854, 2 June 1855; *Milford Journal*, 13 Oct. 1854.

5. *Practical Christian*, 11 Feb. 1854 ("Annual Report of the Council of Religion"); Hopedale Community, "Record Book No. 2," 1, 15 Nov. 1854.

6. *Practical Christian*, 11 Feb. 1854, 27 Jan. 1855.

7. Ballou, *Milford*, 610, 1108–10.

8. Hopedale Community, *Constitution, By-Laws, Rules and Regulations* (1853), 19, 31; *Hopedale Reminiscences*, 26–29; *Practical Christian*, 7 May 1853; 25 Mar., 3 June, 15 July 1854.

9. *Liberator* 26 (1856); 184.

10. Personal though not entirely accurate glimpses of community life can be found in *Hopedale Reminiscences*, memories of people who had been children at Hopedale in the 1850s compiled a half century later.

11. *Practical Christian*, 16, 30 July, 27 Aug., 17 Dec. 1853.

12. Ibid., 3 June 1854, 27 Jan. 1855; Hopedale Community, "Record Book No. 2," 29 Apr. 1856; Hopedale Community, "Account Book—Cabinet Branch, Jan. 2, 1854–July 31, 1855."

13. William Chase, *Five Generations of Loom Builders*, 2–6.

14. Ballou, *Concise Exposition of Hopedale*, 2; Hopedale Community, "Record Book No. 2," 12 Jan. 1853; *Practical Christian*, 4 Apr., 5, 19 May, 22 Sept. 1855; 3 Nov. 1855.

15. Hopedale Community, "Record Book No. 2," 7 Feb. 1855; *Practical Christian*, 22 Sept. 1855; Ballou, *Hopedale*, 274.

16. Ballou, *Hopedale*, 129, 173, 210, 225, and *Concise Exposition of Hopedale*, 2; *Practical Christian*, 31 Jan. 1852.

17. *Practical Christian*, 11 May 1850.

18. Ibid., 5 May, 14 July 1855.

19. Ibid., 30 June, 14 July 1855; Hopedale Community, "Record Book No. 2," 18, 22 Dec. 1853; 4 Jan. 1854; Ballou, *Hopedale*, 362–63.

20. *Practical Christian*, 3 June 1854; 17 May, 14 July 1855; 22 Mar. 1856.

21. Ibid., 27 Mar. 1852; Ballou, *Practical Christian Socialism*, 340–45.

22. *Practical Christian*, 7, 23 Oct. 1854.

23. *Hopedale Juvenile and Collegiate Home School*, 7–8; *Practical Christian*, 19 Apr. 1856; *Liberator* 26 (1856): 72.

24. Hopedale Home School, *Catalogue of Teachers and Pupils*, 1–5, 14–19; *Liberator* 29 (1859): 147.

25. Hopedale Home School, *Catalogue of Teachers and Pupils*, 5–14, and *Reunion of Teachers and Pupils . . . 1867*, 50–63; Ballou, *Practical Christian Socialism*, 186.

26. U.S. Census 1850, Milford. There is little available evidence relating to stock ownership at Hopedale. Reportedly, in 1855 the stock was "now owned almost entirely by resident stockholders." *Practical Christian*, 22 Sept. 1855. In 1850 a committee appointed to devise a plan to "secure greater interest in Joint Stock" reported that because of "the many difficulties with which they met in the investigation," they had no plan except to urge everyone to take an interest in the stock. Hopedale Community, "*Records*," 6, 22 Nov. 1850.

27. *Liberator* 26 (1856): 184; *Practical Christian*, 22 Sept. 1855.

28. Ballou, *Hopedale*, 255.

Chapter 9

1. *Practical Christian*, 22 Sept. 1855.
2. Ibid., 24 Mar. 1855, 4 Oct. 1856. On the ownership of the joint stock, see n. 26 of chap. 8.
3. *Practical Christian*, 29 Dec. 1855.
4. Ibid., 9 Feb., 8 Mar. 1856; Hopedale Community, *Compact of Commune No. 1*, and "Record Book No. 2," 4 Jan. 1856, and "Records Regarding the Organization of Commune No. 1, Jan. 2–April 6, 1856".
5. *Practical Christian*, 17 May 1855; 9 Feb. 1856; 30 May, 27 June 1857.
6. Ballou, *Hopedale*, 281. Ballou says nothing about the Whipple block in this history.
7. *Practical Christian*, 29 Dec. 1855.
8. *Ibid.*, Ballou, *Hopedale*, 408. Ballou says nothing about the Judicatory of Commerce.
9. Chase, *Five Generations of Loom Builders*, 4–6. Probably, Draper accepted stock in payment for the circular sawmill and attached land which the community purchased from him in 1851. Hopedale Community, "Record Book No. 2," 22 Nov. 1851; U.S. Census 1850, Milford.
10. Ballou, *Autobiography*, 513, and *"Funeral Register, 1823–1889"* (Munyan).
11. *Practical Christian*, 27 Jan. 1855.
12. Ibid., 27 Jan., 22 Sept. 1855.
13. Ibid., 9 Feb. 1856; Ballou, *Hopedale*, 284–85; Hopedale Community, "Record Book No. 2," 9 Jan. 1856.
14. Hopedale Community, "Record Book No. 2," 5 Feb. 1856; Ballou, *Hopedale*, 286–87.
15. Hopedale Community, "Record Book No. 2," 22, 23, 24, 27, 28 Feb. 1856; Thomas R. Navin, *The Whitin Machine Works since 1831*, 37–38.
16. William F. Draper, *Recollections of a Varied Career*, 5–7; Chase, *Five Generations of Loom Builders*, 6–7; Thomas H. West, *"The Loom Builders,"* 18–20; Ballou, *Milford*, 723–24, and *Autobiography*, 402.
17. Ballou to Theodore Weld in Benjamin Thomas, *Theodore Weld*, 229; Ballou, *Hopedale*, 289; *Practical Christian*, 22 Sept. 1855.
18. Draper's son William recalled that his father had said that while he was ready to give his best for the public good, he was unwilling to "have business questions decided by a majority vote of people who had not the capacity to understand them." Draper, *Recollections*, 22.
19. Ballou, *Hopedale*, 288–89; Hopedale Community, "Records," 28 Mar. 1851.
20. Ballou, *Hopedale*, 289–91; Hopedale Community, "Record Book No. 2," 2, 7, 8, 15, 21, 23, 28 Mar. 1856.
21. *Practical Christian*, 19 Apr., 2 May 1856; *Leading Businessmen of Milford . . . Embracing Also . . . Hopedale*, 30–31.

22. *Practical Christian*, 1 May, 4 Sept., 2 Oct. 1858.

23. Hopedale Community, "Records Regarding the Organization of Commune No. 1.," 10–11. Of the members of the commune, only Charles Price participated in the community vote on dissolution, and he voted in favor of the plan. Ballou's most notable action at the time of dissolution was to procure the continuation of the enactment establishing communes. Hopedale Community, "Record Book No. 2," 8, 14 Mar. 1856.

24. Ibid., 14 Jan. 1857, 2 Oct. 1859, 7 Jan. 1863; *Progressive Age* 4 (1862–63): 45; 6 (1864–65): 79.

25. *Practical Christian*, 3, 9, 31 May, 10 Oct. 1856.

26. Ballou, *Hopedale*, 289–91, and *Milford*, 260, 269–70; Hopedale Community, "Record Book No. 2," 8 Mar. 1856.

27. *Practical Christian*, 15 Nov. 1856; 7, 21 Mar. 1857; Ballou, *Autobiography*, 414.

28. *Practical Christian*, 17 May, 6 Sept., 4 Oct. 1856; 22 Aug. 1857.

29. Ibid., 15 Nov. 1856, 2 May 1857.

30. Ibid., 6 Sept. 1856, 25 July 1857.

31. Ibid., 4 Oct. 1856; Ballou, *Autobiography*, 407.

32. *Practical Christian*, 1 May 1858; Ballou, *Autobiography*, 406.

Chapter 10

1. *Practical Christian*, 16 May, 13 June, 25 July 1857.

2. U.S. Census 1850, Milford; ibid., 1860, Milford, households #623–664.

3. *Practical Christian*, 16, 30 May, 8 Aug. 1857; 6 Mar. 1858; "Lands for Sale," *Liberator*, Sept. 26, 1859; *Spiritual Reformer* 2 (1860–61); 23: obituary clipping for Richard Walker, in Ballou, "Funeral Register, 1823–1889," 40.

4. *Liberator* 26 (1856): 118, 130; 27 (1857): 122, 130, 132; *Practical Christian*, 9, 23 Aug. 1856; *Milford Journal*, 2 Aug. 1856.

5. *Practical Christian*, 11 July, 26 Dec. 1857; Hopedale Community, "The Inductive Communion Festival, June 24, 1857."

6. *Spiritual Reformer* 2 (1860–61): 29.

7. Fish, *Orthodoxy versus Spiritualism*, 16–20; *Practical Christian*, 12, 27 June, 3 Oct. 1857.

8. *Practical Christian*, 7, 21 Mar., 2 May 1857; 23 Jan., 30 Feb., 20 Mar., 17 Apr. 1858.

9. Perry, *Radical Abolitionism*, 276; Whitney, *Inductive Communion*, 7–8. Butts wrote his own biographical sketch in Ballou, *Milford*, 610. B. J. Butts, "The Man of Content," *Practical Christian*, 7 May 1853.

10. *Practical Christian*, 10, 24 Jan., 7, 21 Feb., 13 June 1857; 24 Nov. 1858.

11. Ibid., 3 Apr. 1858, 11 June 1859.

12. *Radical Spiritualist* 1 (1859–60): 4, 20, 92; *Spiritual Reformer* 2 (1860–61): 15.

13. Ballou, *Autobiography*, 416–20; *Practical Christian*, 1 May 1858; 3 Sept., 29 Oct. 1859.

14. See, e.g., Garrison, *Letters* 4:401, 404–9.

15. *Practical Christian*, 3 June, 1 July 1854; 18 Oct. 1856; 14 Apr. 1859.

16. *Practical Christian*, 13 Dec. 1856; 6 Mar., 3 Apr. 1858; 17 Mar. 1860; *Liberator* 26 (1856): 194.

17. Perry, *Radical Abolitionism*, 241, 261–63; *Practical Christian*, 3 Sept. 1859; *Liberator* 29 (1859): 145.

18. *Practical Christian*, 29 Oct., 12 Nov., 10 Dec. 1859; *Liberator* 29 (1859): 174.

19. *Practical Christian*, 23 Nov. 1859; 14 Apr. 1860.

20. Ibid., 17, 31 Mar., 14 Apr. 1860; Ballou, *Hopedale*, 322–33.

21. Ballou, *Hopedale*, 306–7; Hopedale Community, "Record Book No. 2," 12 Jan. 1859; Adin Ballou, *Remarks . . . at the Annual Meeting of the Hopedale Community*, 3–6.

22. Ballou, *Remarks at the Annual Meeting*, 6–8.

23. Adin Ballou, *Discourse on Christian Non-Resistance in Extreme Cases*, 27; *Spiritual Reformer* 2 (1860–61): 71.

24. Ballou, *Hopedale*, 310–16; Hopedale Community, "Record Book No. 2," 15 Sept. 1861; also, Adin Ballou, *Christian Non-Resistance Defended Against the Rev. Henry Ward Beecher.*

25. Willie Lee Rose, *Rehearsal for Reconstruction*, 48; Hopedale Community, "Record Book No. 2," 8 Jan. 1862.

26. Hopedale Community, "Record Book No. 2," 27 Aug. 1862; Ballou, *Hopedale*, 317–20.

27. Ralph Waldo Emerson, *Emerson in His Journals*, 512; Garrison, *Letters* 4:49n.; Ballou, *Autobiography*, 429, and *Milford*, 140–41; Perry, *Radical Abolitionism*, 272–74. William F. Draper's account of his wartime experiences can be found in his *Recollections.*

28. *Progressive Age* 4 (1862–63); 28, 38. Ballou said that the Home School closed soon after the outbreak of the war, but the Heywoods continued their school throughout 1862. See the *Liberator* 33 (1863): 2.

29. *Modern Age* 7 (1865–66): 128, 151–52; Ballou, *Primitive Christianity* 2:405. Perry, *Radical Abolitionism*, 268–69.

Chapter 11

1. Adin Ballou, *Monitorial Guide*, iii–iv, 5, 7; *Spiritual Reformer* 3 (1861–62): 54, 77.

2. *Spiritual Reformer* 3 (1861–62): 75–79, 86–87; *Progressive Age* 4

(1862–63): 28, 38, 70; 5 (1863–64): 55, 77; 6 (1864–65): 20, 76; *Modern Age* 7 (1865–66): 111–12.

3. *Progressive Age* 4 (1862–63): 28; 5 (1863–64): 68; *Modern Age* 7 (1865–66): 111–12.

4. *Progressive Age* 4 (1862–63): 93; 6 (1864–65): 55, 70, 85; *Modern Age* 7 (1865–66): 34, 144.

5. *Spiritual Reformer* 2 (1860–61): 79; 3 (1861–62): 68–70. *Progressive Age* 4 (1862–63): 77; 6 (1864–65): 38, 40, 46, 89; *Modern Age* 7 (1865–66): 10–11, 26, 45–46, 63, 149–51. Ira Steward was a vice president of the Social Science Association, and he attended at least one meeting of the Progressive Group in 1862. *Progressive Age* 4 (1862–63): 46. For Steward's career and thought, see David Montgomery, *Beyond Equality*, 90, 123, 249–60. Mary B. Steward, the "Librarian" of the association, also took a strong interest in the welfare of workers. Perry, *Radical Abolitionism*, 274.

6. *Modern Age* 7 (1865–66), prospectus, 7–8. The attack on the "State Street monopoly," etc., was first made in a set of resolutions submitted to the Boston convention apparently by Butts and subsequently reprinted in the *Modern Age* 6 (1864–65): 104–5, 152; Butts uses it, without attribution, in his "On Earth, Peace," 15–16.

7. *Modern Age* 7 (1865–66): 13, 26, 28, 52, 69–70, 91–93, 95, 138–41, 174, 178–80, and the title sheets of the Feb. and June issues.

8. Ibid., 2–3, 112, 117–18, 127, 188, 191; Butts, "On Earth, Peace," 14–16.

9. Adin Ballou, *Human Progress in Respect to Religion*, 3, 5–7, 8–14, 19–22, 29–30, and *Autobiography*, 500.

10. Ballou, *Primitive Christianity* 1: iii, 7.

11. Ibid., 2: 237–46.

12. Ballou, *Autobiography*, 469–75, 502, and *Hopedale*, 333–36, 344; *Spiritual Reformer* 2 (1860–61), 78; Hopedale Community, "Record Book No. 2," 20 Aug. 1862, 8 Jan. 1868, and "Agreement of the Transfer of the Books of the Hopedale Community . . . 1871."

13. *Opening Arguments . . . In Remonstrance Against the Incorporation of Hopedale*, 149; Mrs. Harriet Greene Butts, *Bertha and Willie: A Story for the Young*, end paper; Ballou, *Milford*, 610.

14. Ballou, *Hopedale*, 339–48.

15. Ibid., 350–52.

16. Ibid., 349–50, 352–58.

17. Ibid., 355–60.

18. Ibid., iii, xii-xiii, 366–67.

19. Adin Ballou, "Milford," 67, 78, 96–97.

20. In his voluminous letters, Emerson referred to Ballou only once, in February 1841, when he wrote that "a Mr. Ballou . . . is here to christianize us children of darkness in Concord with his Non Resistance." *Letters* 2:379. Wilson, ed., "Christian Doctrine of Non-Resistance," 4.

21. Ballou, "Funeral Register, Book 2," 22, 26.

22. Ballou, *Autobiography*, 476, 523; *Practical Christian*, 4 Oct. 1856.
23. *Memorial of Adin Ballou*, 87–98.
24. Ballou, *Christian Non-Resistance*, 271–77.
25. Lewis G. Wilson, "Funeral Sermon of Mrs. W. S. Haywood [sic]," and "Christian Doctrine of Non-Resistance."

Chapter 12

1. John S. Garner, *The Model Company Town: Urban Design through Private Enterprise in Nineteenth-Century New England* (Amherst: University of Massachusetts Press, 1984), 123–24. Garner gives special attention to Hopedale, esp. for the decades between 1890 and 1910. *Practical Christian*, 19 Apr. 1856; Ballou, "Milford," 97–98.
2. Draper, *Recollections*, 181–88; Navin, *Whitin Machine Works*, 11–17; U.S. Census Office, "Textiles," in *Eleventh Census, 1890*, 169; *Report of the Industrial Commission on the Relations and Conditions of Capital and Labor* 14:460–61.
3. U.S. Census 1850, Milford; *Incorporation of Hopedale*, 104, 117, 143; Hopedale (town), *First Assessor's Report*, 2–7; Lilla Bancroft, *To the Blessed Memory of Joseph Bubier Bancroft, 1821–1909*.
4. Ballou, *Milford*, 261; *Dedication of the Adin Ballou Memorial*; Hopedale (town), *First Annual Report of the School Committee*, 10–11, and *First Annual Report of the Public Library*, 3–8.
5. Garner, *Model Company Town*, 136–43, 181; Hopedale, *First Assessor's Report*, 21, 33.
6. Garner, *Model Company Town*, 137, 145, 182.
7. Ibid., 205; T. Edwin Brown, *Studies in Modern Socialism*, 11, 26, 123, 127–28, 151–52.
8. Ballou, *Autobiography*, 496, 564–65, and *Primitive Christianity* 2: 239.
9. Draper, *Recollections*, 11–28; Ballou, *Milford*, 275.
10. Bancroft, *Memory of Joseph Bancroft*, 20–23; *Practical Christian*, 29 Mar. 1851.
11. Bancroft, *Memory of Joseph Bancroft*, 17–19.
12. West, *Loom Builders*, 12; Navin, *Whitin Machine Works*, 273–74; U.S. Census Office, "Cotton Manufactures," *Twelfth Census, 1900*, 28; *Report of the Industrial Commission* 462.
13. *Report of the Industrial Commission* 14:467, 470–71; Garner, *Model Company Town*, 205–16; Budgett Meakin, *Model Factories and Villages*, 404–6; Paul R. Smith, "An Instance of Practical and Aesthetic Housing," 474–75.
14. Garner, *Model Company Town*, 149–52, 161–62; Meakin, *Model Factories*, 406–7
15. Hopedale (town), *First Annual Report*, 17; Bancroft, *Memory of Jo-*

seph Bancroft, 18; Hopedale Community, "Industrial Army Record," 44, 46, 50; Garner, *Model Company Town*, 183–84, 189.

16. Garner, *Model Company Town*, 143, 152–56, 192–94.

17. Ibid., 192–94; James Church Alvord, "What the Neighbors Did in Hopedale," 61–62, 84, and "Hopedale's Glorified Mill-Pond," 36.

18. Garner, *Model Company Town*, 189, 195–97; Smith, "Practical and Aesthetic Housing," 475; Alvord, "Neighbors in Hopedale," 61.

19. *Practical Christian*, 25 July 1857; G. Sherman Johnson, "A Massachusetts Garden Spot."

20. Garner, *Model Company Town*, 169, 181; Lewis G. Wilson, "Milford and Hopedale," 503, 506; *Dedication of the Adin Ballou Memorial*.

21. Ballou, *Autobiography*, 505–6; Garner, *Model Company Town*, 169; Lewis G. Wilson, "Hopedale and Its Founder," 206; Johnson, "Massachusetts Garden Spot," 607–8.

22. Wilson, "Hopedale and Founders" 209–10; George L. Cary, "Adin Ballou and the Hopedale Community," 683; Alvord, "Neighbors in Hopedale," 61.

23. *Hopedale Reminiscences*, 12, 39, 56ff.

24. Irwin Feller, "The Draper Loom in New England," 324.

25. Johnson, "Massachusetts Garden Spot," 612–13; Draper, *Recollections*, 220 passim, 365–73, 379, 390–98; *New York Times*, 29 Jan. 1910.

26. Garner, *Model Company Town*, 175; *New York Times*, 10 Apr. 1914.

27. Garner, *Model Company Town*, 175, 180; *Report of the Industrial Commission*, 465; *New York Times*, 10 Apr., 4, 24 May, and 1 June 1913.

28. *New York Times*, 10, 17 Apr. 1914; 22 Dec. 1915; 24 Apr. 1924.

29. Ibid., 10, 25 July, 13 Nov. 1926; 19, 30 Sept. 1928; 27 Mar., 19, 30 Sept. 1930.

30. For the textile depression, see Navin, *Whitin Machine Works*, 336–54. According to Irwin Feller, Draper sales were relatively low between 1914 and 1924 but then increased during the rest of the 1920s. *Draper Loom*, 325.

31. West, *Loom Builders*, 29–31; Garner, *Model Company Town*, 17, 118, 126–27, 222; U.S. Bureau of the Census, *Eighteen Census, 1960: Population*, vol. I, part 23, pp. 219–20; Michael Knight, "Hopedale, Mass.," *New York Times*, 1 May 1981.

Bibliography

Manuscripts

Hopedale Community

In Bancroft Memorial Library, Hopedale, Massachusetts. Also available in Jack T. Ericson, ed., *Hopedale Community Collection, 1821–1938*. Glen Rock, N.J.: Microfilming Corporation of America, 1976:1.

"Account Book—Cabinet Branch, Jan. 2, 1854–July 31, 1855."

"Agreement of the Transfer of the Books of the Hopedale Community . . . 1871."

"The Hopedale Industrial Army: Record of Its By-Law, Rules, Regulations and Proceedings." 1849–54.

"The Inductive Communion Festival, June 24, 1857."

"The Inductive Harbinger." 1851–58.

"Minutes of the Hopedale Sewing Circle and Tract Society." 1848–62.

"Proceedings of the Trustees and Executive Council of Fraternal Community No. 1. Book 1. Commenced Jan. 29, 1841 [to 1847]."

"Records of the Proceedings of Fraternal Community No. 1. Book 1. Commencing January 28, 1841 [to 1851]."

"Record Book of the Hopedale Community. No. 2. Commencing June 17, A.D. 1851 [to 1868]."

"A Record of the Hopedale Inductive Communion." 2 vols. 1849–50, 1851–56.

"Records Regarding the Organization of Commune No. 1. January 2–April 6, 1856."

Adin Ballou

Available in Ericson, *Hopedale Community Collection*: "Funeral Register, 1823–1889," and "Record of Marriages, 1823–1889."

U.S. Census Office

Population schedules for Worcester County, Mass., Milford: Seventh Census, 1850, microfilm, reel 344; Eighth Census, 1860, reel 529.

Nineteenth-Century Periodicals

Christian Examiner.
Dial.
Diamond (Hopedale).
Harbinger.
Independent Messenger.
Liberator.
Mammoth (Hopedale).
Milford Journal.
Non-Resistant.
Practical Christian (Hopedale).
Present.
Radical Spiritualist (Hopedale), later called *Spiritual Reformer, Progressive Age,* and *Modern Age.*
Universalist Quarterly.

Articles

Adams, John Coleman. "The Universalists." In *The Religious History of New England,* 295–321. Cambridge, Mass.: Harvard University Press, 1917.

Alvord, James Church. "Hopedale's Glorified Mill-Pond," *Independent* 86 (3 Apr. 1916): 16.

———. "What the Neighbors Did in Hopedale," *Country Life* 25 (Jan. 1914): 61–62.

Ballou, Adin. "Milford." In *History of Worcester County, Massachusetts,* 2:64–99. 2 vols. Boston, 1879.

Birdsall, Richard D. "The Second Great Awakening and the New England Social Order," *Church History* 39 (1970): 345–64.

Cary, George L. "Adin Ballou and the Hopedale Community," *New World* 7 (1898): 670–83.

Caswell, Jerry V. " 'A New Civilization Radically Higher Than the Old': Adin Ballou's Search for Social Perfection," *Journal of the Universalist Historical Society* 7 (1967–68): 70–96.

Coffey, David M. "The Hopedale Community," *Historical Journal of Western Massachusetts* 4 (1975): 16–26.

Draper, William F. "Testimony of Hon. William F. Draper." In *Report of the Industrial Commission on the Relations and Conditions of Capital and Labor,* 14: 460–71. Washington, D.C.: Government Printing Office, 1901.

Emerson, Ralph Waldo. "The Chardon Street Convention." In *Collected Works,* vol. 10. Boston and New York: Houghton Mifflin, 1904.

Feller, Irwin. "The Draper Loom in New England," *Journal of Economic History* 26 (1966): 320–47.

Greeley, Horace. "The Idea of Social Reform," *Universalist Quarterly* 2 (1845): 146–47.

Johnson, G. Sherman. "A Massachusetts Garden Spot," *New England Magazine* 40 (1909): 606–14.

Knight, Michael. "Hopedale, Mass.: How to Live with Less," *New York Times*, 1 May 1981.

Moore, R. Laurence. "Spiritualism." In *The Rise of Adventism*, edited by Edwin S. Gausted, 79–103. New York. 1974.

Parker, Theodore. "Primitive Christianity," *Dial* 2 (1841–42): 293–313.

Peabody, Elizabeth P. "A Glimpse of Christ's Idea of Society," *Dial* 2 (1841–42): 266–67.

Perry, Lewis. "Adin Ballou's Hopedale Community and the Theology of Anti-Slavery," *Church History* 39 (1970): 372–89.

Reichert, William O. "The Philosophical Anarchism of Adin Ballou," *Huntington Library Quarterly* 27 (1964): 257–74.

Rollins, Richard M. "Adin Ballou and the Perfectionist Dilemma," *Journal of Church and State* 17 (1975): 459–76.

Smith, Paul R. "An Instance of Practical and Aesthetic Housing," *American City*, town and country ed., 13 (Dec. 1915): 474–76.

Thomas, John L. "Antislavery and Utopia." In *Antislavery Vanguard*, edited by Martin Duberman, 240–69. Princeton, N.J.: Princeton University Press, 1965.

Wilson, Lewis G. "Funeral Sermon of Mrs. W. S. Haywood [*sic*]." In *Hopedale Community Collection*.

———. "Hopedale and Its Founder," *New England Magazine*, n.s., 4 (1891): 197–212.

———. "Milford and Hopedale," *New England Magazine* 27 (1902–3): 487–508.

———, ed. "The Christian Doctrine of Non-Resistance. By Count Leo Tolstoi and the Rev. Adin Ballou. Unpublished Correspondence," *Arena* 3 (1890–91): 1–12.

Books and Pamphlets

Andrews, Edward D. *The People Called Shakers*. New York: Oxford University Press, 1953.

Ballou, Adin. *An Address at the Funeral of Mrs. Anna T. Draper*. Hopedale, Mass., 1870.

———. *Address before the Thwing Family Annual Meeting*. Hopedale, Mass., 1849.

———. *Autobiography, 1803–1890*. Edited by Wm. S. Heywood. Lowell, Mass., 1896.

———. *Christian Non-Resistance*. Appendix by William S. Heywood. 1910. Reprint. New York: Da Capo, 1970.

———. *Christian Non-Resistance Defended Against the Rev. Henry Ward Beecher.* Hopedale, Mass., 1862.

———. *A Concise Exposition of the Hopedale Community.* Hopedale, Mass., 1853.

———. *Discourse on Christian Non-Resistance in Extreme Cases.* Hopedale, Mass., 1860.

———. *An Exposition of Views Respecting the Principal Facts, Causes and Peculiarities Involved in Spirit Manifestations.* Boston, 1853.

———. *The Furious Priest Reproved: A Letter to the Reverend Abial Fisher of Bellingham.* Providence, R.I., 1823.

———. *History of the Hopedale Community.* 1897. Reprint. Philadelphia: Porcupine Press, 1972.

———. *History of the Town of Milford.* Boston, 1882.

———. *Human Progress in Respect to Religion.* Hopedale, Mass., 1867.

———. *The Inestimable Value of Souls.* Boston, 1830.

———. *Memoir of Adin Augustus Ballou.* Hopedale, Mass., 1853.

———. *Monitorial Guide: For Use of Inductive Conferences, Communities, etc. in the Practical Christian Republic.* Boston, 1862.

———. *Non-Resistance in Relation to Human Governments.* Boston, 1839.

———. *An Oration Delivered Before the Citizens of Blackstone.* Providence, R.I., 1830.

———. *Practical Christianity in Relation to Education and Amusements.* Hopedale, Mass., 1860.

———. *Practical Christianity in Relation to the Superiority of Moral Power over Political Power.* Hopedale, Mass., n.d.

———. *Practical Christian Socialism.* 1854. Reprint. New York: AMS Press, 1974.

———. *Primitive Christianity and Its Corruptions.* Vol. 1. Boston, 1870. Vols. 2, 3, edited by William S. Heywood. Lowell, Mass., 1899, 1900.

———. *Remarks of Adin Ballou at the Annual Meeting of the Hopedale Community.* Hopedale, Mass., 1861.

———. *True Love Vs. Free Love: Testimony of A True Hearted Woman.* Hopedale, Mass., 1855.

———. *Violation of the Federal Constitution in the Irrepressible Conflict.* Hopedale, Mass., 1861.

Ballou, Adin, ed. *The Hopedale Collection of Hymns and Songs for Use of Practical Christians.* Hopedale, Mass., 1850.

Bancroft, Lilla. *To the Blessed Memory of Joseph Bubier Bancroft, 1821–1909.* Boston: Beacon Press, 1930.

Beers, F. W., et al. *Atlas of Worcester County, Massachusetts.* New York, 1870.

Berthoff, Rowland T. *An Unsettled People: Social Order and Disorder in American History.* New York: Harper & Row, 1971.

Bestor, Arthur. *Backwoods Utopias.* 2d ed. Philadelphia: University of Pennsylvania Press, 1970.

Bodo, John R. *The Protestant Clergy and Public Issues, 1812–1848*. Princeton, N.J.: Princeton University Press, 1954.

Brock, Peter. *Radical Pacifists in Antebellum America*. Princeton, N.J.: Princeton University Press, 1968.

Brown, T. Edwin. *Studies in Modern Socialism*. New York, 1886.

Buhle, Mari Jo, and Paul Buhle. *The Concise History of Women's Suffrage*. Urbana: University of Illinois Press, 1978.

Butts, Bryan J. "On Earth, Peace." Hopedale, Mass., n.d.

Butts, Mrs. Harriet Greene. *Bertha and Willie: A Story for the Young*. Hopedale, Mass., n.d.

Cassara, Ernest. *Hosea Ballou: The Challenge to Orthodoxy*. Washington, D.C.: University Press of America, 1982.

Catalogue of the Private Library of the Late Adin Ballou. N.p: C. F. Libbie & Co., 1916.

Cayleff, Susan E. *Wash and Be Healed: The Water-Cure Movement and Women's Health*. Philadelphia: Temple University Press, 1987.

Chase, William. *Five Generations of Loom Builders*. Hopedale, Mass.: Draper Corporation, 1950.

Codman, John T. *Brook Farm*. Boston, 1894.

Coleman, Peter J. *The Transformation of Rhode Island, 1790–1860*. Providence, R.I.: Brown University Press, 1969.

Curti, Merle E. *The American Peace Crusade, 1815–1860*. Durham, N.C.: Duke University Press, 1929.

Dana, Richard Henry, Jr. *Journal*. Edited by Robert F. Lucid. 3 vols. Cambridge, Mass.: Harvard University Press, 1968.

DeBendetti, Charles. *Peace Reform in American History*. Bloomington: Indiana University Press, 1980.

Dedication of the Adin Ballou Memorial. Cambridge, Mass.: Riverside Press, 1901.

DeWitt, Francis. *Statistical Information Relating to Certain Branches of Industry in Massachusetts*. Boston, 1856.

Doherty, Robert. *Society and Power: Five New England Towns, 1800–1860*. Amherst: University of Massachusetts Press, 1977.

Draper, William F. *Recollections of a Varied Career*. Boston: Little, Brown & Co., 1908.

Dubois, Ellen Carol. *Feminism and Suffrage*. Ithaca, N.Y.: Cornell University Press, 1978.

Emerson, Ralph Waldo. *The Early Lectures*. Edited by Robert E. Spiller and William E. Wallace. 3 vols. Cambridge, Mass.: Harvard University Press, 1966–73.

———. *Emerson in His Journals*. Edited by Joel Porte. Cambridge, Mass.: Harvard University Press, 1982.

———. *Journals and Miscellaneous Notebooks*. Edited by A. W. Plumstead and Harrison Hayford. Vol. 7. Cambridge, Mass.: Harvard University Press, 1969.

――――. *Letters*. Edited by Ralph L. Rusk. 6 vols. New York: Columbia University Press, 1939.

Faulkner, Barbara Louise. "Adin Ballou and the Hopedale Community." Ph.D. diss., Boston University, 1965.

Fish, William Henry. *Memoir of Butler Wilmarth, M.D.* Boston and New York, 1854.

――――. *Orthodoxy versus Spiritualism and Liberalism*. Hopedale, Mass., 1857.

Friedman, Lawrence J. *Gregarious Saints: Self and Community in American Abolitionism*. Cambridge: Cambridge University Press, 1982.

Garner, John S. *The Model Company Town: Urban Design through Private Enterprise in Nineteenth-Century New England*. Amherst: University of Massachusetts Press, 1984.

Garrison, William Lloyd. *Letters*. Edited by Walter M. Merrill and Louis Rochames. 4 vols. Cambridge, Mass.: Harvard University Press, 1971–75.

Goodell, William. *Come-Outerism: The Duty of Secession From A Corrupt Church*. New York, 1845.

Greeley, Horace. *Recollections of A Busy Life*. New York, 1868.

Hardinge, Emma. *Modern American Spiritualism*. New York, 1870.

Hayden, Dolores. *The Grand Domestic Revolution: A History of Designs for American Homes, Neighborhoods, and Cities*. Cambridge, Mass.: MIT Press, 1981.

Higginson, Thomas Wentworth. *Letters and Journals*. Edited by Mary T. Higginson. 1921. Reprint. New York: Negro Universities Press, 1969.

Hopedale (town). *First Annual Report*. Milford, Mass., 1887 .

――――.*First Annual Report of the Hopedale Public Library*. Hopedale, n.d.

――――. *First Annual Report of the School Committee*. Milford, Mass., 1887.

――――. *First Assessor's Report*. Milford, Mass., 1887.

Hopedale Community. *Communal Songs and Hymns*. Hopedale, Mass., 1856.

――――. *Compact of Commune No. 1*. Hopedale, Mass., 1856.

――――. *Constitution, By-Laws, Rules, and Regulations*. Hopedale, Mass., 1849, 1853, 1861.

――――. *Declaratory Resolution of the Hopedale Community with Reference to the Existing Civil War . . . Sept. 15, 1861*. N.p., n.d.

Hopedale Home School. *Catalogue of Teachers and Pupils*. Boston, 1859.

――――. *Reunion of Teachers and Pupils . . . 1867*. Cambridge, Mass., 1868.

Hopedale Juvenile and Collegiate Home School. Hopedale, Mass., 1855.

Hopedale Reminiscences. Hopedale, Mass.: Hopedale School Press, 1910.

Hutchinson, John Wallace. *Story of the Hutchinsons*. 2 vols. Boston, 1896.

Kraditor, Aileen. *Means and Ends in American Abolitionism*. New York: Random House, 1969.

Kulik, Gary, Roger Parks, and Theodore Z. Penn, eds. *The New England Mill Village, 1790–1860*. Cambridge, Mass.: MIT Press, 1982.

Leading Businessmen of Milford . . . Embracing Also . . . Hopedale. Boston, 1890.

Longfellow, Henry Wadsworth. *Letters.* Edited by Andrew Hilen. 4 vols. Cambridge, Mass.: Harvard University Press, 1967–72.

May, Samuel J. *Some Recollections of Our Antislavery Conflict.* 1869. Reprint. New York: Arno Press, 1968.

McBee, Alice Eaton. *From Utopia to Florence.* Northampton, Mass.: Smith College, 1947.

McKivigan, John R. *The War against Proslavery Religion.* Ithaca, N.Y.: Cornell University Press, 1984.

McLoughlin, William C. *New England Dissent, 1670–1833.* 2 vols. Cambridge, Mass.: Harvard University Press, 1971.

Meakin, Budgett. *Model Factories and Villages.* Philadelphia: George W. Jacobs, 1905.

Memorial of Adin Ballou. Cambridge, Mass., 1890.

Miller, Perry, ed. *The Transcendentalists: An Anthology.* Cambridge, Mass.: Harvard University Press, 1950.

Miller, Russell E. *The Larger Hope: The First Century of the Universalist Church in America, 1770–1870.* Boston: Unitarian-Universalist Association, 1979.

Montgomery, David. *Beyond Equality: Labor and the Radical Republicans, 1862–1872.* New York: Oxford University Press, 1967.

Navin, Thomas R. *The Whitin Machine Works since 1831.* Cambridge, Mass.: Harvard University Press, 1950.

Nelson, Geoffrey K. *Spiritualism and Society.* New York: Schrockin Books, 1969.

Nichols, Thomas Low. *Forty Years of American Life.* New York, 1864.

Noyes, John Humphrey. *History of American Socialisms.* Philadelphia, 1870.

Opening Argument . . . In Remonstrance Against the Incorporation of Hopedale. Boston, 1886.

Perry, Lewis. *Radical Abolitionism: Anarchy and the Government of God in Antislavery Thought.* Ithaca, N.Y.: Cornell University Press, 1973.

Podmore, Frank. *Modern Spiritualism.* 2 vols. London and New York: Methuen, 1902.

Post, Albert. *Popular Freethought in America, 1825–50.* New York: Columbia University Press, 1943.

Prude, Jonathan. *The Coming of Industrial Order: Town and Factory Life in Rural Massachusetts, 1810–1860.* Cambridge and New York: Cambridge University Press, 1983.

Report of the Industrial Commission on the Relations and Conditions of Capital and Labor. Vol. 14. Washington, D.C.: Government Printing Office, 1901.

Report of A Select Committee on the Subject of A High School in Milford. Hopedale, Mass., 1848.

Rose, Willie Lee. *Rehearsal for Reconstruction: The Port Royal Experiment.* New York: Random House, 1964.

Sams, Henry W., ed. *Autobiography of Brook Farm.* Englewood Cliffs, N.J.: Prentice-Hall, 1958.

Smith, Timothy L. *Revivalism and Social Reform in Mid-Nineteenth-Century America.* New York and Nashville: Abington Press, 1957.

Spann, Edward K. *Brotherly Tomorrows: Movements for a Cooperative Society in America, 1820–1920.* New York: Columbia University Press, 1989.

Steinberg, Sheila, and Cathleen McGuigan. *Rhode Island: An Historical Guide.* Providence: Rhode Island Bicentennial Foundation, 1976.

Thomas, Benjamin. *Theodore Weld: Crusader for Freedom.* New Brunswick, N.J.: Rutgers University Press, 1950.

Tyrrell, Ian R. *Sobering Up: From Temperance to Prohibition in Antebellum America, 1800–1860.* Westport, Conn.: Greenwood Press, 1979.

U.S. Bureau of the Census. *Eighteenth Census, 1960: Population.* Vol. 1, part 23. Washington, D.C.: GPO, 1963.

U.S. Census Office. "Cotton Manufactures." *Twelfth Census, 1900.* Bulletin no. 215. Washington, D.C., 1902.

———. "Textiles." In *Eleventh Census, 1890: Report on Manufactures.* Washington, D.C., 1894.

West, Thomas H. *"The Loom Builders": The Drapers as Pioneer Contributors to the American Way of Life.* New York: Newcomen Society of North America, 1952.

Whitney, Susan E. *The Inductive Communion.* Great Barrington, Mass., 1909.

Index